Library of
Davidson College

Erratum

Line 9 on page 42 should read:
payments can be unambiguously labelled 'right' or 'wrong'.

INTERNATIONAL MONEY

ISSUES AND ANALYSIS

Andrew Crockett
International Monetary Fund Washington

ACADEMIC PRESS

New York San Francisco A Subsidiary of
Harcourt Brace Jovanovich, Publishers. 1977

© Andrew D. Crockett 1977

First published 1977

All rights reserved. No part of this publication may be reproduced, stored in a retrieval system, or transmitted, in any form or by any means, electronic, mechanical, photocopying, recording or otherwise, without the prior permission of the publisher.

Library of Congress Catalog Card Number 77–75302

ISBN 0–12–195750–0

Filmset in Baskerville by Computacomp (UK) Ltd., Fort William

Printed by The Camelot Press Ltd, Great Britain

Contents

   Preface
1 **Features of the International Monetary System**   1
   Introduction   1
   The balance of payments   2
   Features of the international monetary system   4
   The adjustment mechanism   6
   The reserve standard   10
   Integration and the monetary system   14
   The management of the system   16
   Conclusion   18
   Selected further reading   19
2 **The Contradictions in the Bretton Woods System**   20
   Introduction   20
   The adjustment mechanism   21
   Gold and the dollar   27
   Capital flows   30
   The management of the system   34
   Conclusion   36
   Selected further reading   37
3 **The Balance of Payments**   38
   What is payments equilibrium?   38
   The determination of the balance of payments   40
   The price-specie-flow mechanism   42
   Purchasing power parity   45
   The elasticities approach   47
   The absorption approach   50
   The monetary approach   52
   The 'New Cambridge' view   55
   Selected further reading   57
4 **Fixed and Flexible Exchange Rates**   58
   Introduction   58

	Fixed exchange rates	59
	Free floating	64
	Optimum currency areas	68
	Selected further reading	73
5	**Controlled Flexibility of Exchange Rates**	74
	The adjustable peg system	75
	Wider bands and crawling pegs	81
	Managed floating	85
	Selected further reading	92
6	**Adjustment Policies**	93
	Adjustment under fixed rates	93
	Adjustment under floating	97
	The exchange rate regime and developing countries	102
	The options for developing countries under floating	104
	Selected further reading	111
7	**International Liquidity**	112
	The development of reserve assets	113
	Gold	114
	Reserve currencies	118
	IMF-based liquidity	119
	New valuation of the SDR	123
	The Link	128
	Selected further reading	132
8	**The Control of World Liquidity**	133
	Assessing reserve needs	135
	Reserves under fixed rates	139
	Reserves under managed floating	144
	Controlling liquidity	145
	Selected further reading	149
9	**The Control of Capital Movements**	150
	The argument for liberalization	150
	The argument for control	151
	Methods of control	154
	Capital movements and monetary reform	164
	Selected further reading	166
10	**The Euro-currency Market**	167
	The growth of the euro-currency market	169
	Analyzing the euro-markets	172
	The euro-currency market and inflation	180

	Regulation of the euro-currency market	181
	Selected further reading	183
11	**Inflation and the International Monetary System**	184
	The transmission mechanism	185
	Effects of exchange regimes on the price level	191
	Effects on inflation	196
	Conclusions and welfare implications	202
	Selected further reading	205
12	**The International Monetary Fund**	206
	Origins	206
	Structure	208
	The Fund as custodian of monetary order	212
	The Fund's financial role	215
	Lending facilities	217
	Selected further reading	225
13	**Reform**	226
	The collapse of the Smithsonian arrangements	238
	The Jamaica accords	242
	Selected further reading	245
	Index	246

Preface

This book is an attempt to review the theoretical and policy issues involved in the organization of the international monetary system. This is a subject which has to be dealt with on several different levels. First, international monetary economics is an established branch of economic theory, and a proper understanding of international monetary questions requires a prior familiarity with the state of received theory. But more than most branches of economics, international monetary questions have become bound up with political relationships and are greatly influenced by current economic developments.

It is not possible to fully appreciate present controversies unless one sees them against the background of the monetary history of the post-war period. Negotiating positions of countries are influenced by what they see as being in their particular interest; and the preoccupations of monetary officials have been, perhaps excessively, dictated by what seems to be the crisis of the moment.

A book on international monetary economics that aims to provide the reader with a basis for understanding current controversies has to draw heavily on what has come to be called the "reform exercise" of 1971–76. This exercise, which was to fail in most of its more ambitious objectives, succeeded at least in focusing more concentrated attention than had previously been brought to bear on international monetary questions. The debate revealed that many of the issues which it had been hoped could be resolved by collective decision were intractable. The reform of the monetary system was therefore left as an evolutionary process.

To see the present state of the international monetary system as a stage in an evolutionary process is one of the objectives of this book. This evolution is shaped by events and by political forces outside the field of economics, as well as by economic laws and the deliberate decisions of economic policy-makers.

The most pleasant task in a preface, but the one to which it is least adequate, is that of thanking all those who contributed directly or indirectly to the writing of the book. Although an insider for most of the reform discussion, I was more of a spectator than a participant. However, the influence of all those who were participants in the development of my views will be quite evident. I hope I will be forgiven for not identifying particular sources of influence here or in the text. I do, however, owe a particular debt to those who cheerfully accepted the tedious chore of reading part or all of the book in manuscript form and offering valuable comments. These include Morris Goldstein, Larry Officer, Jacques Polak, and Bill White. Large chunks of Chapters 6 and 11 were the product of collaboration with Saleh Nsouli and Morris Goldstein respectively; they cannot, however, be held responsible for the way in which I have interpreted our joint work in this book. To Florence Manges, Adriana Vohden, and Veronica Samson, thanks are due for patient and efficient typing of successive drafts. To the American University Park babysitting cooperative, I owe many evenings of more-or-less undisturbed peace during which the bulk of the work was carried forward. And to my wife, Marjorie, I owe the deepest debt for her constant encouragement at times when I was more than ready to give up the project.

It goes without saying that the views expressed in the book, and the manner of expressing them, cannot be attributed to my employer, the International Monetary Fund.

I Features of the International Monetary System

Introduction

International monetary economics has a relatively short history as a distinct branch of economic theory; just as international monetary relations (as opposed to trade relations) have a relatively short history as a central concern of policy makers. The arrangements under which international payments were conducted in the nineteenth century did not seem complex enough to be dignified with the name 'system'; nor were they the subject of more than passing reference (a chapter at most) in economics treatises and textbooks. The balance of trade, as later research has shown, was frequently out of equilibrium; but in the absence of statistics, rarely if ever did this fact attract attention, and no governments fell because of their actions or inactions in this area. Best of all, some might say, newspapers were unpreoccupied with the gloomy science; finance ministers did not have to meet, in crisis or even at leisure, in selected watering spots; central bankers never went to Basle, and there was one fewer index with which to measure the economic and moral condition of the nation.

Despite this apparent tranquility, however, the factors which now cause concern in the international monetary sphere were not absent in the nineteenth century. They appeared in a different guise, and were attributed to different causes, but their underlying nature was much the same. Just as divergent national policies could lead in the post-war period to balance of payments disequilibria that had to be corrected, so too in the nineteenth century would a country which found its trade cycle out of phase with its trading partners gain or lose reserves, and have to adjust its policies accordingly if it was to keep the value of its currency pegged to gold. The difference was that, before the First World War, the management of reserves was seen as a technical matter of preserving the gold convertibility of domestic currency—something which could normally be achieved by a relatively modest adjustment of interest rates. Larger questions of economic welfare were either not considered or judged subordinate to the primary objective of preserving the gold parity. The cycle of boom and slump was accepted as largely inevitable, and governments did not consider it to be within their power, or their responsibility, to try to prevent it.

The present preoccupation with international monetary problems arises, in large measure, because it is now realized that the nature of the international monetary system, and how it is managed, has a great deal to do with international prosperity. It is also recognized that governments have considerable scope for good or ill in the way they manage arrangements governing international trade and payments. It is the purpose of this book to investigate how this management has been conducted; to set forth what the relevant policy choices are, and to suggest ways in which the system might most fruitfully develop.

The Balance of Payments

As a starting point, it is worth asking why the exchange of goods across national frontiers should pose problems which are different in nature from those caused by exchanges taking place within a domestic economy. In each case, a payment has to be made because a buyer has purchased goods or services from a seller or because a lender has lent money to a borrower. In each case, purchasing power has to be transferred from the purchaser or lender to the seller or borrower. Why then should we regard a sale of English goods to a Frenchman as creating a different kind of problem from the sale of English goods to a Scotsman?

One answer, only partly relevant, lies in the fact that international transactions affect the balance of payments. This presents the need first to finance the deficits or surpluses which may occur, and second to take action to eliminate the imbalance.

But while the balance of payments is a concept which is usually applied to transactions between countries, problems of financing and adjustment can also arise between regions, and indeed between individual economic units. When the spending of an individual, or a region, exceeds income, the deficit must first by financed, and ultimately closed by increasing income or lowering spending.

Within an economy, however, the monetary authorities do not feel that they need to have a *policy* with regard to the balance of payments problems of individuals. This is because, in the normal course of events, financing of such internal disequilibria will be automatic, and will give rise to its own adjustment incentives. An individual cannot spend in excess of his income unless he has acceptable financial assets, or credit, to transfer to sellers. And as his stock of assets, or his creditworthiness declines, he will become unable or unwilling to continue the deficit, and will be forced to tailor his coat according to his cloth.

For regions within a country, the mechanism of financing and adjustment is similar. A deficit will result in the transfer of financial claims to residents in other parts of the country. So long as the rest of the country is prepared to accumulate claims on the deficit region, the deficit may continue. But eventually a point will be reached where individuals and firms within the deficit area are forced, by the decline in their net worth, to bring their spending in line with their resources. One way of making that adjustment is the physical movement of workers from the region in which funds are no longer being spent to the region for whose output expenditures have been increased. Regional balance of payments adjustment can pose economic and social problems that require government policies to alleviate the hardships involved (as witness the regional development programmes in many countries). There is no *monetary* problem of adjustment, however, because different regions within a country use the same currency, issued and backed by the same government.

The difference in the case of international transactions lies in the fact that different currencies are involved. When an Englishman sells goods to a Scotsman, settlement can be simply made by the transfer of money balances from one account to another. When he sells goods to a Frenchman, he will expect to be paid in pounds, while the French buyer will expect to pay in francs. It is evident that an additional transaction is needed to complete the sale. There must be a market where the Frenchman can sell his francs for pounds in order to pay the Englishman.

Since the supply of pounds is, in the last analysis, determined by the policies of the Bank of England, and the supply of francs by the policies of the Bank of France, governments inevitably influence developments in the foreign exchange market, whether deliberately or as a by-product of their other actions. And since the mobility of labour, noted above as one means of securing *regional* adjustment, is more limited across national frontiers, a greater part of the burden of adjustment to disequilibrium has to be borne by changes in relative prices—i.e., in the real purchasing power of one currency in terms of another. These facts make international payments different from domestic payments, and explain the concern of economists and policy makers with international monetary questions. International monetary economics, therefore, is the study of the network of institutions, rules and conventions which govern the conditions under which currencies are exchanged, and international payments disequilibria are eliminated.

Features of the International Monetary System

For a long time it was customary to describe the international monetary system in terms of the reserve asset which was at its base. Thus, the system which prevailed in the period before the First World War, and which was revived for a time in the inter-war period, was normally referred to as the gold standard. By analogy, the system established at the Bretton Woods Conference in 1944, and lasting until 1971, was sometimes referred to as the gold-exchange standard, reflecting the fact that the basic reserve asset was gold, but that foreign exchange, whose price was fixed in terms of gold, was also used as a medium of settlement of international imbalances.

Such a shorthand description is deficient in that it describes only one feature of the monetary system. This need not be a particularly important analytical shortcoming if the feature described is the only one with respect to which monetary authorities have any choice. Under the gold standard, for example, the choice which countries faced was to adhere to the gold standard by fixing the value of their currencies in terms of gold, or not to adhere to it.[1] Once on the gold standard, questions of how to manage a currency did not arise, since policies were largely determined by the decision to peg to gold.

Nowadays, it is recognized that a given monetary system actually involves a number of features, and that these features can be combined in different ways to achieve different objectives. For this reason it is not very illuminating to categorize alternative systems in terms only of the reserve asset which is used. This is, perhaps, the reason why it has become common to refer to the monetary system that existed from the end of World War II until the early 1970s by the rather less specific term: 'the Bretton Woods system'. This designation is not particularly descriptive, however, and some further analysis is needed of what the characteristics of the Bretton Woods system were, and how they differed from those of alternative systems.

There are, perhaps, four major features of international monetary arrangements which deserve separate analysis. The two most important are:

(1) the nature of the mechanism by which the imbalances in international payments are eliminated;

(2) the nature of the asset in terms of which currency values are expressed, and in which settlement of payments imbalances takes place.

In addition two other features also deserve attention:

(3) the degree to which the monetary system promotes an integrated 'one world' economy through multilateral payments arrangements, and

(4) the degree to which the monetary system is centrally managed, rather than being the consequence of individual national decisions.

The Adjustment Mechanism

Perhaps the most important aspect of the international monetary system is the mechanism which is employed to adjust payments deficits and surpluses.

The amount of goods and financial assets which residents of a country can acquire from abroad is limited by the amount of goods and financial assets they are able to sell abroad. The balance between the two, as in any other market where supply and demand have to be equilibrated, is achieved by an appropriate structure of relative prices. But whereas, in the long run, only one set of relative prices and interest rates will produce lasting balance of payments equilibrium, deviations from such a pattern are quite possible in the short run. An overall balance of payments deficit can be financed by running down reserves or a deficit on goods and services can be covered by raising interest rates so as to enable more financial assets to be sold to foreigners.

The choice of adjustment mechanism involves the method employed to restore an equilibrium pattern of relative prices, when disturbances which inevitably affect the balance of payments cause a departure from such a pattern. Choice is introduced by the fact that relative prices among countries can change for two reasons: because of a change in the price of goods in domestic currency, and because of a change in the price of domestic currency in terms of foreign currency (the exchange rate). Under the gold standard, primary emphasis was placed on the adjustment of domestic prices, while under pure gold standard was reflected in an export of gold coinage. adjustment. Intermediate systems involve some sharing of the means of relative price adjustment.

The Gold Standard

Under the pure gold standard, individual countries were, as far as their money was concerned, no more free to have an independent policy, than regions of a country are today. When gold coinage circulated freely as the principal medium of exchange, the fact that coins might be given different names, and bear the imprint of different crowned heads was basically unimportant. Since coinage was 'full-bodied' (i.e., its value as money corresponded to its value as metal), the exchange rate between coinage issued by different countries depended solely on weight.

As a result of this, a balance of payments deficit under the pure gold standard was reflected in an export of gold coinage. Now it is a law of economics, which is as old as serious study of the subject itself, that the nominal value of output in an economy will tend to adjust, by one means or another, to the volume of monetary assets available for the finance of trade. Thus, the resulting shortage of gold in the deficit country caused a contraction of internal trade, downward pressure on prices, and ultimately an improvement in the balance of payments. (None of this was recorded in statistical form, of course, but the mechanism is quite easy to see.) The pure gold standard was, therefore, an example of rigidly fixed exchange rates, under which adjustment to balance of payments disequilibria could take place only through the adjustment of domestic spending in money terms.[2]

The pure gold standard, under which gold was the principal medium of exchange for domestic as well as international transactions, was more of a theoretical construct than an actual historical experience. Almost as soon as gold became generally accepted in the Western world as a means of payment, mechanisms were sought to economize on the transportation and exchange of actual gold. By the mid-nineteenth century, gold had been superseded in importance by bank money as a means of domestic payment. Gold remained the ultimate store of value, however, and central banks retained reserves of gold to preserve the convertibility of their currencies into gold. Since the gold backing was invariably less than the total of liabilities issued, however, the guarantee could not be absolute. Even in the heyday of the gold standard (the period from the Franco-Prussian War of 1870 until the First World War) only three countries—Britain, Germany and the United States—maintained full convertibility of their currencies into gold on demand. Conversion of other currencies into gold had to take place through prior acquisition of one of these major currencies.

Because the major part of the money supply of most countries was backed not by gold but by financial securities and loans to domestic residents, the link between the balance of payments and the domestic money supply under the nineteenth century gold standard was not an automatic one. A balance of payments deficit could lead to an outflow of gold, but the effect of this on the domestic money stock could be offset by the creation of more bank credit.

By and large, however, this did not happen. This was because most countries observed what later came to be called the gold standard 'rules of the game'. Under this set of conventions, countries which experienced a loss of reserves raised their internal interest rates, which both attracted foreign liquid funds in the short term and served to damp down domestic demand, thus improving competitiveness in the longer run. Because of the importance of having a fixed gold value in determining access to both international short term credit, and the London capital market, most major countries adhered to the 'rules of the game' set out above. But it was recognized that currencies *were* different, and their relative values could change in the wake of important disturbances such as wars and revolutions.

Floating
At the opposite extreme from fixed exchange rates (or almost fixed rates, as under the gold standard) is free floating. Free floating is a situation in which the monetary authority does not intervene in the market for its own currency against others; and is not influenced in its economic policies by considerations related to the exchange value of its currency. Balance of payments equilibrium is ensured automatically by the interaction of supply and demand forces in the foreign exchange market causing a change in the exchange rate. If the balance of payments of a country has a tendency to move into deficit at a given rate of exchange, more of its currency would be offered than demanded at that rate. Consequently, as in the case of any other market, the price (exchange rate) would have to adjust in order to ensure a continued equilibrium between demand and supply. For a country with a weak balance of payments a lowering of its exchange rate would discourage imports and other payments abroad, by making foreign purchases more expensive in terms of domestic currency; conversely it would encourage exports and inward investment by making its domestic currency cheaper for foreigners to acquire. So long as the demand for and supply of foreign exchange respond in the usual way to changes in its price, equilibrium can be continuously maintained without any government interference or regulation in the market.

Thus defined, there have been very few cases of free floating. Floating had been resorted to under the gold standard when countries had found themselves unable to maintain the convertibility of paper money into gold. This happened in both France and Britain during the Napoleonic Wars, although in both countries gold and paper continued to circulate, with the latter at a discount. And there are many other examples in the nineteenth century of paper currencies circulating at a varying discount on their official gold value. Rarely under the gold standard, however, was floating free. Countries were usually motivated by a desire to restore eventually the value of their paper currency to its gold parity.

During the First World War, most countries left the gold standard, but again, not to float freely. They invariably attempted to control the extent to which their currencies depreciated; and after the war many, most notably the United Kingdom, made considerable sacrifices to restore the pre-war gold parity. The floating which was resorted to in the 1930s was even further away from the textbook case of non-intervention. Most countries attempted to manipulate their exchange rates to secure advantage over their foreign competitors through large depreciations which would stimulate exports and thereby promote domestic employment.

The most pure examples of floating, in the sense of being the ones that come closest to the textbook case of non-intervention, were some of the floats in the 1970s, though even here most have been subject to some degree of management. And it must be remembered that even where a country does not intervene directly in the exchange market, it can manage other instruments of economic policy (e.g., interest rates) in such a way as to have a strong indirect effect on exchange rates.

Controlled Flexibility
Between the two extremes of rigidly fixed and freely flexible rates is a more or less continuous spectrum of greater or lesser degrees of official intervention in the exchange market. The Bretton Woods system, as it operated during most of the period of its existence, placed a high premium on fixed exchange rates (though it was frequently emphasized that such fixity need not be permanent).[3] The reasons why it was designed in this way can be fairly briefly recapitulated. The experience of the 1930s seemed to show that to allow individual countries a substantial measure of discretion in the determination of exchange rates for their currencies could

result in competitive depreciation and related measures designed to safeguard domestic employment. The use of such external policies to improve trade positions was recognized to have benefited the countries which adopted them only by penalizing their trading partners. In designing the post-war system, therefore, it was thought advisable to place obstacles in the way of such policies by encouraging countries to use exchange rate adjustment only as a last resort, and by requiring international agreement for such adjustments.

This was achieved by the mechanism of having countries establish par values for their currencies, which they were obliged to defend in exchange markets and were expected to change only after international consultation and agreement, and then only when other means of adjustment would involve excessive cost in terms of domestic objectives for employment or price stability. The par value system worked reasonably well in the quarter century following the end of the Second World War, and for the better part of that period, par value changes by major countries were rare. Trade grew rapidly, and incipient imbalances were for the most part rectified by modest changes in the setting of domestic economic policies. Only when divergent economic developments in different countries became large, in the later 1960s, was strong pressure placed on par values.

After the breakdown of this 'par value' system, there was still widespread acceptance of the proposition that exchange rates were matters of international concern. The problem, however, was to find a means by which the influence of the international community could be brought to bear. The approach that seemed most fruitful was to prescribe a set of broad guidelines for countries' external policies that would be designed to permit a measure of choice in the selection of adjustment policies, while nevertheless providing safeguards against actions that would be contrary to the general interest. This is the essence of the exchange system of 'managed floating'—though it is clear that the system is still in its experimental stages.

The Reserve Standard

After the mechanism by which equilibrium is restored and maintained in international payments, the second major feature of the international monetary system is the nature of the asset used for settling payments imbalances, and as the unit of account among currencies.

Gold
The principal source of international liquidity at the beginning of the post-war period was, as it had been since international trade assumed significant proportions, gold. Gold had acquired its importance as an international medium of exchange as a result of its role as a domestic monetary asset, but it retained this role long after it had ceased to play any significant part in the money supply of individual countries. It is instructive to recapitulate why gold was phased out as a national monetary asset, and why a similar phasing out process did not take place at the international level.

It is well known that the use of a commodity as money imposes resource costs in the production of the commodity concerned. In addition, it renders the stock of money subject to the various factors affecting the production of that commodity. Because of these disadvantages, national monetary systems witnessed the growth of financial intermediation which economized on the use of physical gold. This process was initiated by the expansion of banking systems based on fractional reserve holdings. With the development of central banking in the last part of the nineteenth century, gold reserves passed increasingly into the hands of central banks, and the fractional reserves of the banking system were held, almost entirely, in the form of liabilities of the central bank. Thus, the twin advantages were achieved of (a) a reduction in the use of a resource-based asset, and (b) the extension of deliberate control over the volume of bank reserves and, therefore, the supply of money.

The phasing out of gold from national monetary systems depended essentially on the superior attractiveness of claims on banks as a form of wealth holding. Eventually, individuals could transfer claims through adjusting their balances at commercial banks, and commercial banks could transfer claims by adjusting their balances at the central bank, at lower cost and with greater convenience and safety than if gold had been used as the medium of exchange.

When it came to the transfer of claims at an international level, i.e., between countries, the process of financial intermediation was more complex. It would, in theory, have been possible for one country to perform a banking function on behalf of other countries in the world economy. Thus, country A could settle a deficit with country B by transferring claims to assets which were the liability of institutions in country C. To some extent the London financial market performed this function for the world economy in the period before the First World War. Many less advanced countries chose to maintain the convertibility of their currencies by holding reserves in the form of sterling, or other 'gold' currencies. By and large, however, the major countries preferred, at least in the gold standard period, to hold their reserves in a form which was directly under their control and in this sense inalienable. One does not have to seek beyond obvious political considerations for an explanation of this preference. But holding reserves directly in gold was also felt to be important in maintaining 'confidence' in the stability of a currency, partly because its convertibility was then not dependent on the position of any other currency.

Clearing and Credit Arrangements
When the convertibility of national currencies into gold collapsed in the 1930s some other means of financing deficits and surpluses was clearly required. Free floating could, in theory, have obviated the need for international reserves, since the demand and supply for each currency could be continuously equated by market forces—with speculators financing temporary excesses or shortfalls. However, as noted earlier, the 1930s experience was very far from the free floating paradigm. The device that grew up at that time, and continued both during and after the Second World War, was that of bilateral clearing arrangements. These arrangements usually prescribe that any currency earned by the exporters of country A in country B can be used only to purchase goods in B for export to A. This kind of arrangement can in principle be multilateralized in order to permit a large number of, or all, countries to participate, with clearing being effected by an adjustment of credits or debits in a central clearing house, instead of through the exchange of gold or other assets. Such was the essence of the scheme proposed by Keynes to the Bretton Woods Conference.

A scheme in which payments imbalances are settled by adjusting national credit balances has the advantage of making the volume of international liquidity (i.e., the maximum size of such balances) subject to international control. Furthermore, such liquidity would not be dependent on commodity money, or on previously acquired balances of national currencies. As such, it would avoid the resource costs of using gold, and the asymmetrical consequences of singling out one or a few currencies for use in reserves.

In fact, the choice made at Bretton Woods was to continue to use gold, both as the unit of account in which par values were measured, and as the principal reserve asset. The role of credit operations was limited to lending, in fairly modest amounts, by the International Monetary Fund, to finance payments deficits. Despite the modesty of the Fund's resources (at least by comparison with the proposals of Keynes) the inclusion of a mechanism to supply internationally controlled conditional liquidity through the Fund was an important and novel part of the Bretton Woods arrangements.

Foreign Exchange Holdings
The most significant feature of the liquidity arrangements of the Bretton Woods system, however, was the growth of holdings of foreign exchange in reserves. The use of foreign exchange in reserves was made necessary by the inadequacy of gold supplies. In the period since the end of the Second World War, the world economy has grown more rapidly than the stock of monetary gold. In addition there has been an expansion of trade even more rapid than the growth in production, and over most of the period there has also been a gently rising level of prices. Eventually, there arose a need to supplement gold, a need that was not fully met by conditional liquidity available under the Fund's articles.

Immediately after the war, there were considerable holdings of sterling by countries in the sterling area. But this situation was due less to a shortage of global liquidity than to the specific nature of the reserve-pooling and exchange control arrangements in the sterling area.[4] It also reflected the acquisition of bilateral balances in sterling by countries which had been major suppliers of the United Kingdom during the war. More significant was the growth of dollar holdings in reserves, which began in the late 1950s and continued steadily until, by 1971, dollars were a greater proportion of reserves than gold.

This development was not foreseen by the creators of the Bretton Woods system, and it created difficulties as the continued convertibility of dollars into gold came into question. To overcome these problems, the Bretton Woods Articles were amended (in 1969) to permit the creation of an international fiduciary asset (Special Drawing Rights), which would supplement gold in reserves. Although this development came too late to save the system, the creation of owned reserves by international agreement was an important addition to the conditional liquidity facilities already available through the IMF.

Integration and the Monetary System

Another important aspect of monetary arrangements is the extent to which they further multilateral financial and trading relationships. The gold standard was essentially a multilateral, one-world system, since all countries adhering to it were on the same monetary standard, and their residents could freely make payments to residents of other countries whose currencies which were also on the gold standard. By contrast, the system which sprang up during the 1930s—sometimes called Schachtianism after its chief exponent, Dr Hjalmar Schacht, the German central banker and finance minister—was essentially autarkic. Foreign exchange was rationed for approved priorities which were determined by central decision. Access to needed imports was acquired through the negotiation of quasi-barter deals with suppliers; preferential treatment was given to suppliers who would take domestically produced goods in exchange.

It is, perhaps, so obvious that allocative efficiency requires that trade and investment be allowed to take place freely across national frontiers that one may wonder why it is necessary to make a point of stressing this feature of the system. However, seen from a national standpoint, it is less clear that all trade and investment flows are beneficial. In market economies, individual transactions are governed by private considerations of cost and price, as seen by the traders or investors involved; and these may not always correspond with the government's perception of the broader national interest. This will be particularly the case where capital flows of a speculative or political character are thought to be undermining a country's domestic policies, or where an apparently inappropriate exchange rate maintained by a trading partner seems to threaten domestic competitiveness. These fears constitute the rationale for restrictions on certain types of transactions, and for bilateral arrangements between countries designed to ensure a mutually equitable sharing of the benefits of trade. The experience of the 1930s shows, however, that it is likely that uncoordinated restrictions can quickly degenerate into a system of trading or currency blocs under pressure of events.

The Bretton Woods system is in intent a 'one-world' system, and there can be little doubt that such a broadly liberal framework is in the mutual interest of all nations. However, it has been recognized that to permit any and all international transactions to take place might, in certain circumstances, impose intolerable strains on the system. Thus possibilities for agreed departures from complete freedom were allowed for. In fact, the Articles of Agreement of the International Monetary Fund, drawn up at Bretton Woods, placed much greater emphasis on freedom from restrictions for payments for goods and services on current account than for capital transfers. This was partly because freedom for current account transactions was seen to be quantitatively more important for the efficient allocation of real resources, and partly because experience had shown that capital movements could take place for reasons other than the relative productivity of investment, and could, on occasion, run counter to the objective of allocative efficiency. In principle, however, it was clear that the free movement of capital could contribute to an optimum allocation of resources, and in particular was important for economic development in the poorer countries. It was a natural, if not a necessary, corollary of the increasing freedom for current transactions that capital account transactions should be liberalized also.

The gradual reduction of exchange control barriers, coupled with the rapid growth in the network of international financial claims, revealed, however, a potential for instability in the system. Fixed exchange rates could be threatened by movements of speculative funds, even when policy authorities did not believe there was an underlying disequilibrium. In the later years of the Bretton Woods system, it came to be realized that a par value adjustment mechanism could only coexist with freedom of national monetary policy if exchange controls on capital movements were accepted at least as a stand-by feature of the monetary system.

The Management of the System

A fourth way in which the international monetary system can be categorized is in terms of the degree of discretionary management which it requires. The achievement of agreement between sovereign powers is never an easy matter, particularly when national economic interests may differ; and the difficulty generally increases with the number of parties among which agreement has to be reached. There is, therefore, a considerable advantage in having a system which provides for the automatic harmonization of policy decisions made by national monetary authorities, rather than one which requires continuous international surveillance to achieve international consistency.

From this point of view, rigidly fixed exchange rates and free floating both have attractions. In neither case is there much need for countries to reach accommodations with each other on their external policies. Rigidly fixed rates place the entire onus of adjustment on a country's domestic policies, while floating, if it is genuinely free, allows market forces to achieve the necessary harmonization of policies. At a time when the mechanisms of international cooperation are either weak or under strain, there are considerable practical advantages in each of these two extreme types of exchange rate regime.

The gold standard represents the extreme of a self-regulating system. Each country has an individual responsibility to manage its affairs so as to maintain the gold value of its currency; and the system, i.e., relations between currencies, takes care of itself. Such a philosophy accorded well with the 'hidden hand' principle which underlaid laissez-faire economics, and preached a minimum of interference by governments.

However, the 'hidden hand' approach assumes the existence of equilibrating tendencies in market forces that did not always exist—or if they did, did not work fast enough to avoid considerable economic hardship. For example, it was not the case that output tended easily or quickly to its full employment level. Changes in demand caused by changes in the economic climate overseas could have serious effects on domestic employment and incomes. Once it was realized that the monetary system played a role in the transmission of these influences, it was inevitable that governments would seek ways of controlling them.

The effect of overseas developments on the domestic economy can be offset by floating; and genuinely free floating is another way of avoiding the need for central management of the system. If countries eschew any specific balance of payments or exchange rate targets, there is no need for mechanisms to ensure that national policies are in harmony. They always are, by default.

Perfectly floating rates, however, have proved an unattainable objective, since countries may always perceive a national advantage in intervening, directly or indirectly, to influence their exchange rate. To the extent that they do, a floating system can have the result both of failing to harmonize economic policies and of provoking international political tensions. This certainly was the consequences of floating in the 1930s.

In the absence of a system which provides for the automatic harmonization of national economic policies, there is an obvious need for an 'internationalization' of decision-making. This was the overriding concern of the founders of the International Monetary Fund, and it is a concern which has underlain much of the recent discussion on monetary reform. Relative currency values, it is recognized, should not be the result of uncoordinated national actions. Decisions on exchange rates should be acknowledged to have international importance, and there should be a designated forum for the arbitration of conflicting views. This principle is reaffirmed in the amended provisions of the IMF charter on exchange rates, agreed in 1976.

In this sense, the international monetary system that has existed since the end of the Second World War has been a 'managed' system. It has also been managed in that the international community has accepted a collective responsibility for controlling international liquidity. This again is a departure from earlier systems, though as was noted above, no very successful mechanisms for actually performing the control function have yet been devised.

These objectives of internationalized decision-making are now widely accepted, and in themselves provide a sound basis for international economic cooperation. They require, of course, a willingness on the part of individual countries to give up a certain amount of freedom over their own policies in order to obtain, indirectly, a measure of influence over the policies of others. This is more than simply a question of laying down ground rules concerning decision making procedures and voting rights. As in other fields of international relations, monetary cooperation has to tread a delicate path between the need for rules and the desire of sovereign states to retain as much authority as possible in their own hands.

Conclusion

In this chapter we have examined four features of the international monetary system in which the Bretton Woods system differed from its predecessors. By and large, the system established at Bretton Woods constituted a remarkably successful framework for international monetary cooperation over much of the post-war period. The adjustment mechanism worked reasonably well within the framework of a par value system, and trade and payments restrictions were progressively reduced. World output and trade grew at unprecedented rates and full employment was, with minor departures, well maintained. However, as the system came under increasing strains in its later years, it became apparent that the features of the system could not easily be adapted to meet the needs of a changing world economy. This was not a matter of a single aspect of the system which was malfunctioning. Rather, it was becoming increasingly difficult to continue with a system designed for different circumstances, and whose very success was, as will be seen, making it obsolete.

It will be the purpose of the next chapter to examine in more detail how and why the Bretton Woods system broke down. This will then serve as background for a more detailed study in the later chapters of the particular features of the international monetary system, and the alternative ways in which they might be adapted.

[1] There was also the possibility of choosing some other commodity standard such as silver, but this was only seriously discussed in countries when the silver-mining lobby was strong.

[2] It is worth noting in passing that, as Hume pointed out, in his essay *On the Balance of Trade*, the gold standard mechanism made a policy of mercantilism fruitless. Mercantilism was a policy of expanding national wealth by attracting gold from abroad through a balance of trade surplus. From the foregoing analysis, however, it can be seen that an inflow of gold would simply lead to an expansion of trade and rising prices which would eventually reverse the original surplus.

[3] See e.g. *International Monetary Fund Annual Report*, 1951, p. 36.

[4] The sterling area countries had pooled their reserves in London in the pre-war period and continued to do so for several years after the war. Many of these countries had accumulated substantial claims on the United Kingdom during the war, which could not be transferred into hard currency, but were blocked in sterling balances.

Selected Further Reading

Aufricht, Hans, *The Fund Agreement: Living Law and Emerging Practice*, Princeton Studies in International Finance No. 23, 1969.

Hirsch, Fred, *Money International*, Allen Lane, London, 1969.

Machlup, Fritz, *Plans for the Reform of the International Monetary System*, Princeton Special Papers in International Economics No. 3, 1964.

Morse, C. Jeremy, 'The evolving monetary system,' International Monetary Fund, *Survey*, June 17, 1974.

Officer, L.H., and Willett T.D., (eds) *The International Monetary System*, Prentice Hall, Englewood Cliffs, N.J., 1969.

Triffin, Robert, *The Evolution of the International Monetary System: Historical Reappraisal and Future Perspectives*, Princeton Studies in International Finance No. 12, 1964.

Triffin, Robert, *Our International Monetary System: Yesterday, Today and Tomorrow*, Random House, New York, 1967.

Yeager, Leland B. *International Monetary Relations: Theory, History and Policy*, 2nd edn, Harper and Row, New York, 1976.

2 The Contradictions in the Bretton Woods System

Introduction

In the previous chapter, a number of the characteristic features of the Bretton Woods system have been analyzed, and comparisons have been made with alternative types of arrangement. This analysis has suggested areas of potential weakness in the Bretton Woods system, and it is the purpose of this chapter to explore these in more detail. In fact, each of the features noted in the last chapter began to present problems as the world economy developed in the post-war period.

An adjustment mechanism based essentially on fixed exchange rates imposed severe strains at a time when the relative economic position of countries was rapidly changing. The simultaneous existence of different reserve assets became increasingly untenable as the primary reserve asset, gold, became a smaller and smaller proportion of total liquidity. An integrated one-world system developed contradictions when individual countries sought, for domestic reasons, to pursue divergent politics. Capital flows induced by different policy developments could not be accommodated in a fixed rate system with limited liquidity except by resorting to exchange control measures more stringent than most countries were willing to accept. And finally, a managed system was unable to adapt in a timely manner to changing circumstances since individual countries were unwilling to surrender the necessary autonomy to enable the International Monetary Fund to adapt to new realities. Each of these tendencies played their part in the breakdown of the Bretton Woods system and each one deserves further attention in what follows.

The Adjustment Mechanism

The exchange rate regime which was established as a result of the Bretton Woods Conference was, essentially, a fixed rate system. Of course, it was recognized that circumstances could arise in which the relative competitiveness of countries had become so out of line that some kind of exchange rate adjustment would be necessary to enable the system to continue functioning. This was a lesson which had been well learned from the breakdown of the gold standard in 1931. The fixed rate system was, therefore, modified to permit exchange rate adjustment, by international agreement, under conditions of 'fundamental disequilibrium'.

There were three ways in which the adjustment mechanism actually worked that were unsatisfactory. Firstly, it did not operate in a sufficiently timely way. Domestic measures of adjustment were delayed in their implementation and often sluggish in their effect on the balance of payments; and exchange rate changes were frequently resisted even after substantial disequilibrium in the external accounts was evident. Secondly, there was an asymmetry between the adjustment pressures on surplus countries and those on deficit countries. Thirdly, there was an asymmetry, both of rights and obligations, between the major reserve centres (the United States, and, to a lesser extent, the United Kingdom) and all other countries.

Speed of Adjustment
The conditions required for a system of fixed exchange rates to work well can be summarised as follows. First, and most importantly, the external position of countries must be sensitive to the instruments of domestic economic policy. This involves two aspects: the domestic price level must be responsive to relatively minor changes in aggregate demand

policies, and the trade balance must be responsive to those induced changes in the domestic price level. Secondly, countries must be prepared to modify their domestic economic objectives to meet external objectives such as balance of payments equilibrium and exchange rate stability.

The responsiveness of the balance of payments to shifts in domestic demand conditions seemed to vary between countries. Some, such as Japan (in 1967) and Italy (in 1963–64) were able to divert resources into the balance of payments quite efficiently by means of a domestic monetary squeeze. Others, such as the United Kingdom and the United States, found that their external position was much less sensitive to domestic measures. In the case of the United Kingdom, a series of stop-go cycles had only very temporary effects on the balance of payments, and then mainly through slump-induced reductions in inventories of imported goods and raw materials. In the United States, very tight monetary policy in 1966 and 1969 achieved a rapid improvement in the capital account while credit conditions remained tight, but did little to improve the underlying current account position.

One of the main reasons for the ineffectiveness of domestic demand policy in achieving any lasting effect on the balance of payments lies in the resilience of inflationary pressures. Because of price inflexibility in a downward direction, slack demand, unless it is unduly protracted, cannot actually push prices down, merely retard their rate of growth. This fact in itself does not necessarily make demand management ineffective in influencing the balance of payments. A favourable differential in inflation rates might achieve a substantial improvement in the trade accounts if the relevant elasticities of demand in international trade were sufficiently high. In fact, they turned out to be quite low (most estimates of the price elasticity of demand for manufactured goods are around two).

It also turned out to be the case that there was an unwillingness on the part of countries to orientate their policies to the needs of the balance of payments, at the expense of domestic objectives. Friedman undoubtedly reflected an increasingly important American view when he stated in 1967 'it is undesirable that the United States put major reliance on this adjustment mechanism [domestic deflation] partly because foreign trade is so small a part of our economy—it is absurd to force 95 per cent of the economy to adjust to 5 per cent rather than the other way around'.[1]

An important factor in the increasing unwillingness of countries to try to preserve fixed rates was the growing importance attached to monetary policy in domestic stabilization. In the 1950s and early 1960s, it had been generally assumed that fiscal policy was a more powerful tool for domestic stabilization, while monetary policy had its main impact on capital flows in the balance of payments. This broadly Keynesian view was reflected in the Radcliffe Report,[2] and formally set out in an influential article by Robert Mundell in 1962.[3]

Later in the 1960s, however, monetarist views gained ground, and many countries sought to use monetary policy as an instrument of domestic stabilization. This meant that surplus countries were increasingly unhappy about the effects of inflows of funds on their domestic money supply. Exchange controls provided only a partial answer, since in the form in which they were employed, they were not able to be fully effective.

Despite the difficulties in using domestic measures to achieve adjustment, a par value system could still work reasonably well if timely changes in parities were made when countries found themselves in situations of 'fundamental disequilibrium'. Fundamental disequilibrium was a deliberately vague concept, and in retrospect it seems fair to say that for most of the life of the Bretton Woods system it was interpreted by most countries rather restrictively—more restrictively, indeed, than the authors of the Articles of Agreement intended. As Oort put it: 'The lack of flexibility before 1972 was always more a matter of governments' attitudes than of international constraints'.[4] Between 1949, when there was a general realignment of currencies following the immediate reconstruction phase of the postwar period, and 1967, which began a period of rather greater use of the exchange rate instrument, there were only two major instances in which important countries used par value changes as a mechanism of adjustment. The first was a pair of devaluations of the French franc in 1956 and 1958, reflecting an intractable problem of domestic inflation under conditions of successive weak governments. The second was the revaluation of the German mark and Dutch guilder in 1961, when the two countries concerned had a large and growing current account surplus. Apart from these two instances, and the case of Canada, which floated from 1950 to 1962, the major countries adhered quite strictly to fixed exchange rates.

In the last years of the Bretton Woods system, there was general agreement that more timely par value changes were needed.[5] However, there continued to be resistance. Partly, this could be attributed to the desire to avoid the appearance of a defeat to government policies—resulting in what Oort has termed 'the political asymmetry between action and inaction on exchange rates'. Partly it reflected an unwillingness to concede a profit to speculators and thus store up further trouble for a situation in which the exchange rates to be defended were more reasonable.

Whatever the reason, it is clear in hindsight that the parity for sterling was defended long after a change was needed; and that a change in the franc/mark rate, mooted in October 1968 but vetoed by President de Gaulle, was also necessary. (The change came the following year, after de Gaulle's departure from power.) Even as late as 1971, when the need for more flexibility of rates was widely conceded, countries were unwilling for it to be *their* rates which changed. The United States, for example, initially resisted adjusting the par value of the dollar following its departure from gold; for political reasons, it preferred a realignment to be achieved by revaluations on the part of other countries.

Asymmetries between Deficit and Surplus Countries
Related to, but separable from, the difficulties posed by the sluggishness of the adjustment mechanism, were the alleged asymmetries in the way in which the mechanism worked. This defect had an important political dimension since, depending on one's viewpoint, it seemed to place an unfair portion of the burden of making the system work on one party or the other.

In the first place, the asymmetry of financial discipline placed a more visible constraint on the policies of deficit countries than on those in surplus. A country which had been losing reserves, and did not have an infinite borrowing capacity, had no choice but to adjust its domestic policies or devalue. A surplus country, on the other hand, could continue to run a surplus for as long as it was willing to accumulate reserves.

The possibility of asymmetry in adjustment discipline was foreseen in the Bretton Woods articles, which attempted to guard against it by the 'scarce currency' clause. It was assumed that the currency of a persistent surplus country would become scarce in the Fund, because other countries would be withdrawing it for use in making payments.[6] In such a case, various kinds of discrimination against payments to a 'scarce currency' country were permitted. In fact, however, the scarce currency clause was never invoked—partly because of a political reluctance to sanction restrictions in what was intended to be a liberal system, and partly because the scarcity or otherwise of a currency was a fallible guide to the need for adjustment action.

As a result, deficit countries felt the mechanism of adjustment bore disproportionately on them. The developing countries were the chief sufferers, since events over which they had little control, such as downturns in world trade, forced adjustments on them that could not easily be attributed to errors of domestic policy. But in the latter stages of the Bretton Woods system, other countries felt constrained too. The United States, in particular, was unwilling to be forced into a painful domestic adjustment in 1971, when it saw the non-appreciation of the European currencies as being just as responsible for its payments difficulties. The situation was not helped any by the penchant of some European leaders to equate balance of payments deficits with economic mismanagement, and surpluses with financial rectitude.

Part of the problem, too, was due to the fact that under the Bretton Woods articles, the IMF could only concur in an exchange rate change proposed by a member; it had no formal power to propose a change itself.[7] Thus there was no way for the international community to encourage the correction of a disequilibrium which had arisen because of *inaction* on the exchange rate.

Asymmetries between Reserve Centres and Other Countries
The second type of asymmetry in the Bretton Woods system was that between reserve centres (the United States and, to a much lesser extent, the United Kingdom) and the rest of the world. Since dollars and sterling were held in reserves, it was obviously possible for a deficit on private transactions by Britain or the United States to be financed by an increase in

dollars and pounds held by central banks overseas. To countries which were not reserve centres, this appeared to be an uncovenanted advantage. since the reserve centres could run deficits at will, and simply pay for them by printing claims on themselves.

The political dimension of this complaint became evident when the United States deficit reached sizable proportions, and particularly when the deficit was partly accounted for by American expenditures of a kind which other countries did not approve. The Vietnam war was one example of United States overseas expenditure which, it was claimed, was 'financed' by the dollar's reserve role. American direct investment in European industry was another.

There was often an element of demagoguery in these assertions; a balance of payments deficit cannot be attributed to one component of the accounts any more than to another; and there is no evidence that if the United States had been forced to balance its external accounts it would have significantly curtailed expenditure on either the Indochina war or on foreign investment. Still, we are dealing here with political economy, and these factors played a role in the acceptability of the system to the countries involved.

But even the advantages to the reserve centres of their reserve currency role are far from being unqualified benefits. Their domestic policies must be conducted in such a way so to prevent the sudden withdrawal of foreign-owned balances, especially when their reserves are limited. For the United Kingdom, for example, domestic policy was constrained over much of the post-war period by the need to avoid a loss of confidence in sterling—given that Britain's short-term liabilities far exceeded its reserves. In the case of the United States, the role of the dollar as numeraire of the system diminished the power of the United States to influence its own exchange rate. Since other countries pegged their rates in terms of dollars, it was not clear that a change in the United States par value would actually achieve a reduction in the dollar's exchange rate against the currencies of other countries.

Because it was difficult for the United States to achieve adjustment by devaluation, and unnecessarily wasteful to achieve it by payments restrictions or domestic deflation, many observers recommended a policy of 'benign neglect' of the balance of payments. If the rest of the world really wanted an improvement in the United States' current account, the argument ran, they could revalue their own exchange rates. If, on the other hand, they wanted to protect their export industries, they would have to pay the price by accumulating the dollars their exporters earned. By abjuring a specific policy with respect to its own balance of payments, the United States would place this choice squarely on the shoulders of its trading partners.

In the end, the asymmetry of the reserve currency feature irked both sides. Surplus countries felt they were subsidizing the reserve centre, and at the same time suffering unwanted inflation, as their accumulation of reserves fuelled the growth of the money supply. On the other hand, the United States felt that undervalued exchange rates by other countries were undermining the current competitiveness and long-term viability of important sectors of American industry.

Gold and the Dollar

Another contradiction in the Bretton Woods system (not in its conception, but as it actually operated) related to reserve supply arrangements. The intention of the founders of the IMF was that world liquidity should consist of gold, plus international borrowing rights.

As was noted in the last chapter, however, the stock of monetary gold was not rising in the post-war period anywhere near fast enough to keep pace with the world's need for liquidity. The one method of increasing liquidity sanctioned in the IMF Articles of Agreement—a uniform devaluation of currencies in terms of gold—was unsatisfactory. The redistribution of wealth would be both arbitrary and unwelcome; the use of such a means of increasing liquidity would likely give rise to speculation over a further change in the gold price at some future date; and the ratification procedure by national legislatures was cumbersome and by no means guaranteed to be successful.

But if gold itself could not provide the basis for an expansion in world liquidity, what could? Borrowing facilities in the IMF were one possibility, but had the disadvantage that drawing rights were circumscribed by conditions. It was therefore natural that countries should seek to supplement reserves held in gold with holdings of foreign exchange. The currency that was most in demand was that of the world's strongest economy and largest trading nation—the United States dollar.

It is sometimes implied that dollar holdings were merely the passive reflection of the United States' balance of payments deficit. This is a considerable simplification of the casual factors at work, however. If the European countries, which became the main holders of dollars, had really been unwilling to hold them, they could have adopted policies to avoid such accumulation. One possibility would have been to increase the exchange rate for their domestic currencies which would have reduced their accumulation of dollars and at the same time counteracted inflationary tendencies within their own economies. Alternatively, they could have converted their dollars into gold, which by reducing American reserves would eventually have forced the United States to change its domestic policies or to devalue. The fact that most major countries did not follow either of these courses of action implies that the growth of dollar balances was just as much the result of the holders' desire to acquire them as of American policy in permitting a deficit to occur.

Seen from an American perspective, the growth of dollar holdings abroad was no more than a natural consequence of the banking function performed by the United States economy. Because of the central role of the United States dollar, it was natural that foreigners should hold a growing volume of short-term claims on the United States. These claims, although individually all withdrawable at short notice, were really an essential store of liquidity for the finance of world trade. So long as the world economy was expanding, this stock of short-term claims was not likely to be run down—any more than the demand to hold domestic bank deposits is likely to decline in an expanding economy. Therefore, additions to the stock of American short-term liabilities should not be considered as a deficit requiring correction, but as the natural expansion of a banker's balance sheet in a growing economy. This argument was originally applied to the growth of private holdings of dollars but one could, indeed, go further and argue that a portion, at least, of the growth of official claims on the United States could also be regarded a normal phenomenon, satisfying as it did a need for expanding liquidity that could not be met from any other source.[8]

This argument was not accepted by European countries, because, as mentioned above, it seemed to imply an asymmetry of obligations. As a result, the growing role of the dollar in fulfilling world reserve needs posed a difficult problem of reconciling the external objectives of the United States and those of its major trading partners. In a growing world economy, particularly one where real growth was augmented by inflation, it was natural that most countries should seek a rising level of external reserves. Under the Bretton Woods system, however, reserves could only be acquired by running a surplus in the balance of payments. This is not an objective that can be pursued successfully by all countries at the same time.[9] If the countries which were free to pursue independent exchange rate policies sought to have rising reserves, it was inevitable that the United States, as the principal reserve centre would either have to accept a decline in its own reserves, or witness an increase in its liabilities vis-à-vis the rest of the world.

Although the deficits of the United States reflected in part the success of the monetary system in providing a suitable environment for the post-war rehabilitation of the economies of the rest of the world, the situation spelled danger for a system in which the United States dollar played the key role. So long as the American economy was clearly the dominant one, and the American dollar was strong, it made sense for other currencies to fix their exchange rates in terms of the dollar, to conduct their intervention in dollars, to formulate their monetary policy in the light of United States policy and so on. When the assumption that the American dollar would remain strong indefinitely was called into question, it became more doubtful that countries would be willing to accumulate liabilities in a currency which, according to the conventional definition of the balance of payments, was out of equilibrium. There was an element of Catch 22 in this. If the dollar was strong, other countries would accept dollars but they would not be available; if the United States was in deficit, dollars would be available, but other countries would be less willing to accept them.

So long as United States liabilities were small in relation to the United States gold reserves, there was no particular difficulty in maintaining a fixed value for the dollar in terms of gold. As American liabilities grew, however, it became clear that convertibility of dollars into gold could only be maintained in principle so long as conversion in fact was not exercised. It was the realization of this basic contradiction that prompted the search for a new supplementary reserve asset whose value in terms of the primary asset, gold, would be more assured. The result of this search was the creation of Special Drawing Rights with a value fixed (at least theoretically) in terms of gold.

This development came too late to save the system, since existing holdings of dollars had reached a level at which the United States could not guarantee their conversion into gold if the dollar came under pressure in exchange markets. Furthermore, SDRs could only supplement gold satisfactorily if there was confidence that they would in practice be at least 'as good as gold'. This basic requirement had already been called into question in 1968, when central banks ceased selling gold to the public at the official price—a development which resulted in the free market price of gold going up while the value of the SDR stayed still. It was doubtful whether the SDR–gold relationship would continue to be credible in circumstances where the declared monetary price of gold was becoming increasingly out of line with the price determined by supply and demand in the private market. A growing world economy simply could not exist based on a reserve of gold which was fixed in price and growing only slowly in quantity. And the attempt to preserve the central role of gold, while supplementing it with other assets whose gold value could not be indefinitely guaranteed was likely sooner or later to encounter the constraint of Gresham's Law.[10]

Capital Flows

Parallel with the weakening of the dollar, but separate from it, there was a rapid growth in the outstanding quantity of short-term, mobile capital which was also casting a shadow over the working of the par value system. The reconstruction and modernization of the economies of Western Europe and Japan had made possible the liberalization of their payments systems during the post-war period. The culmination of this trend was the restoration of non-resident convertibility in 1958.[11] The growing ease with which payments could be made across national frontiers, coupled with the expanding volume of world trade, and increasing interdependence of national economies, added greatly to the volume of funds that could move out of one currency into another at short notice. The integration of international capital markets, and particularly the growth of euro-currency banking after the late 1950s, served to increase the institutional efficiency of foreign currency financial markets, and thus facilitated short-term capital mobility.

There is no inherent reason, of course, why movements of short-term funds should necessarily be destabilizing, even under a fixed rate system. It is in principle quite possible for governments to manage their domestic monetary policies in such a way as to encourage an inflow of funds when this is needed to counteract a deficit on the current and long-term capital account. On the whole, however, the nature of a fixed exchange rate system is such that it is very easy for destabilizing speculation to be set in train. Any balance of payments disequilibrium of significant size is bound to raise questions as to whether the exchange parity of the country concerned is appropriate. Whether or not a change in parity is judged to be likely, wealth-owners can best protect themselves by moving some at least of their assets into the currency which is a candidate for appreciation and out of the currency which it is thought might devalue.

There were bouts of currency speculation in the 1950s and early 1960s, but they were generally quite easily weathered by the authorities. For one thing, the funds at the command of speculators were limited. For another, the par value edifice which had been erected after the war was still sufficiently imposing to convince most observers of its basic resilience. And the disequilibria that arose on current account were relatively modest. After the establishment of convertibility, however, things began to change. Balances held in foreign currencies began to grow quite rapidly, and the euro-dollar market, established in London in the late 1950s, facilitated transfers of funds between currencies. The expansion of international banking and growth of multinational corporations also played their part in increasing the volatility of short-term capital. About the same time, the size of payments disequilibria of some important countries became larger.

The first clear warning that speculative pressure could not be checked by tightening domestic credit and borrowing abroad came in 1964, when the new British Labour government attempted to stem an outflow of short-term funds by a two per cent increase in bank rate. Significantly, for the first time since the war, such a measure failed to have the desired effect on confidence in sterling. It was seen as, first, underlining the gravity of the situation, and second, insufficient to prevent a devaluation in the event that a bandwagon against sterling began to roll. The situation was eventually retrieved by a further package of measures, an even clearer political commitment by the government against devaluation, and an until then unprecedented credit line of some $3,000 million negotiated by the Bank of England with a group of central banks.

The 1964 episode was just the beginning of a steady escalation of the power of private short-term capital to threaten officially maintained exchange rates. The euro-dollar market, which was then in its infancy, continued to grow rapidly, averaging an expansion of over 20 per cent per annum for the remainder of the decade. At the same time, incipient payments disequilibria became greater, as the gap between countries' economic performances widened. Sterling was successfully defended against speculative runs in 1965 and 1966, but forced to devalue in 1967. In March of the following year, a run on the dollar forced the United States to suspend the convertibility of the dollar into gold other than for central banks. France withstood speculative pressure in October 1968, but had to devalue in August 1969. The German mark was revalued in October of the same year, after a short upward float, and Canada floated in 1970. In 1971, the dam burst, and after the German and Dutch currencies were allowed to float in May, the United States suspended, on August 15, the residual convertibility that still existed for central banks.

The common theme of these events is a continuous growth in the volume of private funds able to move across the exchanges; an increase in the underlying payments disequilibria that provided the incentive for such movements, and an inability on the part of the authorities either to finance such flows, or to take adjustment action of a kind that would effectively discourage them. Policies to affect the balance of payments on current account were recognized to be too slow-acting to have much effect on exchange market pressures in the short run. And shifts in monetary policy in an attempt to stabilize flows of short-term capital would have meant a subordination of domestic policy objectives to external constraints—a subordination which most countries were unwilling to accept.

In an attempt to reconcile the conflicting goals of fixed exchange rates and independent domestic monetary policies, capital controls of varying kinds were resorted to; but none proved effective. In the early 1960s, the United States imposed an Interest Equalization Tax, which effectively closed the New York market to foreign borrowers, and followed this up in 1966 with a voluntary programme of restraint on overseas investment. The United Kingdom ceased the trend to liberalization on its exchange control arrangements in the mid-1960s and began to reimpose restrictions of a quite far-reaching kind. Surplus countries, too, used exchange controls to try and prevent inflows of funds, or at least to offset their domestic monetary effects. The most popular of these instruments was the adjustment of reserve requirements against bank deposits by non-residents.

Although these measures presumably had some effect on the capital flows of the countries which adopted them, they were certainly not sufficient to prevent speculation when a change in par value was anticipated. For one thing, very large changes in net payments could be achieved by quite small shifts in the timing of payments for current transactions. Then in the case of deficit countries, there was very little that could be done to prevent the withdrawal of funds by non-residents, short of the drastic step of 'blocking' balances. For surplus countries, it was not acceptable to refuse to accept deposits by non-residents; and the disincentive of a low, zero, or even negative interest rate was insufficient to keep funds out when expectations of revaluation were strong.

The Management of the System

It would have required a very strong institutional structure to have preserved the Bretton Woods system in the face of the economic strains placed on it by the developments mentioned above. Such a structure did not really exist. Although the Articles of Agreement of the IMF constituted a remarkably successful framework for international cooperation over much of the post-war period, they came under increasing strain as the system developed and changed. In the later years of the Bretton Woods arrangements, it became apparent that the mechanisms for international management of the system were not sufficiently strong to preserve it from the centrifugal tendencies of divergent national policies.

In retrospect, it seems to have been the case that the success of the system in the early post-war period was due not only to the ability of its institutional mechanisms to resolve conflicts among nations, but also to the absence of basic sources of conflict. Most countries had, by and large, been successful in achieving high levels of employment and relative stability of domestic prices. They were, therefore, less tempted to pursue external policies that would lead to conflict with other countries. The rapid growth of the world economy also allowed countries to expand their overseas markets without coming into serious conflict with the interests of others. The assistance extended by the United States, under the Marshall Plan, in the post-war recovery of Europe and Japan contributed to this harmony. Even when, in the 1960s, the growing strength of the trading position of countries outside North America began to weaken the United States' external position, there was still little feeling of conflicting interests. Because of its strong domestic economy and minor dependence on foreign trade, the United States was initially not much concerned about the deterioration in its balance of payments. Thus, to an important extent, countries other than the United States were able to pursue exchange rate policies of their own choice, while the United States, by virtue of the central reserve role of the dollar, was able to adopt a policy of 'benign neglect' of its payments position. The growing need of the rest of the world for reserves meant that a United States deficit lubricated the international financial mechanism by providing dollars for other countries to hold.

When surplus countries began to become concerned about their accumulation of dollars, however, and the United States itself began to worry about its deteriorating trade position, the difficulties of harmonizing external policies came into sharper focus. The desire of many European countries to have a strong balance of payments for themselves was not compatible with the objective, widely shared, that the United States deficit should be eliminated through an improvement in the American competitive position. Just as one relative price determines the quantities of two products that exchange for each other, so in a monetary system of n currencies, there are only $n-1$ independently determined exchange rates. For most of the life of the Bretton Woods system it was accepted that the United States dollar was the residual currency of the system, whose authorities could not unilaterally change its exchange rate. Once this axiom came into doubt, and the American authorities insisted on an equal right to pursue an active external policy, the question of how to reconcile national policies came very much to the fore.

The Bretton Woods articles tended to gloss over this difficulty of harmonizing policies. It was assumed that the appropriateness of exchange rates could be considered on a case-by-case basis, and that the need for all countries to pursue payments equilibrium would make the resulting pattern of rates broadly correct. However, because of the asymmetries noted above in the way the adjustment system worked, it became clear that individually determined payments objectives would not necessarily be mutually consistent.

Various attempts were made to find a suitable forum in which the effective reconciliation of divergent targets could be pursued. These included the OECD, where a special working party of the Economic Policy Committee was established in 1961; and the Group of Ten, which was composed of the ten major trading nations, plus Switzerland. In neither case, however, was there any machinery to carry discussion forward from 'multilateral surveillance' to effective harmonization of policies. Thus the Bretton Woods arrangements found themselves handicapped by the fact that they were a managed system in which the major countries were not prepared to concede much authority to the instruments of centralized management.

Conclusion

With the benefit of hindsight, it is not difficult to see the contradictions in the Bretton Woods system. A fixed exchange rate system could not operate where there was a large volume of mobile capital ready to flow in response to expectations of exchange rate changes; at least not unless the adjustment mechanism was working in a particularly efficient and timely way. And the distinction between reserve currencies and others, concerning both rights and obligations, became increasingly difficult to sustain in a world of greater economic and political equality among nations.

In the end the system was brought down by overwhelming speculative flows, prompted by a basic disequilibrium in the balance of payments position of major countries, and encouraged by the clear lack of will by many countries to make the domestic sacrifices necessary to preserve the fixed rate system.

The Bretton Woods system can be said to have collapsed on August 15, 1971. It is true that a fixed rate system, though without formal convertibility, was re-established in December 1971 and lasted, without the participation of Canada and with the defection of sterling in June 1972, for some fourteen months. It was always a fragile system, however, and was seen by its architects as providing a breathing space until more permanent arrangements could be worked out. Accordingly, its history belongs more to the story of the reform, which is the subject of Chapter 13.

---

[1] Friedman, M., and Roosa, R.V., *The Balance of Payments: Free versus Fixed Exchange Rates*, American Enterprise Institute, 1967, p. 12.
[2] *The Committee on the Working of the Monetary System: Report*, London, H.M.S.O., Cmnd. 827, 1959.
[3] Mundell, R.A., 'The appropriate use of monetary and fiscal policy for internal and external stability', IMF *Staff Papers*, March 1962.
[4] Oort, C.J., *Steps to International Monetary Order: The Exchange Rate Regime of the Future*, Per Jacobsson Foundation Lecture, 1974.
[5] See, for example, the 1970 Report of the IMF Executive Directors on *The Role of exchange rates in the Adjustment of International Payments*, IMF, Washington, D.C., 1970.
[6] The mechanism of IMF operations is dealt with in Chapter 12. Here we need only note that the Fund operates as a revolving pool of currencies.

[7] Although the staff of the Fund could, of course, make informal recommendations concerning the exchange rate.
[8] See, for example, Kindleberger, C.P., *Balance of Payments and the International Market for Liquidity*, Princeton Essays in International Finance No. 48, 1965.
[9] Except to the extent that gold production is adding to world reserves.
[10] Gresham's Law is based on the observation of Sir Thomas Gresham (in Elizabethan times) that bad money tends to drive out good—i.e., where two forms of money circulate with the same nominal value, the one which is considered to have the greater real value (the 'good' money) is hoarded, while the other (the 'bad' money) is the one exclusively used for transactions purposes.
[11] *De facto* convertibility was achieved in 1958, although the acceptance of the obligations of Article VIII of the IMF Agreement came only in 1961 for most European countries and in 1964 for Japan.

Selected Further Reading

De Vries, Tom, *An Agenda for Monetary Reform*, Princeton Essays in International Finance No. 95, 1972.

De Vries, Tom, 'Jamaica, or the non-reform of the international monetary system', *Foreign Affairs*, March 1976.

Dunn, Robert M., Jr., *Exchange Rate Rigidity, Investment Distortions and the Future of Bretton Woods*, Princeton Essays in International Finance No. 97, 1973.

International Monetary Fund, *The Role of Exchange Rates in the Adjustment of International Payments*, Report by the Executive Directors, Washington, D.C., 1970.

International Monetary Fund, *The Reform of the International Monetary System*, Report by the Executive Directors, Washington, D.C., 1972.

Strange, Susan, *International Monetary Relations*, Oxford University Press, London, 1976.

Triffin, Robert, *Gold and the Dollar Crisis*, Yale University Press, New Haven, Conn., 1960.

3 The Balance of Payments

The previous two chapters have dealt with, respectively, the nature of the Bretton Woods system, and with the problems and contradictions which led to its downfall. This serves as a background for a more detailed discussion, in the chapters which follow, of specific features of the monetary system, and the alternative arrangements which are possible in respect of them.

Since the principal purpose of the international monetary system is to promote international trade and to facilitate the smooth adjustment of payments positions, it is important to begin a review of international monetary issues with a discussion of how balance of payments disequilibria arise and are eliminated. It is the purpose of this chapter to do that, and thus lay the groundwork for an analysis of policy choices in the chapters which follow.

What is Payments Equilibrium?

The balance of payments of a country is simply a statistical presentation of all the transactions of residents of that country with foreigners. By the principles of double-entry bookkeeping, each credit in the account is matched by a corresponding debit: for example, the import of goods and services is a debit, the transfer of assets to pay for goods and services is a credit. Overall, the balance of payments, net of errors and omissions, must sum to zero.

What the foregoing means is that it is strictly meaningless to say *the* balance of payments is in deficit. When such statements are made, what is meant is that one part of the accounts, judged by the speaker to be of analytical importance for a particular purpose, is in deficit, and is being financed by the surplus produced elsewhere in the accounts.

Of course, it will happen all the time that parts of the accounts will be in surplus and parts in deficit without this being anything to worry about. A disequilibrium can be said to exist when the balance between surpluses and deficits in different parts of the accounts is not sustainable. Whether a situation, which represents an equilibrium at a point in time, is considered sustainable over a longer period is naturally a subjective question. There are, however, a number of rather more objective criteria that can be employed.

As far as the policy authorities of a country are concerned, their foreign exchange reserves can be considered to be the ultimate limiting factor on their freedom of action. Gross reserves cannot be run down below zero, and they cannot be increased indefinitely. Over the long haul, therefore, a country cannot expect to finance, through continuing changes in reserves, a deficit or surplus arising elsewhere in its external payments. There is a strong presumption, therefore, for saying that balance of payments equilibrium requires equilibrium in the 'overall balance'—that is the balance on all transactions before taking account of reserve movements.

Some analysts believe this is sufficient and that it is unnecessary to concern oneself further with the distribution of deficits and surpluses between components of the overall balance. On the other hand, it can be argued that this distribution is an important aspect of the sustainability of a particular payments position and exchange rate. It can be argued that a country which is financing a heavy current account deficit by sales of financial assets, or borrowing abroad, will eventually be forced to adjust its policies. Since the current account measures whether a country's net external worth is increasing or decreasing, it can be argued that this component of the accounts has a special significance.

There are also a number of intermediate points in the accounts at which the line can be drawn. These have the common characteristic of attempting to distinguish between 'autonomous' flows, i.e., transactions which take place for their own sake, and 'accommodating' flows, which take place to finance flows elsewhere in the accounts.[1] Such a distinction cannot of course be watertight, but it can be a handy frame of reference in discussing whether or not a given payments position requires adjustment.

Analyses of the balance of payments sometimes fail to distinguish *which* balance of payments is being considered. This can lead to confusion, both in the interpretation of the underlying forces at work, and in the formation of policies to achieve adjustment. The following discussion will try to keep the various categories distinct, with the help of the following schema:

Construction of Balance of Payments Accounts

Credit(+) / Debit(−)	Transaction	Balance
+ −	Exports of goods Imports of goods	= Trade balance
+ −	Trade balance Invisible receipts Invisible payments	= Current balance
+ −	Current balance Long-term investment inflow Long-term investment outflow	= Basic balance
+ −	Basic balance Private short-term lending Private short-term borrowing	= Official settlements balance
+ −	Official settlements balance Official lending Official borrowing	= Overall balance
−	Overall balance Reserve increase (+ decrease)	= Zero

The Determination of the Balance of Payments

It has been recognized by economists since at least the time of David Hume, that there exist natural forces tending to restore equilibrium in the overall balance of payments. This mechanism works through the impact of foreign payments on the domestic money supply and in turn on domestic demand. Having been developed, however, to explain the balance of payments under a pure gold standard, the 'price-specie-flow' mechanism set out by Hume ignores the power of governments to neutralize the impact of international monetary flows on domestic monetary conditions; and this must be considered an important limitation on its general applicability.

An alternative, more direct, more intuitive approach is to explain trade flows by looking directly at relative price levels. A simple version of this approach is the purchasing power parity doctrine, which in its pure form hypothesizes that exchange rates are in equilibrium only when prices (i.e., the purchasing power of currencies) are equalized across countries.

A more sophisticated approach using prices concentrates on the trade balance (or occasionally the current balance) and views it as being determined by changes in relative price levels working through the elasticity of demand and supply for traded goods. Domestic prices under this 'elasticities' approach, and indeed also under the purchasing power parity approach, are often taken as given, and the analysis concentrates on the effect of exchange rate adjustments in stimulating changes in the demand for and supply of traded goods.

However, while it may have been reasonable in the underemployment conditions of the 1930s to regard the balance of payments as determined by the effects of exchange rate changes on relative prices, such an assumption was no longer tenable in the seller's market of the post-war period. A devaluation could only improve the trade accounts if steps were taken to see that it resulted in additional supplies, rather than rising prices. An alternative theoretical framework to one based on relative prices is one based on relative 'absorption', i.e., one which explains the balance of trade as the difference between the overall output of an economy, and domestic demands on resources.[2]

Finally, the wheel has come almost full circle with the most recent development in balance of payments theory, the monetary approach. This approach is essentially an elaboration of the Humean mechanism, in which the balance of payments is explained by discrepancies in the demand for, and supply of, money. The so-called 'New Cambridge' approach (at the time of writing not fully articulated) has features of the monetary approach, but resembles the absorption approach in its use of national income relationships.

None of the theoretical approaches to the balance of payments. To this end, mercantilists favoured measures They are essentially different ways of looking at the same phenomenon, and each has its usefulness for a particular purpose. As in the case of the Keynesian and monetarist explanations of income determination, however, different approaches, while not necessarily inconsistent with each other, provide very different insights and suggest radically different policy prescriptions. It is therefore important from a practical, as well as from a theoretical, point of view to subject the various approaches to the balance of payments to closer scrutiny. This will enable us, in later chapters, to examine the specific questions of policy choice which face individual governments, and also the general question of whether and how the international community can prescribe guidelines for balance of payments adjustment policies.

The Price-Specie-Flow Mechanism

The earliest attempt to explain the natural mechanism of balance of payments adjustment under the gold standard was by David Hume, in his essay on *The Balance of Trade*, published in 1752.[3] Hume was mainly concerned to dispute what was then the mercantilist orthodoxy, and which held that the objective of commercial policy ought to be to accumulate treasure from abroad, through a surplus in the balance of payments. To this end, mercantilists favoured measures designed to restrict imports and encourage exports.

Hume's refutation of this role ran in terms of the constancy of the velocity of circulation of money. A surplus in the balance of trade would produce an inflow of money (specie) from abroad, which would increase the ratio between money and income in the economy concerned. Individual economic units, finding themselves with excess cash balances would attempt to restore equilibrium in their holding of assets by spending their excess money. To the extent that this additional spending was on imports, the balance of payments would move back directly towards an equilibrium position.

Even if the additional spending was on domestic goods, however, the end result would be the same, though the route by which it was achieved would be somewhat more indirect. Additional demands on domestic output would tend to displace supplies from existing purchasers. In their attempt to continue to obtain supplies, these purchasers would bid up the price of domestically produced goods. Higher prices would reduce the demand for domestic products, thus discouraging exports and encouraging imports. Equilibrium would be restored when the money supply in each country was restored to the desired ratio with income, at which point there would be no tendency for specie to flow either in or out.

(It should be noted in the above example that a surplus in the balance of payments has to be offset by a subsequent deficit before the balance of payments can return to an equilibrium position. This is because the initial surplus will cause an increase in the money supply which tends to give rise to an increase in the price level in the surplus country. This higher price level will eventually generate a deficit in the balance of payments, which will persist until both the domestic money supply and the domestic price level have returned to their original values.)

The price-specie-flow mechanism was developed to explain a situation in which gold was the only form of money, and was used in its metallic form both for domestic and for international transactions. However, it requires only minor theoretical adjustment to adapt it to the reality of the nineteenth century gold standard, with its fractional reserve banking systems. In practice, most monetary authorities, deliberately or incidentally, manipulated domestic monetary conditions to be consistent with the requirements of external adjustment. Thus, a loss of gold from the central reserves was usually the occasion for an increase in interest rates to protect the reserves. As Bagehot[4] wrote in the mid-nineteenth century, 'The principal precaution [against a loss of gold] is a rise in the rate of discount and such a rise certainly does attract money from the continent and from all the world much faster than could have been anticipated'.

Although an increase in interest rates was primarily intended to attract short-term funds from abroad, it had the additional consequence of limiting the expansion of credit domestically, and putting a brake on the growth of the money supply. This, in turn, improved the balance of payments directly through curtailing imports, and also tended to depress the domestic price level which improved longer-term competiveness.

The lesson of Hume's interpretation of the price-specie-flow mechanism, which was drawn most clearly by Bagehot, was that if central banks followed the gold standard rules of the game, the balance of payments would take care of itself. Like much of nineteenth century economics, the lessons it produced for policy makers were that a minimum of interference with economic phenomena was to be desired. Since equilibrium was a natural state, nature should be left to pursue its beneficial course.

It was not until the inter-war period that the price-specie-flow mechanism, along with much of the rest of classical economics, came under fire. The burden of the criticism was not that the equilibrium tendencies of the price-specie-flow mechanism did not exist, but that they worked too uncertainly and too slowly to be acceptable. A shortage of money, for example, was not easily and quickly translated into a decline in the price level which smoothly restored the desired ratio between real money balances and real income. In practice, prices turned out to be sticky in a downward direction, and the recessions of the late nineteenth century tended to be long drawn out affairs in which a downward price adjustment was achieved only at the expense of protracted stagnation and unemployment.

The first systematic attempt to look at the balance of payments in a different way was the purchasing power parity doctrine, developed by the Swedish economist Gustav Cassel during the First World War, and applied mainly to the question of determining equilibrium exchange rates. It is to this that we now turn.

Purchasing Power Parity

The purchasing power parity doctrine came to the fore during and after the First World War, when economists and policy-makers addressed themselves to the question of the parity at which countries which had left the gold standard because of wartime upheavals should re-adhere to it. (It was at the time taken as axiomatic that a return to 'normalcy' required a resumption of pre-war international moneary arrangements.)

Since, in equilibrium, the level of prices in different regions of a country tends to be more or less equalized, it may seem to constitute a minor and uncontroversial extension of this observation to conclude that international payments will be in equilibrium when international prices (i.e., the relative purchasing power of different currencies) have been similarly equalized.

This simple proposition bristles with practical difficulties, however, when an attempt is made to infer equilibrium exchange rates from price indices. In a world of free trade, without transport costs or other imperfections, it would be impossible for prices of the same commodity to be different in different countries. The mere equalization of prices for traded goods does not ensure trade equilibrium, however. If the price level of nontraded goods in country A is higher than that in country B, it will be more profitable to employ factors of production in A to produce nontraded goods; while it will be more profitable to employ factors of production in B to produce traded goods. The disequilibrium in trade flows will reveal itself not in a disparity of prices of traded goods but in a disparity of supplies of such goods called forth from the respective countries at the given world price.

The foregoing may seem obvious and straightforward, but it was not so to some of those who attempted to use purchasing power parity concepts in the 1920s. When the British pound had appreciated just prior to its return to the gold standard in 1925, the advisers of the then Chancellor, Mr Churchill, observed that the wholesale price index in Britain stood at about its 1913 relationship with that of the United States and they concluded that it was therefore safe to resume convertibility at the prevailing exchange rate. What they overlooked was that, by using an index heavily weighted with traded goods, observed prices were bound to conform with those in other countries, whatever the underlying disequilibrium. As Keynes noted[5] 'since the systems of weighting and the grades and qualities of the selected articles are various, there has been just that degree of discrepancy to make the theory seem prima facie interesting'.

In order to tell observers something useful about equilibrium exchange rates, therefore, the purchasing power parity doctrine must be able to say something not only about the prices of traded goods, but also about relative costs and prices for goods which are *not* traded internationally and which *can* vary among countries. To do this, it relies on the proposition that traded and nontraded goods are competing sources of employment for factors of production. A change in their relative price will therefore induce factors to switch from one form of employment to the other. If the technological constraints on production remain more or less fixed, and tastes and preferences do not change, then the relative price of traded and nontraded goods in each country will remain constant. Since traded goods prices are, by hypothesis, equalized across countries, this means that prices of nontraded goods must also be equalized if the flows of goods entering world trade are to remain the same.

To state the conditions under which purchasing power parity will identify an equilibrium exchange rate suggests immediately that in many cases the proposition will not hold. For one thing, the differential in technological progress between traded and nontraded goods industries need not be the same in all countries. For another, the pattern of demand may change. Either will necessitate changes in relative prices between products so as to maintain a balance between supply and demand. If relative prices are changing at different rates in different counties—which is only to be expected since the changes in their tastes are independent, as also may be the technological possibilities they face—then purchasing power parity will not hold. A common international price level for traded goods will require a different change in domestic prices to maintain unchanged incentives to produce for export.

In addition, there are other reasons why price levels in different countries may not be equalized. International trade is never costless, and frequently transportation and distribution will add substantially to prices. Then tariffs, quotas and subsidies interfere with the working of the price mechanism.

For all these reasons, it is not surprising that empirical attempts at verification of the basic purchasing power parity postulate have had very mixed results.[6]

Despite the obvious limitations of purchasing power parity, there is probably an important residual category of situation in which it has analytic value. When price changes result primarily from inflation or deflation (i.e., money has changed in value against all other commodities, with little change in the relative value of commodities other than money) then it is reasonable to expect purchasing power parity to be useful. In equilibrium, the adjustment of an exchange rate to compensate for this kind of inflation should not affect the relative prices of real goods, and should be large relative to the adjustment required to compensate for change in the slow-moving factors: technology and tastes.

Although there are therefore circumstances in which the purchasing power parity approach has validity, and can be a useful guide to policy, it is probably more often the case that changes in the general level of prices are accompanied (and perhaps superseded in importance) by changes in relative prices. For this reason, more powerful techniques than mere comparison of relative price levels have been sought to explain changes in trade flows.

The Elasticities Approach

The elasticities approach represented an attempt to find an analysis which would have more practical value in policy decisions than the price-specie-flow mechanism, or purchasing power parity. The gold standard mechanism placed the entire responsibility for balance of payments adjustment on prices and production in the domestic economy—an equilibrium tendency which was felt to be too slow and uncertain in its effect. On the other hand, the purchasing power parity approach, particularly in light of the unfortunate consequences of Britain's return to the gold standard in 1925, was recognized by the economics profession to be too simplistic to constitute a satisfactory explanation by itself.

The elasticities approach was developed during the inter-war period when economists addressed the question of whether, and under what conditions, exchange rate changes would restore balance of payments equilibrium. The analysis usually assumed that traded goods were in almost perfectly elastic supply—not an unreasonable assumption given the underemployment and excess capacity which characterized that period. With the further assumption that product prices were fixed in domestic currency, this meant that changes in balance of the payments were entirely determined by the responsiveness of the demand for traded goods to changes in their price.

The consequence of this view of the balance of payments adjustment mechanism was that attention was naturally focused on the exchange rate as the means of adjustment. Analysis was directed at estimating the relevant demand elasticities and specifying the conditions under which a devaluation would improve the balance of payments, and by how much.

Devaluation reduces the foreign currency price of exports and thus stimulates purchases by foreigners; at the same time it tends to increase the domestic price of imports, thus restraining domestic spending on foreign goods. A revaluation, of course, has precisely the opposite effect, but in both cases, the consequences for the *volume* of goods traded are unambiguous. When it comes to judging the effects of an exchange rate change on the balance of trade, however, it is necessary to express flows of goods in value rather than volume and thus to use a single numeraire currency. If this is the foreign currency, then the value of imports will certainly be reduced, since their price (in foreign currency) will not rise, and their volume will drop. The value of exports may go up or down, however, depending on whether the higher volume of sales is sufficient to offset the reduced price in foreign currency. If the elasticity of demand for exports is greater than one, then export receipts will go up, in foreign currency terms, following a devaluation. With perfectly elastic supplies of tradable goods, a devaluation will only improve the balance of payments when the sum of the elasticity of demand for imports and the elasticity of demand for the country's exports is greater than one.

The elasticities approach to the balance of payments suggests exchange rate adjustment as the most potent (though not the only) mechanism of adjustment, and suggests the computation of demand elasticities as the analytical tool by which policies in the exchange field can be chosen so as to conform with equilibrium. The difficulty with the elasticities approach, however, is that it implicitly assumes that domestic prices are stabilized, and that there are no obstacles to channeling additional resources into production for export or import substitution.

This is a reflection of the partial equilibrium nature of an analysis of elasticities. Partial equilibrium analysis ignores the feedback effects of a price change in one good on real incomes and therefore on the demand for goods in general. Where one is interested in the market conditions for a product which represents a very small proportion of total demand and output, this is perhaps not very serious. In the case of foreign trade, however, the omission is much more troublesome.

If an exchange rate change succeeds in its objective of improving the balance of payments, it will presumably increase domestic incomes in export and import competing industries. But these higher incomes will affect the payments situation directly, through enlarging the demand for importables, and indirectly by adding to overall demand and thus tending to push up prices. As Harry Johnson notes, this prompts the question 'why doesn't the expansion of income and therefore demand go on and on until the initial improvement in the trade balance is exactly offset by reductions in exports and increases in imports induced by the cumulative expasion of income kicked off by the initial improvement?'[7]

Because of the partial equilibrium nature of the elasticities approach, its use was more suited to the inter-war period, characterized by worldwide depression, than to the post-war world characterized initially by chronic shortage of supply, and then by approximate equilibrium at full employment.

Faced by the problem of giving the elasticities approach meaningful empirical content in a world of overfull employment, analysts developed refinements designed to calculate total rather than partial elasticities. In other words, instead of merely considering demand elasticities for imports and exports, supply elasticities had also to be taken into account, and also the pattern of substitutions generated by the change in relative prices. The difficulty with this approach to making theory more realistic was that the elasticities themselves depended on demand conditions. In a fully employed economy, it is clearly harder to divert resources into the balance of payments than in an economy where there is a substantial measure of spare capacity.

The Absorption Approach

In the immediate post-World War II period, the failure of many European economies to respond more vigorously to devaluation was initially ascribed to low elasticities of demand for their exports. (The economists who propounded this theory were known as 'elasticity pessimists'.) Later, however, alternative explanations were offered, which were general equilibrium in character and exploited the national income relationships developed by Keynes. The balance of payments implications of Keynesian analysis were first drawn explicitly by Harrod and repeated by Sidney Alexander.[8] Their analysis started from the national income accounting identity in which income is equal to expenditure, *plus* the balance of payments surplus (or *minus* the deficit):

$$Y = C + I + X - M$$

where:

Y = Income
C = Consumption
I = Investment
X = Exports
M = Imports

Turning this equation around, the balance of payments can be seen as equal to domestic income minus domestic expenditure.

$$X - M = Y - (C + I)$$

This was not in itself a new discovery, based as it was on Keynesian national income analysis. But such a presentation did suggest that a more fruitful approach to explaining what was happening to the current account of the balance of payments ought to run in terms of what was happening to domestic income and domestic expenditure (or absorption). A devaluation could not be effective unless it acted either to increase output, and therefore the resources available for export, or to decrease absorption. The lesson for the world economy in the 1950s, where there was, in general, very little unused capacity, was that devaluations to be successful had to be accompanied by measures to restrain domestic demand.

Devaluation in itself will not be neutral with respect to its effect on the pressure of demand. On the whole, it may be expected to increase the pressure of demand (at least as far as price effects are concerned); but in order to determine the extent to which this effect should be accepted or offset, it is necessary to examine some of the other consequences of devaluation. First among these is the effect of devaluation in activating idle resources. Where there are idle resources, devaluation will of course have a direct favourable effect on the balance of payments, and the additional income generated in this way will have second round multiplier effect that will raise domestic income still further, and permit an increase in domestic consumption.

Another influence of devaluation on absorption occurs through the terms of trade. Since devaluation usually results in turning the terms of trade against the devaluing country, it will tend to reduce real income and to that extent reduce absorption (particularly the absorption of tradable goods whose prices will have risen.)

The implication of the absorption approach for policy formation is to place much more emphasis on the level of domestic demand as a determinant of the current account than on relative price levels. To this extent, it tends to emphasize demand management as the principal instrument of adjustment rather than exchange rate policy. Although the foregoing statement is perhaps an exaggeration of the position of Alexander and others who favour the absorption approach, it does indicate one of the practical dangers of relying purely on policies designed to influence domestic absorption.

Merely reducing the level of domestic demand does not guarantee that the resources thus released will be redirected into the balance of payments. Initially, the main result is simply to reduce overall output, with the balance of payments improving only to the extent of the import component of the marginal output. Only gradually are unemployed resources reabsorbed in a way beneficial to the balance of payments. This gradual process requires the transfer of factors of production into new employment, and the creation of demand for their product. The creation of such demand relies either on the pre-existence of unfilled export demand, or on the effect of slack capacity in reducing domestic price levels relative to those of foreign competitors.

The caveats just expressed suggest a synthesis of the elasticities and absorption approaches from the point of view of policy prescription. Direct action on price levels (via exchange rate policy) may be necessary to stimulate the changes in demand necessary to improve the balance of payments. At the same time, domestic demand management should operate on domestic absorption levels so as to free the necessary resources to meet the higher external demand. Neither policy, if applied independently, is sufficiently powerful or quick acting to achieve the results which are possible when both are employed together.

The Monetary Approach

The monetary approach to the balance of payments is similar in spirit to the absorption approach, but extends it to provide an explanation of the overall balance of payments, instead of just the current account. This extension enables the balance of payments to be viewed not in terms of the demand for and supply of goods, services and capital assets, but in terms of the demand for and supply of money which is, after all, the other side of the coin.

The monetary approach is an outgrowth of the monetary (or Chicago school) view of income determination, and has gained a considerable academic following in recent years. It is not a new approach, however, either intellectually or in practical terms. In substance, it is basically a refined and updated version of Hume's price-specie-flow mechanism. It also is consistent with the policies developed earlier under financial programmes of balance of payments stabilization employed by the International Monetary Fund, in that organization's consultations with its member countries.

The monetary approach to the balance of payments rests on two basic empirical propositions. In the first place, the demand for money in an economy is assumed to be a stable function of a few variables. Secondly, the price of traded goods is assumed—at least for a small economy—to be largely exogenous, as is the level of economic output. Taken together, these assumptions imply that in an open economy, the authorities cannot control the quantity of money held by domestic residents. If the quantity of money is below the desired stock, given the level of output and other determining factors, economic units will seek to acquire additional money balances. Individually, they will do this by restricting their expenditure relatively to their income, and collectively, the economy as a whole will restore equilibrium by running a balance of payments surplus and attracting money from abroad.

The process of restoring equilibrium between the demand for money and the available stock of money balances can, under the monetary approach paradigm, be achieved without any sacrifice in the level of economic output. This is because prices of traded goods are assumed to be given, so that producers can sell as much as they produce at an exogenously given price. All that domestic demand management policy (i.e., credit creation policy) can achieve is to affect the level of domestic demand, and thus the size of the foreign trade balance.

The foregoing can be easily expressed in mathematical notation. The demand for money is a stable function of income and the rate of interest:

$$M_d = f(Y, r)$$

The supply of money consists of money created domestically, plus money inflows from abroad (i.e., the surplus on the balance of payments)

$$M_s = D + R$$

Since, in equilibrium the demand for money will equal the supply,

$$M_s = M_d$$

the balance of payments (or the change in reserves) can be expressed as:

$$R = M_d - D$$

In other words, any discrepancy between the volume of money balances demanded, and the stock of money created by the authorities will be eliminated by a reserve movement generated through a balance of payments surplus or deficit.

An interesting and novel finding from the above approach is that economic growth will, *ceteris paribus*, improve the overall balance of payments, since it tends to increase the demand for money vis-à-vis the domestically created supply of money.

Although the monetary approach to balance of payments determination falls in the mainstream of the Hume price-specie-flow theory, it involves several refinements which are particularly significant from the point of view of policy formation in present-day circumstances. Most importantly, modern theory distinguishes between money of domestic origin and money of external origin. In the scheme of things described by Hume, money consisted entirely of precious metals, and the only means of acquiring (or losing) precious metals was through a surplus or deficit in the balance of payments. Thus at all times Hume saw a tendency for the balance of payments to tend towards equilibrium.[9]

In the modern approach, it is recognized that a fractional reserve banking system, on a fiduciary base, has the capacity to create or destroy deposits independently of the availability of money flows from abroad. What is given is the demand for real money balances. What is left to be determined within the system is the extent to which this demand will be satisfied from internal sources, through credit creation in the domestic banking system, or from external sources through surplus or deficit in the balance of payments.

The implication of the monetary approach is that the only way (but a very powerful way) in which the monetary authorities can exercise control over the balance of payments is through limiting the rate of growth of domestic credit, so that domestic economic units will cut back their expenditure relative to their income, in order to rebuild their money balances.

It is easy to see that the monetary approach is quite compatible with the absorption approach, and, indeed, that it is essentially the other side of the same coin. The monetary approach stresses the need for equality in the demand for and supply of money, while the absorption approach stresses the need for equilibrium in the market for domestic output. The monetary approach is perhaps a more general theory, since it explains the overall balance of payments (including the capital account) while the absorption approach is concerned mainly with explaining the current account.

The main criticism which can be levelled against the monetary approach is that, like the absorption approach, it deals in long-run equilibrium forces which, however powerful they may be in explaining secular tendencies, are of limited usefulness in analyzing the short and medium-term developments of primary interest to policy makers. An example of this shortcoming is the demand-for-money function. It is readily documented that the demand-for-money function exhibits remarkable stability over fairly long historical time periods. This is strong evidence that a change in the money supply sets in train powerful forces tending to restore the basic ratio of money balances to incomes. However, over the short-term time horizon of primary interest to policy-makers, the demand for money exhibits less stability. Thus an expansion or contraction in the money supply may initially have its main effect in causing a change in the velocity of circulation of money rather than in levels of income and expenditure.

Another difficulty lies in the likelihood that fluctuations in domestic output will have to be interposed between changes in the money supply and changes in the overall balance of payments. Unless adjustments in the prices and volumes of traded goods occur frictionlessly, monetary policy will first have to affect domestic demand, before the resultant changes in prices and availability of traded goods (and assets) affect the balance of payments.[10]

As a practical matter, however, it seems unlikely that governments will feel able to refrain from intervention to counter the business cycle, and to improve the balance of payments. This being so, they are likely to feel some impatience with policy prescriptions which rely only on long-run equilibrium tendencies. So although monetary and budgetary policies will undoubtedly be used to influence balance of payments deficits, it is unlikely that action through the exchange rate will be abandoned.

The 'New Cambridge' View

The 'New Cambridge' view of balance of payments determination is a by-product of an attempt to explain domestic economic cycles, and has so far been expouned in only a limited number of contributions by economists at Cambridge University. Although the proponents of this view are not monetarists, it resembles the monetary approach to the balance of payments, in that it postulates a stable demand by the private sector of the economy for a particular category of financial assets. The difference lies in the fact that monetarists emphasize the stability of the demand for money, while the New Cambridge school asserts a stability in the demand for net financial worth.

Therefore, while monetarists view the overall balance of payments as being determined by whether the supply of domestically created money is greater or less than the increase in the demand to hold money, the New Cambridge school looks at the current account, and sees it as being determined by whether the public sector's deficit is greater or less than the desire of the private sector to accumulate net financial wealth.

Since it concentrates on the implications of certain national income accounting identities for the current account, the New Cambridge view also has affinities with the absorption approach. Where it differs, however, is in its assumption that the private sector's net absorption is basically stable, so that balance of payments fluctuations are primarily caused by swings in the public sector's net financial position.

One aspect in which the policy prescriptions of monetarists and New Cambridge economists coincide is in the danger of trying to fine-tune the economy over the business cycle. Because of the lags and uncertainties that exist, both schools believe that official counter-cyclical policy has often been counter-productive and has tended to inhibit the natural stabilizing forces within the economy. Monetarists have therefore advocated a policy of stable growth in the money supply over time, while the New Cambridge school advocates a stable budgetary position (though not necessarily a *balanced* budget). The proper choice of this policy target, these economists believe, would ensure balance of payments equilibrium at a stable exchange rate—with monetarists focusing on the overall balance, and the New Cambridge school on the current balance.

[1] This distinction has been made most clearly by J.E. Meade. See his *The Balance of Payments*, O.U.P., London, 1951.
[2] See, for example, Harrod, R.F., *International Trade,* Cambridge, 1939 and Alexander, S.S., 'Effects of devaluation on a trade balance', IMF *Staff Papers*, April 1952.
[3] Reproduced in David Hume *Writings on Economics*, edited by Eugene Rotwein, Nelson, 1955.
[4] Walter Bagehot, *Lombard Street*, London, 1867.
[5] Keynes, J.M., *A Treatise on Money*, Vol. 1, London, 1930. See also Keynes' 'The Misleading of Mr Churchill' reprinted in *Essays in Persuasion*, New York, 1932.
[6] For a thorough review of these studies, see Officer, L.H., 'The Purchasing power parity theory of exchange rates: a review article', IMF *Staff Papers* March 1976.
[7] Johnson, H.G., *Money and the Balance of Payments*, University of Alabama Distinguished Lecture Series, October 23, 1975.
[8] Harrod and Alexander, *opera cit.*
[9] Strictly speaking, this was only true for a country which did not produce specie, or absorb specie in non-monetary uses. These countries would have to run a deficit or surplus on their non-specie trade to offset their continuing absorption of production of precious metals.
[10] In fairness, it should be noted here that many Chicago school economists would not agree with the implication here that the equilibrium tendencies work only in the long run. This, however, is an empirical question on which the available evidence is not conclusive.

Selected Further Reading

Alexander, S.S., 'Effects of devaluation on a trade balance', IMF *Staff Papers*, April 1952.
Cripps, F., Godley, W., and Fetherston, M., *Evidence Submitted to Public Expenditure Committee, Ninth Report from the Expenditure Committee*, 1974, H.C. 328, H.M.S.O., London.
Frenkel, J.A. and Johnson, H.G. (eds), *The Monetary Approach to the Balance of Payments*, Allen and Unwin, London, 1976
Johnson, H.G. 'The monetary approach to the balance of payments', in his *Further Essays in Monetary Economics*, Allen and Unwin, London, 1972.
Meade, J.E., *The Balance of Payments*, Oxford University Press, London, 1951.
Polak, J.J., 'Monetary analysis of income formation and payments problems', IMF *Staff Papers*, 1957.
Robinson, Joan, 'The pure theory of international trade', *Review of Economic Studies*, 1946–47.
Whitman, Marina, 'Global monetarism and the monetary approach to the balance of payments', *Brookings Papers in Economic Activity, No.3,* Brookings Institution, Washington, D.C. 1975.

4 Fixed and Flexible Exchange Rates

Introduction

Chapter 3 has dealt with the various theoretical approaches to analyzing and explaining developments in the balance of payments. Since the restoration and maintenance of balance of payments equilibrium is the primary objective of the adjustment process, this discussion has important relevance for policy decisions concerning international monetary arrangements.

Policies concerning adjustment have both an international and a national dimension. Internationally, the problem is to design a set of rules and practices which facilitate adjustment and share its burdens in an acceptable and equitable manner. Nationally, the problem is one of choosing the mix of policies (within the set that is internationally permitted) which minimizes the domestic costs of achieving adjustment. This chapter and the next will consider the former question which concerns essentially the nature of the exchange rate regime, and the constraints placed on countries in their choice of adjustment measures. Chapter 6 will concentrate on the policy choices facing individual countries.

It is convenient to begin with the polar cases of rigidly fixed and freely floating rates. These are not realistic alternatives, of course, but they constitute a useful analytical starting point. Later in this chapter, we will consider the desirability of regional currency groupings in 'optimum currency areas'. In the next chapter attention is directed to the various forms of controlled flexibility that have been tried or proposed. These include, *inter alia*, the adjustable par value system of Bretton Woods, and the managed floating instituted in 1973.

Fixed Exchange Rates

The case for fixed exchange rates between different national currencies is basically an extension of the case for a unified money within a single economy. The use of money with a fixed value facilitates trade, avoids the costs and inefficiencies of barter, and promotes intertemporal contracts. It is well recognized that the monetization of national economies has played an essential role in the growth of production and in social progress.

When one country's currency has a fixed value in terms of those of its trading partners, the economic result is the same as if one currency was used in all countries.[1] Thus the geographical area within which the special functions of money can be provided is enlarged. In this way, international trade and exchange are promoted, thus contributing to an increase in welfare, both directly through the improved allocation of resources and indirectly as they help to spread technological change and to speed productivity growth. Saving and investment are encouraged, since savers in one country can place financial resources at the disposal of investors in another, without exposing themselves to the risk that the value of their investment will be affected by exchange rate changes.

A second virtue which is sometimes claimed for a fixed exchange rate system is that it imposes a discipline on countries to follow responsible financial policies, because of the need to maintain balance of payments equilibrium. Excessively inflationary policies will drive domestic prices up, thus making local producers uncompetitive in international markets and causing a deterioration in the balance of payments. Excessively deflationary policies, on the other hand, will damp down the demand for imports and perhaps generate a fall in domestic prices relative to those abroad, thus causing an improvement in the balance of payments. Although there can be temporary or cyclical price divergencies between countries in the short run, eventually the price level in all countries adhering to a fixed exchange rate standard (at least the price level of traded goods) must move in broadly the same manner.

It may be asked why conformity in price level developments is considered an advantage. In itself, there is no special virtue in constraining a country to achieve any particular price level, particularly if for domestic political reasons it would prefer to have a somewhat different emphasis in its policies from that of its trading partners. However, it will be readily appreciated that there is a risk of economic considerations becoming subordinated to political necessities, particularly in democracies where governments are subject to dismissal when they lose popular support. The advocates of fixed rates see the discipline of this regime as a useful safeguard against the temptations of mismanagement to which finance ministers might otherwise fall prey.

This argument can be put in a more positive way too. It may be the case that a particular policy prescription is desired by the authorities of a country, but is difficult to implement because of lack of public support. In such circumstances, the need to defend a fixed parity may serve as a focus to rally public support for unpopular policy. The unsatisfying aspect of this line of argument is that it emphasizes simply the public relations value of a fixed rate, and prompts the question whether a better solution might not be to educate the electorate to the economic facts of life.

Another advantage of rigidly fixed rates, cited most recently by Laffer,[2] is that it allows part of the effects of unexpected disturbances in the domestic economy to be transmitted abroad. Suppose, for example, that because of some mistake of domestic policy, shift in the savings ratio, or in the demand for money, there is an increase in the level of effective demand. In a closed economy, which is already at full employment, this increase in demand causes a rise in the domestic price level. In an open economy under fixed exchange rates, however, part of the excess demand 'leaks out' in a balance of payments deficit. This reduces the excess demand for domestic output, and, by reducing the domestic money supply, also tends to offset the effect of the basic disturbance. Thus the adjustment problem in the country where the disturbance originally occurred is minimized.

The corollary of the foregoing is less beneficial, however. While a country may be protected by fixed exchange rates from the full consequences of domestic disturbances and policy mistakes, it has to bear a share of the burden of the disturbances and mistakes of others. For to the extent that excess demand 'leaks out' of the country where it was originally created, it 'leaks in' (via a balance of payments surplus) to that country's trading partners. Whether it is more desirable to be protected against your own or against others' mistakes depends of course on who makes the most mistakes; but from the point of view of equity, it would seem preferable to design a system in which each country had the maximum incentive to avoid policy mistakes itself.

In order for the argument made by Laffer to have validity, therefore, it must be demonstrated that disturbances generated abroad are potentially less damaging than those of domestic origin. This will be the case if foreign disturbances, stemming as they do from a number of different sources, tend to cancel each other out. Even if they do not, there may be advantage in spreading the impact of unexpected developments if countries in general are more able to absorb a series of small disturbances than a single large one. In such cases, the consequences of policy errors abroad for a country adhering to a fixed rate may not be all that great; while the consequences of 'bottling up' domestic errors by flexible rates may be much more serious.

In practice, however, the biggest question mark surrounding the operation of the fixed exchange rate system relates to its ability to ensure the smooth elimination of balance of payments disequilibria. In principle, this adjustment can be achieved by the manipulation of domestic demand. To take the example of a balance of payments deficit: a deficit would lead to an outflow of money from the domestic economy, which would itself exercise a dampening effect on demand. This automatic mechanism (which was the essence of adjustment under the gold standard) can be supplemented in a managed system by discretionary policy measures also intended to reduce domestic demand and free domestic resources for exports and import substitution.

The practical question is whether this adjustment can in fact work smoothly enough to satisfy the domestic objectives of the authorities in the field of full employment and stable prices. It is easy to see that merely reducing domestic demand does not by itself cause the freed resources to be devoted to exports. Resources may have to be switched to export production, and a demand has to be generated in export markets. In the case of manufactured products, the price elesticity of demand is not infinite. Producing more does not ensure that more can be sold. Customers must be attracted by lower price, shorter delivery, better quality or some other positive aspect. In an economy whose price mechanism functioned according to the classical precepts, these incentives might be created relatively easily. A reduction in domestic demand would tend to leave products unsold, which would immediately cause producers to lower prices; the same would be true for workers who, finding no demand for their labour at the existing wage rate would accept work at a lower wage. Lower wages and prices would promote exports and restrain imports, thus tending to restore balance of payments equilibrium, without involving more than frictional unemployment of factors of production.

In fact, however, for a variety of institutional reasons, which are well known and need not be repeated here, prices of both finished products and factors of production tend to be sticky, particularly in a downward direction. Thus a reduction in domestic demand in the first instance reduces imports only to the extent of the import content of output not produced. The rest of the reduction in demand is reflected in lower domestic output. Over time, of course, the lower level of domestic output will have its effect on the domestic price level, and hence upon export competitiveness, and this will tend to restore employment and production to their previous level. Meanwhile, however, the economy will be operating below capacity.

For a surplus country, balance of payments adjustment under fixed exchange rates has to take place through an increase in inflation. This need not involve any immediate direct cost in terms of lost real output, but it will require the country to accept more rapid inflation that it wishes on domestic grounds.

In so far as this undesired inflation is also unforeseen, which is likely, it will result in an unanticipated transfer of wealth from creditors to debtors. This imposes social costs, since it causes income distribution to diverge from the desired pattern; and it will probably also result in resource misallocation, since investment decisions will be made on the basis of wrong forecasts concerning relative prices and real interest rates. Lastly, if the surplus country sees this additional inflationary impetus as being liable to set off a wage price spiral which it is difficult to stop, it will be additionally reluctant to accept this means of adjustment.

This brief review of adjustment problems under fixed rates implies that the costs of such a system depend on several factors:

(1) the degree to which the domestic objectives of various countries diverge. If one country sets a high priority on price stability, even at the cost of some unemployment, while another prefers full employment with inflation, they will find it more painful to have the same policy than if their objectives are more similar.[3]

(2) the extent to which prices have to adjust to compensate for disturbances in the balance of payments. This is largely a question of elasticities. If price elasticities of demand and supply are high, it will take a relatively small change in the domestic price level to have a sizable effect on the balance of payments. On the other hand, if elasticities are low, a much greater price adjustment will be required to eliminate a balance of payments disturbances of given size.

(3) the ease with which prices respond to changes in demand, caused either by monetary conditions or fiscal action. It seems fairly clear that prices are relatively flexible in the upward direction and respond rather rapidly to an intensification of demand pressure. On the other hand, downward price movements can only be accomplished by rather prolonged underemployment of resources.

It was probably the case that in the period in which the gold standard operated, the factors just noted were more favourable to fixed rates than they are now (though it must be recognized that even then adjustment was often painful). In the first place, there was much less opportunity for divergence in the policy objectives of different countries; if only for the simple reason that governments did not have objectives in the field of macroeconomic policy other than preserving the gold convertibility of their currencies. The money supply was allowed to be influenced by balance of payments flows and the availability of gold; and although banking systems were able to create credit to some multiple of available reserves, there was little awareness as to if and how the domestic creation of money might be controlled. On the question of management of real output, classical economics taught that full employment was the natural state of the economy, and that cyclical unemployment was essentially a frictional problem due to residual imperfections in the market mechanism.

In addition to this harmony (by default) in economic objectives, it is also probably true that prices in the nineteenth century were more flexible, and elasticities of demand greater. A larger proportion of total demand was represented by products, such as foodstuffs, for which there were relatively perfect markets in which prices were flexible downwards as well as upwards. Furthermore, the institutional rigidities in the price mechanism, caused in part by monopolistic tendencies in both business and labour organization, were, despite some striking counter-examples, probably fewer in the nineteenth century. Lastly, the kinds of products entering world trade were generally of a more homogeneous nature than today, which would lead one to expect that similar products coming from different countries had a higher measure of substitutability (i.e., a greater price elasticity of demand) than now.

A system of rigidly fixed rates in the circumstances of the 1970s would undoubtedly run into severe difficulties. There is a reluctance to be committed to the harmonization of domestic policy objectives; prices respond only in a limited fashion to fluctuations in the pressure of demand, and elasticities of demand in international trade have in general turned out to be quite low, at least in the short run. For these reasons, a *rigidly* fixed exchange rate regime has never been advanced as a serious possibility in any of the recent discussions on reform of the international monetary system.

Free floating

The opposite pole to rigidly fixed rates is a system in which exchange rates are left free to be determined by the interplay of supply and demand in the foreign exchange market. In such a system the government does not intervene in this market, nor does it have any need to hold foreign exchange reserves.

The principal advantage of a system of free floating is that it avoids the problems of financing balance of payments disequilibria inherent in a fixed exchange rate system. Since the price of a currency is left free to adjust continuously so as to equate private demand and supply, an overall balance of payments deficit or surplus by definition cannot occur. There is therefore no need for central banks to maintain reserves of international liquidity, and no need for governments to formulate explicit objectives with regard to their balance of payments.

The absence of any problem of financing does not, however, mean that countries do not have to adjust to changing economic relationships with the rest of the world. But the needed adjustment is brought about automatically, without any need for discretionary decision-making on the part of governments. If a country's exports are tending to become uncompetitive, say because its price level is rising more rapidly that that of its trading partners, then the resulting tendency for its balance of payments to move into deficit will be checked by a downward movement in the country's exchange rate. There will be no need to manipulate the level of domestic demand for any reasons other than the country's own economic welfare. Similarly, there will be no need to place artificial restraints on trade and payments in order to protect the balance of payments.

Freedom for the exchange rate to move does not, it should be stressed, imply that the rate will in fact fluctuate to any substantial degree (any more than the freedom of the price of Fords to fluctuate against those of Vauxhalls means that the fluctuation will take place). Under normal circumstances most countries may be expected to aim at reasonable stability in their price level. Divergent trends will usually accumulate only gradually over time, so that the underlying exchange rate which will equilibrate the demand and supply for currencies will be steady or slowly changing. Any tendency for a temporary current account disequilibrium, say for seasonal reasons, to cause a substantial movement in exchange rates will be checked by short-term capital movements, stimulated by the possibility of profit when the rate movement is reversed.

The main advantage of floating rates in a world in which governments accept responsibility for the performance of the domestic economy, is that it frees the authorities from the need to make the balance of payments a constraint on policy. A country can therefore undertake whatever measures it deems necessary to achieve its domestic objectives, without having part of the effect 'leak out' abroad, or worrying about the consequences for the balance of payments. Similarly, a government need not have its domestic objectives upset by the imported consequences of deflationary or inflationary policies among its trading partners.

The disadvantage of freely floating exchange rates lies in the possibility that market mechanisms may not achieve an appropriate exchange rate. The exchange rate which achieves equilibrium in the foreign exchange market at any moment in time may not be the one that it is conducive to equilibrium in the medium term. If it is not, then the price mechanism will be giving wrong signals to those who have to make future contracts, or invest now for returns in the future. These wrong signals will result in wrong decisions concerning the allocation of resources.

Although no one would disagree that private markets can be wrong about the relative value of currencies, it can be claimed that in most circumstances, they are usually the best guide there is. Given the uncertainties surrounding the future, governments' views of what constitutes an appropriate medium-term exchange rate are just as likely to be in error as those of private markets. One can even argue that, since government officials do not have to back their judgment with their own money, perhaps less weight should be attached to their views. These objections have force, and should give pause to officials when they propose intervention in opposition to market tendencies. Nevertheless, there may be circumstances when, even after making due allowance for modesty in their own forecasting abilities, the monetary authorities believe the market-determined rate is generating a resource misallocation. One example of such a circumstance might be when market behaviour is based on an expectation of official action which the authorities know to be false. Another might be when an exchange rate is bid down or up because of risks which affect individual speculators, but which should be ignored from the view point of the economy as a whole. Still another might be when private transactors do not have sufficient resources to stabilize the exchange rate at an equilibrium level; or, saying much the same thing, when they require the probability of sizable profit to induce them to commit funds to a particular currency.

In any event, the exchange rate is an economic variable which has such fundamental importance for the working of an economy, and for domestic objectives in the field of prices, employment and income distribution, that democratically elected governments cannot easily ignore it. Furthermore, since an exchange rate involves two parties, countries cannot be unconcerned about the policies of their trading partners. It is now well accepted that exchange rates are matters of international concern.

Another problem in the operation of a freely floating exchange rate system is defining just what free floating means. Non-intervention in the foreign exchange market turns out to be a definition whose apparent simplicity is deceptive in practice. The fact that governments do not intervene in the foreign exchange market directly does not mean that their actions in other financial markets do not affect conditions in that for foreign exchange. After all, central banks, when they intervene in the domestic money market, recognize and expect that their actions will have repercussions across the whole range of domestic markets for real and financial assets. It is not surprising that such intervention should also have an impact, and quite a sizable one, on the market in which domestic money is exchanged for foreign currency.

Indeed, one can go further. The whole range of government policies affects prices, levels of demand, and the distribution of expenditure between saving and consumption. This latter distribution is particularly important because, as has been noted in the previous chapter, changes in absorption affect the current account. If domestic saving runs ahead of domestic investment, this means the country concerned is a net investor overseas. The outflow of capital will tend to force down its exchange rate, which in turn will help to generate the current account surplus which pays for the foreign investment. Although all this may happen without direct intervention in the foreign exchange market, it cannot be said to be independent of government policies. There is no guarantee that the consequences of policies adopted by one country will be economically desirable or politically acceptable for its trading partners. Politically, countries may be unwilling to see their domestic industries passing into foreign hands because of decisions taken elsewhere. Economically, the expansion of one country's export industries, and contraction of another's may impose real resource costs particularly if it has to be reversed at some future date.

A final problem in the operation of floating rates is the fear that speculative activity will not in fact be stabilizing, but will lead to substantial rate fluctuations. Proponents of this view point to the experiences of the 1930s, and more recently, the developments in exchange markets since the introduction of floating in 1973. These fluctuations, it is claimed, lead to additional uncertainties in trade, and therefore to reduce the level of trade, and the benefits associated with the international division of labour.

An objection to drawing such conclusions from previous experience is that floating rates have usually been implemented when a disturbed situation has led to the breakdown of a fixed rate regime. It is therefore difficult to disentangle the effects on trade and exchange markets stemming from the original disturbance from those directly attributable to floating. As Milton Friedman has noted ' ... floating exchange rates have often been adopted as a last resort by countries experiencing financial crises when all other devices have failed. That is a major reason why they have such a bad reputation.'[4]

It is reasonable to conclude that neither rigidly fixed nor freely floating rates are a realistic likelihood in the foreseeable future. The reasons for this are political as well as economic, but they are nonetheless compelling. It is now necessary, therefore, to consider possible exchange regimes which combine elements of fixity and of flexibility. In the next chapter, we will discuss the numerous proposals which provide a greater or lesser measure of controlled flexibility for all currencies. Here we consider the proposal to have fixed rates between certain currencies (optimum currency areas) with free floating between currency blocs.

Optimum Currency Areas

Perhaps the simplest way of developing the case for optimum currency areas is as follows: it is accepted that a single currency promotes specialization, trade and economic integration will outweigh the costs if factors of production are sufficiently mobile to ease adjustment difficulties when costs in one area of the country diverge from those elsewhere. Nation states, however, were not designed primarily in order to derive the maximum benefit from a unitary currency. Thus it may be the case that benefits can be reaped from widening (or conceivably, narrowing) the area within which a single currency is used. How far such a process should be extended is essentially an empirical question. It is a matter of trading off the advantages of currency union in promoting integration against the disadvantages of fixed exchange rates in constraining the adjustment mechanism and thus imposing additional adjustment costs. The analysis of optimum currency areas must therefore proceed in terms of an analysis of the factors which go to make up these advantages and disadvantages.

The advantages of using a single currency are greater the greater the amount of trade between the countries or areas concerned (strictly, this should be the greater the *trading potential*, rather than the amount of trade conducted). The need to convert one currency into another at an exchange rate whose future value cannot be predicted with certainty is an inconvenience (even if it is no more) which discourages international specialization and trade. The greater the field of production to which such an inconvenience applies, or could apply, the greater the real economic costs of maintaining separate currencies.

The disadvantage of a single currency lies mainly in the fact that an external disequilibrium of one member of the currency union has to be corrected by changes in its domestic supply and demand conditions, and cannot be aided by changes in the exchange rate. This will add to the real 'costs' of balance of payments adjustment. How much it will add will depend in part on the degree of price rigidity. The more rigid price levels are, the more difficult (and thus the more costly in real terms) will be adjustment without an exchange rate change. Several factors bear on the ease with which a payments disequilibrium can be eliminated by a country observing a fixed exchange rate. One is the share of tradeable goods in total output. The greater this is, the easier it will be to divert marginal output to alternative uses to meet the requirements of payments balance. A related consideration is the mobility of factors of production. If factors are free to move within a geographical area to regions where their marginal product is higher, there will be less need to use exchange rate changes to equalize the value of marginal product. Thirdly, a high degree of financial integration among regions means that payments disequilibria within the area can be more easily financed, meaning that real adjustment can be spread over a larger period.

The factors which facilitate adjustment between countries which have reasonably highly integrated trade structures and fixed exchange rates would tend to add to the cost of adjustment through exchange rate flexibility. The more open a country is, the less able are its monetary authorities to influence relative prices through devaluation. This is because a given exchange rate change will tend to be 'passed through' in domestic prices to a greater degree, thus resulting in more price instability for a given degree of control over the balance of payments. Furthermore, if a large foreign trade sector can be taken to imply a lack of domestic substitutes (something that may not always be true), then the volume of imports will probably not be very responsive to changes in price.

The foregoing implies that countries which trade extensively with each other and make use of the same capital market would benefit from coming together in a common currency area. Areas where the intensiveness of trading relationships is less, and which have essentially separate capital markets, would on the other hand benefit from retaining flexibility between their currencies.

This conclusion is strengthened by the fact that a common currency area implies a common monetary policy within the area. In countries which are highly integrated with respect to trade or factor mobility, fluctuations in the level of business activity are naturally highly correlated. There is therefore less need for independent monetary policy and a better case for the uniform discipline of a common currency. In countries whose trading interdependence is at a lower level, there is much less reason to expect them to experience the business cycle in unison, and therefore there are higher costs associated with abandoning monetary independence.

This line of reasoning has led the proponents of optimum currency areas to suggest that continental Europe and the Western Hemisphere should form the two main currency areas in the world, with the United Kingdom and Japan, perhaps with associated countries, as subsidiary blocs. Other countries would presumably align themselves with whichever major bloc was closer to them in trading relationships. It is often assumed that a development along these lines would lead to a very limited number of currency areas, perhaps eventually only two. This overlooks the fact that many smaller nations trade heavily with a variety of major countries; and it would be difficult and perhaps undesirable for them to align themselves with one bloc, and thus constrain their monetary policy to follow that of the rest of the bloc. It also overlooks the fact, pointed out by Kenen,[5] that smaller economies are often less diversified, and therefore more likely to find themselves in disequilibrium as a result of special factors not shared by a currency group as a whole. Where this is the case, it may be that small open economies have an even greater need for the monetary independence that only a separate exchange rate can give.

Because participation in a common currency area involves a considerable sacrifice of national sovereignty, a certain harmony of objectives in the monetary area is highly desirable. As Tower and Willett state:

'Perhaps of primary importance for a successful currency area with a less than perfect internal adjustment mechanism is that there be a reasonable degree of compatibility between the member countries' attitudes toward growth, inflation and unemployment and their abilities to "trade-off" between these objectives'.[6]

Even an initial harmony in overall economic objectives will seldom be sufficient to ensure that the realized level of economic activity and rate of growth is satisfactory to all members of the currency area. Because of this, loss of sovereignty in such an important area of economic policy as monetary management will only be accepted if there is some means of protecting those regions of the currency area that are adversely affected by a common policy. If one country within a currency area is experiencing recessionary tendencies at a time when the bloc as a whole does not need expansionary policies, something must be provided to compensate for its loss of the exchange rate instrument. However, satisfactory mechanisms for income redistribution are usually found only within nation states, not between them. The regional programmes of the European Economic Community are one example of compensatory income flows on an international level, but the difculties in making these programmes acceptable to all members of the community serves as a warning against expecting too much from such policies. So long as these other weapons of economic policy are not employed to compensate countries for not being able to adjust their exchange rates, there will be a strong case for making optimum currency areas coterminous with the boundary of political decision-taking in the broader sense.

The beginning of an approach to an optimum currency bloc may be seen in the Common Market. The EEC Narrow Margins Arrangement in effect binds participant countries to hold their currencies within a narrow band of their parity vis-à-vis other participants' currencies. The aim was that barriers to capital flows would be gradually lifted, and the permissible margin of fluctuation gradually reduced, until monetary union was achieved. The difficulties of such an arrangement can be easily seen from the fact that three of the four largest countries in the EEC at one time were outside the narrow margins arrangement. At the same time, negotiations on regional assistance under the Community budget continue to be difficult and protracted. It is to be expected that political cooperation within the EEC will have to proceed to a much more advanced stage before the present joint float can be consolidated and transformed into a genuine common currency.

---

[1] Provided there is no expectation of a change in the relative value of the various currencies.
[2] Laffer, A.B., 'The phenomenon of worldwide inflation: a study in international market integration', in Laffer, A.B. and Meiselman, D. (eds), *The Phenomenon of Worldwide Inflation,* American Enterprise Institute, Washington, D.C. 1975.
[3] A number of economists believe that the trade-off between unemployment and inflation is a false antithesis in the longer term, since expectations are adjusted to take account of the rate of inflation. Since they would consider that there is only one rate of unemployment that is sustainable, without causing accelerating inflation or deflation, they would argue there is no reason for countries to have different objectives for prices. However, it must be noted that there is strong evidence that a trade-off does exist in the short term, and anyway governments certainly act as though they had different objectives in the field of price stability.

[4] Friedman, M., and Roosa, R.V., *The Balance of Payments: Free vs Fixed Exchange Rates,* American Enterprise Institute, Washington, D.C., 1967.
[5] Kenen, P.B., 'The theory of optimum currency areas: an eclectic view', in Mundell, R.A. and Swoboda A.K.(eds), *Monetary Problems of the International Economy,* University of Chicago Press, Chicago, 1969.
[6] Tower, E., and Willett, T.D., 'The concept of optimum currency areas and the choice between fixed and flexible exchange rates', in Halm, G.(ed.), *Approaches to Greater Flexibility,* Princeton, 1970, pp. 407–415.

Selected Further Reading

Friedman, Milton, 'The case for flexible exchange rates' in his *Essays in Positive Economics,* University of Chicago Press, Chicago, 1953.

Friedman, Milton, and Roosa, R.V., *The Balance of Payments: Free vs. Fixed Exchange Rates,* American Enterprise Institute, Washington, D.C., 1967.

Ishiyama, Yoshihide, 'Optimum currency areas: a survey', IMF *Staff Papers,* July 1975.

Katz, S.I., *The Case for the Par Value System, 1972,* Princeton Essays in International Finance No. 92, 1972.

Kenen, P.B., 'The theory of optimum currency areas: an eclectic view', in Mundell, R.A. and Swoboda, A.K. (eds) *Monetary Problems of the International Economy,* University of Chicago Press, Chicago, 1969.

Lanyi, Anthony, *The Case for Floating Exchange Rates Reconsidered,* Princeton Essays in International Finance No. 72, 1969.

Meade, J.E., 'The case for variable exchange rates', *Three Banks Review,* September 1955.

Sohmen, Egon, *Flexible Exchange Rates: Theory and Controversy,* University of Chicago Press, Chicago, 1961.

5 Controlled Flexibility of Exchange Rates

Rigidly fixed exchange rates, and completely free floating, as discussed in the previous chapter, represent the two extremes of fixity and flexibility in exchange rate arrangements. Between these two polar cases lies an almost continuous spectrum of possibilities. Because of the drawbacks associated with purely fixed or purely floating rates—noted in the last chapter—most practical attention has been focused on intermediate regimes which attempt to secure, as far as possible, the advantages of each regime without the disadvantages.

Most of the proposals for controlled flexibility, from Bretton Woods onward, have been based on a par value system—the distinction being in the manner by which par value changes are brought about, and the scope for flexibility around fixed par values. Since the breakdown of the par value system, however, more attention has been devoted to defining countries' obligations with respect to the *intervention* they undertake, rather than to the precise *rate* they maintain. This resulted in the enunciation by the IMF of guidelines for the management of floating exchange rates. Later, the 1976 amendment to the IMF Charter required the Fund to adopt specific principles for the guidance of member countries' exchange rate policies.

This chapter will examine a number of the principal proposals which have been made to introduce controlled flexibility into the exchange rate regime. It begins with the adjustable peg system of Bretton Woods, and goes on to consider some of the suggested modifications to this system, still based on the par value concept. Finally, since the prevailing exchange rate regime among major countries is one of managed floating, it needs to be discussed how this system can be made to operate most efficiently, and how policy conflicts between countries can be avoided.

The Adjustable Peg System

The 'adjustable peg' mechanism of the Bretton Woods system was an attempt to capture the advantages both of the stability offered by fixed exchange rates, and the flexibility of a regime in which currency values were able to change. In this way it was hoped to avoid the chaotic exchange rate gyrations of the 1930s, with their competitive external policies, and the rigid adjustment requirements of the latter days of the gold standard.

The principle of the adjustable peg system was that countries should declare par values for their currencies, and permit fluctuations within narrow bands (of 1 per cent) around the declared par values. Short-term disturbances in the balance of payments would be dealt with, either by allowing the exchange rate to fluctuate in the narrow band around par, or by use of exchange reserves (or, of course, by some combination of the two). Larger disturbances which were nevertheless reversible in nature, would be financed by borrowing, and for this purpose the International Monetary Fund would stand ready to supply needed currencies to its member countries.

Only in the case of disturbances which gave rise to 'fundamental disequilibrium' in a country's balance of payments would a change in par value be called for. One of the most difficult operational features of an adjustable peg system is to decide when a fundamental disequilibrium exists, and what magnitude of exchange rate adjustment is necessary to correct it. Too frequent exchange rate adjustments would destroy the confidence with which traders and investors used existing exchange rates to guide their decision-making. International trade and investment would thus become subject to an additional degree of uncertainty—something which would tend to inhibit international specialization and thus diminish the economic advantages associated with it.

On the other hand, too rigid an exchange rate structure would impose severe adjustment costs on countries out of equilibrium. It is recognized that domestic cost and price structures tend to be somewhat sticky, particularly in a downward direction, and that when one country's price level has become severely out of line with that of its trading partners, an adjustment policy which does not involve use of the exchange rate can impose very severe costs in terms of domestic underutilization of resources, or unwanted inflation.[1] It is important to the functioning of the adjustable peg regime, therefore, that in cases of fundamental disequilibrium, timely and adequate adjustment of the exchange rate should take place.

No formal definition of what constitutes fundamental

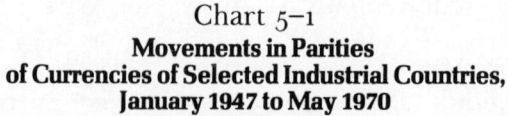

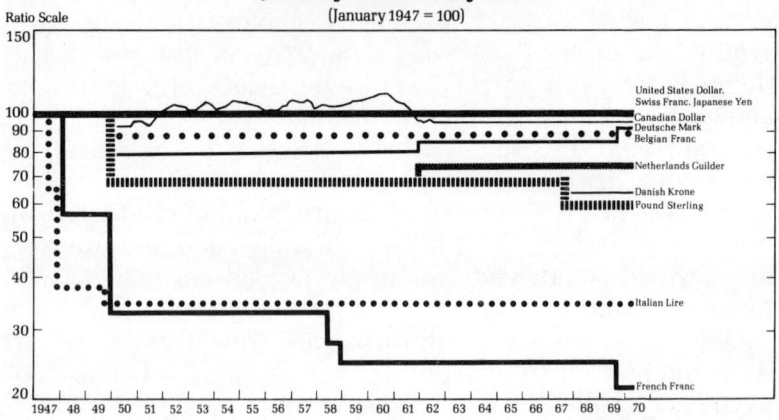

Chart 5–1
**Movements in Parities
of Currencies of Selected Industrial Countries,
January 1947 to May 1970**
(January 1947 = 100)

disequilibrium existed under the Bretton Woods system. It can be seen from Chart 5–1 that exchange rates remained remarkably constant for most of what could be termed the Bretton Woods period. Between 1949, when the main post-war realignment of exchange rates took place, and 1967, when the devaluation of sterling ushered in a period of exchange rate instability that finally resulted in the rupture of the system, there were only two instances of par value changes by major currencies. One was the two devaluations of the French franc in 1956 and 1958—something that was related to the political instability of the last years of the Fourth Republic. The second was the 5 per cent revaluations of the Deutsche mark and Dutch guilder in 1969, in response to the persistent balance of payments strength of these two closely-linked economies.

From this experience, it is clear that the interpretation of fundamental disequilibrium applied in practice during most of the Bretton Woods period was quite a restrictive one. On several occasions, countries experienced severe balance of payments difficulties, and did not devalue. One indication of the restrictiveness of the concept is the size of the devaluations (there were very few revaluations) that did in fact occur. The fact that devaluations tended to be by large amounts indicates that in most cases the underlying disequilibrium was quite substantial before exchange rate change was resorted to.

Fundamental disequilibrium, it should be noted, can be manifested in a number of ways other than a conventional balance of payments deficit or surplus. An underlying balance of payments disequilibrium can be suppressed by a low level of domestic demand, by import restrictions, by controls over capital flows, or cutbacks in aid, or by an aggressive monetary policy aimed at attracting short-term flows of money from abroad. Where any of the above policies have to be applied in a continuing and substantial manner, a disequilibrium may be said to exist even though there is no severe pressure in the foreign exchange market.

None of the foregoing provides much specific guidance for an assessment of when a disequilibrium crosses the threshold from 'transitory' to 'fundamental'. This is essentially a question of judgment which depends largely on the importance attached to rate stability. It is clear that under the Bretton Woods system (as it operated, though not in its conception) exchange rate adjustment was regarded as a late, if not a last, resort of policy. In general, countries were expected to initiate adjustment by using the tools of domestic fiscal and monetary policy. Only if these proved inadequate was a par value change resorted to. In practice, however, countries too often postponed *any* adjustment action until disequilibrium was quite far advanced. This was made possible by the relative ease of *financing* a deficit in its early stages.

When a disequilibrium reaches a certain size, there is a natural doubt in the minds of market participants concerning the ability of the authorities to eliminate it without recourse to a par value change. This gives rise to perhaps the most serious adverse feature of the adjustable peg system—the incentive it offers to destabilizing speculation. Once a disequilibrium becomes apparent, speculators are likely to sell the currency of the country in deficit, hoping to profit (or avoid loss) from a devaluation. The risk involved will be minimal, since there is almost no likelihood that the deficit currency will be revalued. Thus the extent of the loss to which speculators are exposed is the marginal one of the possible appreciation of the deficit currency within the margins.

Given such an attractive one-way option to private speculators, pressure on reserves from capital flows can add to weakness on current account, and present the authorities with a difficult policy choice. Their reserves may not be adequate to resist sustained speculative pressure, and to devalue because of reserve depletion would simply hand speculators an uncovenanted profit and remove all freedom of manoeuvre from the authorities' hands. In such a case, they might be forced to over-devalue for fear that a lesser change in parity would not satisfy speculators. On the other hand, to devalue at an early stage in a disequilibrium undermines the principles of the adjustable peg system by not giving other methods of adjustment time to work.

In the end, it was the volatility of speculative capital that eventually brought down the Bretton Woods system. The increasing integration of the world economy, the introduction of convertibility for the European currencies, the growth of international financial markets, particularly the euro-currency market, all played a role in increasing the volume of mobile funds at the disposal of speculators. At the same time, the amount of the financial resources that national monetary authorities could call on to defend the existing pattern of exchange rates was not growing nearly as fast.

Could the par value system be made to function effectively? And if so what changes would have to be made in its operation? A first necessity would be to reduce the element of speculation associated with par value changes. To this end, such changes would have to be smaller in relation to the margins within which fluctuations normally occurred. Parity changes would also have to be more timely to prevent the build-up of substantial payments disequilibria over time—disequilibria which both encourage speculation and make the choice of an appropriate new par value more difficult.

These modifications in the way in which exchange rate adjustments were used were recognized to be necessary in the 1970 Report of the Executive Directors of the Fund.[2] In themselves, however, they are only palliatives. For a par value system to operate satisfactorily requires a commitment on the part of major countries to resist exchange rate changes where adjustment can be brought about, without undue hardship, by other means. So long as countries acquiesce in divergent cost trends over the long run, adjustments in exchange rates will continue to be necessary. Periodic step-changes in parities are an inefficient and costly way of achieving this adjustment. They are inefficient because they involve a disequilibrium rate

Chart 5–2

Exchange Adjustments under Par Values

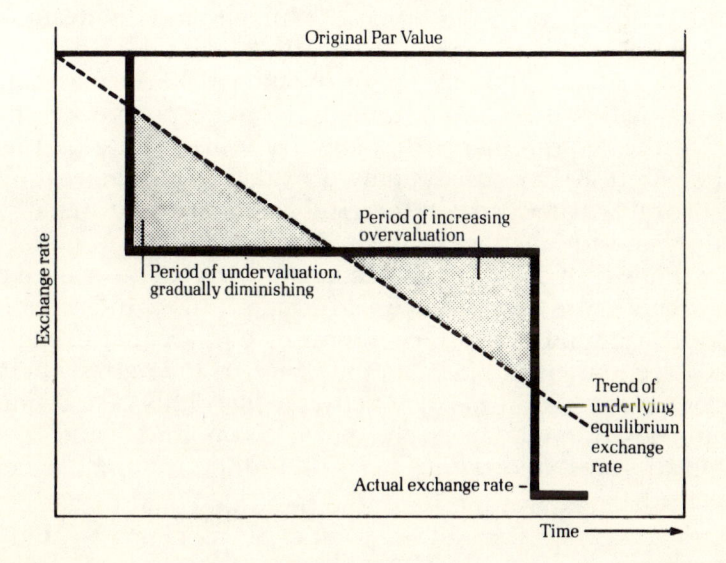

of exchange *most of the time* (see Chart 5-2), and this is costly because the signals which the price mechanism gives for the allocation of resources will be wrong. Not only will they be wrong, but they will change periodically in an apparently arbitrary way. In such circumstances, the adoption of a par value system can *add to* rather than diminish the uncertainties involved in international trade and investment. Thus, only when par values can be established with a reasonable expectation that they will be maintained for a substantial period would it be appropriate to adopt such a system.

In present circumstances conditions are not propitious for a return to par values for two main reasons. Firstly, the underlying divergence in cost trends between countries is so great (and seems likely to remain so) that no structure of par values could endure long enough to perform the intended function of reducing uncertainty in international transactions. Secondly (associated with the first reason), no major country is willing to subordinate domestic economic objectives to external balance to the extent necessary to make a par value system workable. In particular, since policy authorities have rediscovered the power of monetary policy, they are no longer prepared to sacrifice control over the domestic money supply to the maintenance of an external parity.

Before passing on to an examination of some of the specific proposals for modifying an adjustable peg system, it is worth noting briefly the institutional advantages and disadvantages associated with such a regime. On the credit side, a par value provides a focus of attention for the international surveillance of national policies and a frame of reference within which to judge the responsibilities of a country to its trading partners. The Bretton Woods system provided that international approval was needed for the establishment of an initial par value, and for changes in this par value (beyond an initial 10 per cent which could be undertaken unilaterally). The need for international concurrence (through the International Monetary Fund) was a recognition of the fact that exchange rates are matters of international concern, and represented an attempt to strike a balance between the rights of individual countries to manage their own economies, and their obligation to avoid actions harmful to their trading partners.

This balance was, perhaps, the best that could be achieved in the existing state of international cooperation, and it certainly represented a significant advance over the autarkic tendencies of the 1930s. However, the Bretton Woods rules left several difficult cases uncovered. The most important were situations in which a member's exchange rate had got into a disequilibrium situation by *not* changing the par value when such a change was necessary. This 'competitive non-appreciation'—where a country had a substantial payments surplus but did not propose a change in par value so as not to harm its export industries—was very similar in its economic effect to the competitive depreciation specifically proscribed in the IMF Articles.

The Articles of Agreement also appear to overestimate the possibilities of having a considered dialogue, at an international level, on par value changes. In practice, the exigencies of exchange market management mean that the international community can be notified of a proposed change in par value only after the authorities of the country concerned have already decided upon it. Thus the formal role of the IMF in exchange rate changes has in practice been reduced to that of giving an ex-post stamp of approval to decisions made by individual members.[3]

There is very little that can be done at a formal level about this second problem. The only possibility of improved management lies in closer contact and cooperation at an informal level. Concerning the first problem—the 'asymmetry' in exchange rate surveillance, the obvious remedy lies in giving the international community greater authority to pass judgment on all aspects of external policy. This in fact is proposed in the 1976 amendments to the Articles of Agreement. Here, the references to the need to avoid 'competitive exchange alterations' have been replaced by a reference to 'competitive exchange policies'; although the context in the amended articles is no longer that of the par value system.

Wider Bands and Crawling Pegs

As noted above, the most serious shortcoming of the adjustable par value system as it operated in the 1960s was the incentive it offered to destabilizing speculation. The two main modifications to the system that were proposed to alleviate this problem were the adoption of wider bands of permitted fluctuation around par values; and a mechanism by which the parity of a currency would be able to change gradually over time by small amounts. This second proposal is widely known as the crawling peg, though more attractive appellations have been proposed such as 'dynamic parity' or 'gliding parity'.

The *band proposal*[4] was directed at widening the permissible margin of fluctuation around parity from the one per cent in either direction of the International Monetary Fund Articles of Agreement to as much as 5 per cent—though intermediate figures also found favour. By increasing the scope for movements in a currency's value without a change in parity, it was expected that destabilizing speculation would be deterred. With wider bands, speculative pressure would lead to more downward movement in the rate, and the increased scope that this offered for a subsequent upward movement if the parity was successfully defended would, therefore, give rise to counter-speculation of a stabilizing character. In addition, a band as wide as, say, 5 per cent around parity would provide much more scope for exchange rate movements to influence the current account than had been the case when fluctuations were limited to 1 per cent around par. An individual currency could then fluctuate by as much as 10 per cent against the numeraire currency, and by as much as 20 per cent against any other currency. (This would occur when a currency at the top of the band of fluctuation against the numeraire and one at the bottom of the band changed places.)

The principal disadvantage associated with widening the band of fluctuation permitted for currencies lies in the additional uncertainties which such a regime involves for non-speculative transactions. If rate movements are sufficiently great to have an impact on the current account or the long-term capital account, then the uncertainties which are involved for private traders and investors may be such as to reduce the incentive to engage in international transactions. Mainly for this reason, the IMF executive directors concluded in 1970 that a widening of the band to 5 per cent would not be desirable, although their report was cautiously welcoming to some modest widening of margins: ' ... it is not self-evident that the present limit of one per cent in the operational margin is the maximum that can be tolerated without risk of replacing rather than reinforcing the procedure for adjusting exchange rates through the par value mechanism'.[5]

The reference to replacement rather than reinforcement of the procedure for adjusting exchange rates reflects another aspect of the band proposal. Some advocates of the proposal had suggested that if the bands were wide enough, a change in par value could be made without necessarily involving any break in the market value for a currency. For example, if the band was 5 per cent, a currency would undertake a formal devaluation of as much as 10 per cent, while retaining the same market value, simply by moving from the bottom of one band to the top of another. Such an arrangement would clearly reduce destabilizing speculation substantially. It would, however, carry the exchange rate regime so far towards free flexibility that it is perhaps more appropriate to consider a regime with bands of 5 per cent as more akin to a variant of floating. The difference from free floating would be that the international community would retain the power to withhold approval of movements which carried exchange rates outside the established band.

Bands of fluctuation of a somewhat lesser size (say 2–3 per cent) would still involve the problem of discrete changes in market value for currencies. Such changes in market values could be smaller than the case where narrow bands were being observed (since more of the movement would take place 'within the band'). As a result, the incentives to destabilizing speculation would be correspondingly less. Perhaps for this reason, the Bretton Woods system in its later years seemed to be moving toward wider margins ($2^1/_4$ per cent under the Central Rate regime established in December 1971) with smaller changes in par value. And in the amended Articles of Agreement it is provided that in the event of a return to par values, margins should initially be set at $2^1/_4$ per cent.[6]

The *crawling peg* should be regarded as a generic term which applies to a family of proposals whose common characteristic is that declared par values should be adjusted gradually over time, by amounts that could be offset by corresponding changes in domestic interest rates, and which would therefore not generate destabilizing speculation.[7]

Under one set of proposals, a country finding itself in fundamental disequilibrium would, as under the adjustable peg system, propose a change in par value but would approach its new par value gradually, say at a rate of 2 per cent per annum. This proposal retains the feature of the Bretton Woods system that the initiative for a par value change comes from the country concerned. Alternative proposals mostly involve provision for the *automatic* adjustment of par values in response to specified indicators. The trigger for a change in par value could be either (i) the position of the market exchange rate, over some period, within its permitted band, (ii) reserve changes or (iii) some composite indicator made up of a number of variables reflecting external strength.

Such automatic mechanisms for adjusting exchange rates would provide for a response to incipient disequilibria that began sooner and proceeded more gradually than under the adjustable peg regime. This would make adjustment less disruptive than under a system where exchange rate changes occurred less frequently but in larger amounts. By diminishing the possibility of step changes in par values, such an arrangement would also reduce the possibility of destabilizing speculation. Automatic adjustment of par values would serve the purpose of removing decisions concerning exchange rates from the political arena, and thus would remove one barrier that, under the Bretton Woods system, often stood in the way of timely and adequate adjustment. In so far as adjustment was in fact brought about more smoothly and rapidly, this would have the additional benefit of reducing pressure for restrictions over trade and capital flows, as means of suppressing external disequilibria.

To set against these advantages, however, the crawling peg mechanism for adjusting exchange rates has a number of drawbacks. By the time a disequilibrium becomes reflected in the specified indicators, or becomes recognized by the authorities, it may have reached a size where it cannot quickly be corrected by a movement in the exchange rate limited to 2–3 per cent per annum. The authorities of the country then face the choice between constraining their domestic policies over a number of years to conform to the gradual exchange rate adjustment that is taking place, or proposing a step change in the exchange rate. The former course of action may involve a departure from desired domestic objectives for a number of years. For example, if it is known that a country's exchange rate will be 2 per cent lower a year hence, the interest rate on securities of one year maturity will have to be 2 per cent higher than those in other countries to prevent an outflow of capital. On the other hand, to resort to step changes in the exchange rate forfeits the attractive feature of the crawling peg mechanism and, if frequently used, would tend to introduce incentives to speculative capital flows.

There are other, more practical, difficulties in the operation of an automatic adjustment mechanism. No single indicator, and no composite set of indicators, is fully satisfactory as a guide to a country's external performance. Furthermore, as noted earlier, the existence of a disequilibrium cannot be measured solely in terms of a country's external position. It would therefore be necessary to have provision for the authorities of a country to 'override' the exchange rate signal given by the designated indicator. This would reintroduce the problem of surveillance and undermine the attractive simplicity of the automatic mechanism. Finally, the removal of political and psychological constraints on par value changes is not an unqualified advantage. As the 1970 Report of the IMF Executive Directors points out, in some cases: ' ... such constraints have strengthened the hands of the domestic authorities in securing acceptance of necessary domestic adjustments that would otherwise be resisted'.[8]

Managed Floating

Even with additional flexibility provided by wider bands and arrangements for more timely exchange rate adjustment, a par value system would not be workable when there were substantial divergencies in cost and price trends among the major currencies. When, in addition, most countries give priority to the pursuit of domestic objectives in the formation of their demand management policies, there is very little scope for these trends to be brought together. Such a situation has in fact characterized the first half of the 1970s, and seems likely to continue for some time. Beyond this, the 1970s began with substantial disequilibria in the underlying balance of payments of a number of countries (in particular that of the United States), and no clear picture as to the size of exchange rate adjustment necessary to eliminate these disequilibria.

The combination of these factors was sufficient to cause the par value system to falter in 1971 and break down completely in 1973. The accelerating inflation of 1973–74, and the enormous changes in balance of payments positions following the increase in oil prices, merely served to confirm the impossibility of maintaining fixed rates in such circumstances.

At first it was assumed that the optimal way of operating a floating system was simply to refrain from intervention in the foreign exchange market. This value judgment was reflected in the distinction (first made by Professor Schiller, the German Finance Minister) between 'clean' floating and 'dirty' floating. Clean floating implied that a country's exchange rate was left to be determined by market forces, while dirty floating implied manipulation to influence the rate artificially. It soon became obvious, however, that this distinction was oversimplified. There are many ways in which countries can affect supply and demand conditions for their currency without intervening in the foreign exchange market. Domestic monetary expansion, for example, when it increases the supply of domestic currency without increasing the demand for it, is likely to push down the price of the domestic currency in terms of other assets, including foreign exchange.

If clean floating cannot be unambiguously defined as the absence of exchange market intervention, nor should the pejorative connotation of dirty floating be inferred from the presence of intervention. Such intervention can be undertaken out of a desire to prevent undue fluctuations in exchange rates, or to encourage a movement towards a rate conducive to balance of payments equilibrium in the medium term.

If one country chooses to maintain a certain value for its currency through direct intervention in the foreign exchange market, while another manipulates domestic interest rates so as to achieve the same result, it is not clear that one policy should be regarded as more internationally acceptable than the other. The basic question is whether the overall stance of a country's economic policies helps achieve a sustainable balance of payments in the medium term.

One possible way out of the dilemma is to assess policies not in terms of the instruments used but according to the motive for which they are employed. A set of measures employed to meet domestic objectives would, by this approach, be considered within the right of a country to adopt without consultation. On the other hand, measures designed to affect the structure of the balance of payments would be subject to international surveillance.

This distinction is quite clearly more easy to sustain at a conceptual than at an operational level. For one thing there is no way truly to know the motivation for a particular economic policy—and anyway it is likely to be mixed. For another, it is cold comfort for a country's trading partners to know that a particular policy was adopted for domestic reasons, if the actual consequences were harmful to them.

Perhaps the only distinction which is even partly sustainable on operational grounds is between those policies which have a substantial and fairly direct external impact, and those whose external impact is much more muted and indirect. Into the first category would fall use of reserves in intervention, official external borrowing, officially encouraged private borrowing, interest rate policy, capital and exchange controls, and current account restrictions adopted for balance of payments reasons. Most of the other weapons of economic policy would fall into the second category, although the importance for the balance of payments of such instruments as fiscal policy and incomes policy should not be minimized.

The need for some code of conduct to define countries' rights and obligations under floating was reflected in the adoption of the IMF executive directors of the 'Guidelines for the Management of Floating Exchange Rates' in June 1974.[9] At the same time, the difficulties of delineating with precision such rights and obligations are clear from the general language in which the guidelines are couched.

Under Article IV of the proposed amendments to the IMF Charter, the Guidelines for Floating will be replaced by broader obligations applying to all members. Article IV gives Fund members the right to adopt any basic exchange rate practice (except pegging to gold) and focuses the surveillance of the international community on the actual policies adopted by countries under exchange arrangements of their choice.

In the language of the formal Article, members' obligations are couched in terms even more general than those of the Guidelines for Floating. Countries are enjoined to promote domestic economic and financial stability, and to avoid exchange rate manipulation, but no specific guidance is given as to what in practice is implied by these obligations. For this purpose, the Fund is required to 'adopt specific principles for the guidance of the exchange rate policies of all members'. These principles will then become the basis on which the Fund will exercise the required 'firm surveillance' over exchange rate policies.

At the time of writing the Fund is still in the process of working out these principles. It seems reasonable to expect, however, that they will build on experience with the 1974 guidelines, and for that reason it is of interest to review the latter here.

For the most part, the 1974 guidelines are addressed to the question of appropriate market intervention, and they deal with three broad types of situation:

(1) Day-to-day and week-to-week fluctuations in rates.

(2) Exchange rate oscillations of slightly longer duration, say month-to-month or quarter-to-quarter.

(3) The medium-term evolution of exchange rates.

The first two types of exchange rate movement are essentially reversible, and central banks are encouraged to resist them, when stabilizing speculation in the private market is insufficient to do so. These two guidelines do not raise any particular difficulties of principle, only the practical one of distinguishing reversible tendencies from those which are part of a trend. If short-term reversible fluctuations were clearly recognizable as such, there would be no need for official intervention, since the private market would perform the function of stabilization guided by profit incentives. On the other hand, in the more usual case when there is some uncertainty in identifying the nature of factors affecting the exchange rate, official intervention does not simply duplicate the activities of private transactors, but does involve a danger of resisting what will eventually turn out to be a necessary movement of the rate to promote underlying equilibrium.

In the somewhat longer term, the focus in the 1974 guidelines is less on eliminating fluctuations in exchange rates and more on ensuring that rates maintain a relationship which is conducive to sustainable balance of payments equilibrium. The guidelines tentatively suggest that it might be useful to establish exchange rate 'norms', as a point of reference from which to judge at least the direction in which rates ought to be moving. However, central banks are asked only to refrain from intervention that would push the rate further away from the norm, not necessarily to intervene actively to return to the norm.

The principal problem in implementing this guideline lies in judging what rate should be considered a 'norm' at a point in time. By definition, absence of official market intervention means that the overall balance of payments is in equilibrium. To say the exchange rate is in disequilibrium therefore implies that a current account surplus or deficit is being financed by capital flows that are unsustainable in the longer term. While it may well be the case that such situations arise from time to time, it is hard to be confident that the authorities will always know what is a sustainable capital flow, while private market participants remain unable to make the same distinction.

On balance, therefore, the occasions on which the view of the authorities concerning movements in exchange rates is likely to be superior to the collective opinion of participants in the foreign exchange market are probably relatively rare. Only when the authorities are in possession of information that is unavailable to private transactors, or when the authorities are able to pool risks that are too big to be handled by individual dealers in the market, or when the private and social costs of particular exchange rate developments diverge, can it be said with confidence that there is likely to be a strong case for official intervention.

The guidelines acknowledge the difficulties of resisting strong market pressure on exchange rates and absolve member authorities from any obligation to attempt this. They also state that reserve levels should be taken into account in the assessment of intervention policies, and they stress that trade and payments restrictions should be avoided. The principal virtue of the guidelines is that they provide a broad framework, internationally agreed, within which the multilateral surveillance of members' external policies can take place. But they are not sufficiently precise, in themselves, to provide a guide to conduct in particular situations. Two particular questions that arise are: to which countries should the guidelines be applied, and how should exchange rate movements be measured in a floating world?

A case can be made for saying that guidelines should be applied only to those countries that retain absolute discretion over the development of their exchange rates—i.e., those whose currencies are independently floating. For others, which peg their currencies in one manner or another, the appropriate focus of the international community's attention is the initial establishment of the peg, and subsequent changes in it. However, it must be recognized that the exchange rate of a pegged country can become out of equilibrium just as easily as that of a floating currency—more so, perhaps, since there is no need for the exchange rate to be such as to establish a short-run equilibrium of supply and demand in the private market. Thus it is probably more appropriate to subject the external policies of all countries to surveillance, whatever the particular mechanism they select for the management of their exchange rate.

Another problem arises in connection with the definition of exchange rate movements. This concept is relatively unambiguous when all currencies fluctuate within narrow margins around a fixed par value. In such a case, a country which changes its exchange rate changes it by the same amount against all its trading partners. But in a floating world there is not one exchange rate for a currency, but a large number, one for each trading partner. Some way must be found of averaging developments of this large number of exchange rates into a single number. A straightforward average is unsatisfactory, since some exchange rates are much more important for a country than others. Some weighting is needed, and the simplest and most obvious weighting scheme is one based on the importance of other countries in the bilateral trade of the country concerned. This, too, is not wholly satisfactory. Some countries export or import products whose price is, to a large extent, determined in world markets and very little influenced by the geographical pattern of their trade (this applies particularly to the exports of primary producing countries). In other cases, the bilateral pattern of trade is a poor guide to competitive relationships. The United Kingdom and Japan, for example, trade very little with each other, but are important competitors in markets for manufactured goods in Asia and Africa. It is desirable to take this fact into account in measuring the importance of exchange rate movements for a country's balance of payments. Some models try to take account of multilateral trade patterns in arriving at a measure of effective exchange rates. There is, however, no universally agreed and easily measurable concept of an effective exchange rate which can be used for surveillance in connection with the guidelines for floating.[10]

---

[1] This assumes that the country does not resort to controls over trade and payments—in which case the adjustment costs are transferred to its trading partners.
[2] International Monetary Fund, *The Role of Exchange Rates in the Adjustment of International Payments*, Report by the Executive Directors, IMF, Washington, D.C., 1970.
[3] Though the development of close working relations between member countries and the Fund staff has resulted in informal prior consultation on most occasions on which par values were changed.
[4] See, for example, Halm, George N., *Toward Limited Exchange Rate Flexibility*, Princeton Essays in International Finance No.73. Princeton, 1969.
[5] IMF, loc. cit.
[6] It will be clear to readers that the spuriously precise figure of $2^1/_4\%$ has no profound economic significance, but represents simply a negotiating compromise—presumably between the proponents of 2% and $2^1/_2\%$.
[7] For an early exposition of the proposal, see Williamson, *The Crawling Peg*, Princeton Essays in International Finance No.50, Princeton, 1965.
[8] IMF, loc. cit.
[9] Decision No.4232–(74/67) of the IMF, 13 June 1974, reproduced on pp. 112–6 of IMF Annual Report for 1974.
[10] For a more detailed description of the concept of an effective exchange rate, and its statistical derivations, see Rhomberg, R.R., 'Indices of effective exchange rates', IMF *Staff Papers*, March 1976.

Selected Further Reading

Ethier, W., and Bloomfield, A.I., *Managing the Managed Float*, Princeton Essays in International Finance No.112, 1975.

Grubel, Herbert G., 'The case for optimum exchange rate stability', *Weltwirtschaftliches Archiv*, 1973, pp. 351–380.

Halm, G.N. (ed) *Approaches to Greater Flexibility of Exchange Rates*, Princeton University Press, Princeton, N.J., 1970, (The Burgenstock papers).

International Monetary Fund, *The Role of Exchange Rates in the Adjustment of International Payments*, Washington, D.C., 1970.

Kenen, P.B., 'Floats, glides and indicators: a comparison of methods for changing exchange rates', *Journal of International Economics*, 1975.

Marris, Stephen, *The Burgenstock Communiqué: A Critical Examination of the Case for Limited Flexibility of Exchange Rates*, Princeton Essays in International Finance No.80, 1970.

Mikesell, R.F. and Goldstein, H.N., *Rules for a Floating Rate Regime*, Princeton Essays in International Finance No.109, 1975.

Williamson, John, *The Crawling Peg*, Princeton Essays in International Finance No.50, 1965.

Yeager, L.B., 'A skeptical view of the "band" proposal', *National Banking Review*, March 1967.

6 Adjustment Policies

The choice of exchange rate arrangements must take account not only of the ability of different adjustment mechanisms to achieve balance of payments equilibrium, but also the willingness of national authorities to accept constraints on their freedom of policy choice. The successful operation of a par value system presupposes a willingness, within certain limits, to allow external considerations to influence domestic demand management policies. It requires that price trends in various countries exhibit a comparable development, so that individual countries must take the necessary measures to enable their price level to move in line with that of the average of their trading partners. On the other hand, floating requires a framework of international cooperation and consultation if it is not to give rise to self-regarding policies by individual countries which may be contrary to the general interest.

This chapter discusses some of the policy considerations related to the choice of exchange rate regime, both from the point of view of the efficiency of the international adjustment process and from the point of view of an individual country attempting to maximize its domestic welfare, subject to the constraints placed on its freedom of policy choice by international monetary arrangements.

Adjustment under Fixed Rates

Certain conditions can be identified which would be conducive to the maintenance of a system based on par values. In the first place, if countries share similar objectives with respect to price stability and employment, it is more likely that domestic goals will coincide with external goals. For example, a country which found itself experiencing a deterioration in its balance of payments because its inflation was proceeding more rapidly than that of its trading partners would probably wish to introduce measures of demand restraint both to counter inflation and to improve the balance of payments.

Secondly, a high level of price flexibility will enable relatively small changes in the pressure of demand to achieve significant effects on relative price levels. Thus, the amount of domestic output which has to be foregone to achieve the desired change in price levels is minimized, and factors of production can easily be shifted, via the price mechanism, from domestic to external demand.

Thirdly, high elasticities of demand and supply will enable changes in relative price to be quickly translated into an improvement in the balance of payments (provided domestic demand is reduced to permit the shift of resources to take place).

Fourthly, since one country's surplus is another's deficit, it is important that understandings exist regarding the relative responsibilities of surplus and deficit countries in sharing the adjustment burden. If one party is unable or unwilling to take any action to reduce the disequilibrium on its side, it becomes more likely that the adjustment required of the other party is greater than it is politically prepared to accept.

The less the extent to which the first three conditions are met, i.e., the less effective are domestic measures in securing adjustment, the greater the importance of the fourth condition, i.e., political acceptance of where the responsibilities of adjustment lie. This last condition was not adequately spelled out under the Bretton Woods arrangements, but it is clearly an important feature of the successful operation of a par value system. In particular, if par values are ever again accepted as an objective, it would be necessary to provide some guarantee that countries which found themselves in disequilibrium should not be forced into the adoption of measures which were excessively harmful to their domestic objectives. Two means have been suggested to achieve this goal. The first is that any country should be able to float 'in particular situations' (i.e., when the maintenance of a fixed par value became unacceptably onerous in terms of its other economic objectives). The second protection was envisaged as a system of 'objective indicators' which would serve to signal the need for adjustment, and which would apply with equal force to surplus and to deficit countries.

Once the international community has laid down the broad guidelines for balance of payments adjustment, individual countries have the problem of choosing the mix of policies which enables them to achieve adjustment at the least possible domestic costs. Indeed, it is one of the objectives of international rules for adjustment that they should preserve the maximum degree of freedom for individual countries to follow adjustment policies of their own choosing.

Under a fixed exchange rate system, a country has no alternative but to use the instruments of domestic demand management to achieve the goal of external balance. However, it is possible to vary the 'mix' of domestic policies in order to minimize the impact on domestic economic objectives. For example, as was originally pointed out by Mundell,[1] fiscal policy and monetary policy, though both affecting the internal and the external situation, have different relative effects. A fiscal stimulus will normally increase domestic demand by a greater amount than it increases imports. On the other hand, monetary actions are likely to have a greater effect on the balance of payments, since they tend to create interest rate differentials which generate substantial international movements of funds. Mundell's prescription, therefore, was that fiscal policy should be directed to the pursuit of objectives in the domestic field, while monetary policy should be assigned the task of stabilizing the balance of payments.

A variant of this proposition is embodied in the suggestion that monetary policy can, by itself, be used to achieve a dual objective through 'twisting' the yield curve. If by aggressive open market operations, the monetary authorities of a country are able to raise short-term rates and lower long-term rates, this may also allow them to increase the level of domestic demand, while improving the balance of payments. This is because the long-term interest rate is considered to be of central importance for domestic investment decisions, while short-term rates are more relevant in inducing international capital flows.

The use of independent policy instruments is a conceptually satisfying way of achieving objectives which under certain conditions may seem incompatible (e.g., domestic expansion and balance of payments improvement). And it undoubtedly has influenced the formation of policy. However, it is essentially a short-run equilibrium approach. An improvement in the balance of payments based on short-term capital inflows induced by interest rate differentials is transitory in nature. Capital flows take place to restore balance in wealth-owners' portfolios of assets. Once balance is restored, the flow will tend to dry up, and can only be sustained by the *widening* of interest rate differentials in order to create a further portfolio disequilibrium and thus induce a further capital flow to restore balance. Furthermore, capital flows give rise to debt service payments in the opposite direction, which aggravates the initial imbalance on current account. Thus, unless measures are taken to restore the current account balance to some sort of sustainable equilibrium, reliance on manipulation of the capital account to maintain balance will not work.

In a fixed exchange rate system, therefore, there is ultimately no escape for a country from the pursuit of policies designed to harmonize price trends with what is happening in its trading partners, and to limit the growth of real domestic demand to the rate of output expansion. Various alternatives to straightforward demand management have been proposed, however. The most frequently recommended is probably incomes policy, which in its application is usually intended primarily to affect the rate of domestic inflation. Incomes policy is designed to exert a direct effect on factor and product prices, and thus to short-circuit the uncertain, time-consuming, and ultimately wasteful process of allowing a cut in aggregate demand to work its way through the economic system in such a way that downward pressure is exerted on prices. For all its superficial appeal, however, incomes policy has usually encountered strong opposition, and governments have often felt that the political costs of a mandatory incomes policy are too high to pay, other than in time of clear national emergency. It is revealing that most of the countries which have resorted to incomes policy generally consider that its usefulness is essentially short term.

Perhaps because the mechanisms intended to minimize domestic adjustments' costs under fixed rates have proved to be only partially effective in a world of increasing divergence in domestic economic objectives, most major countries resorted to a system of managed floating. It seems unlikely that countries will be prepared in the near future to accept the constraints on their freedom of domestic policy action required by the discipline of a fixed exchange rate. The experience of the recent past is that substantial fluctuations in domestic economic activity are needed to secure a significant impact on the balance of payments in the short term; governments are now sufficiently sensitive to their electorates' preferences in the fields of full employment and price stability that they are unlikely to sacrifice their domestic objectives for the somewhat nebulous advantages of greater exchange rate stability.

Adjustment under Floating

The move to a floating exchange rate, although it removes the balance of payments as a direct constraint on policy formation, does not fundamentally change the contours of the adjustment problem. Whatever the exchange rate regime, resources have to be redirected from domestic to foreign uses to correct an incipient balance of payments deficit. And this can just as easily involve underutilization or wasteful allocation of resources under floating as under any other exchange rate regime.

The first problem is to ensure that the exchange rate adjustment necessary to correct a disequilibrium does not go too far. The risk of over-shooting arises from the lags in the working of balance of payments adjustment, and from the initially perverse effects of an exchange rate change on the current account. These perverse effects arise because of the price effects of, for example, a depreciation, resulting in an immediate worsening of the terms of trade which, with unchanged trade flows, causes a deterioration in the balance of payments. Only with a lag does the new level of relative prices have its effect on trade volumes, and thus generate an improvement in the payments situation. This is frequently referred to as the J-curve effect, since the letter J traces the initial deterioration and subsequent improvement of the balance of payments.

In theory, and ideally, there will be a body of well-informed and well-endowed speculators who will have a clear idea of what constitutes a medium-term equilibrium in a country's exchange rate, and who will back their judgment by heavy intervention to prevent the rate going too far away from this level. In practice, however, speculators are not always sufficiently well informed of likely future developments to perform the smoothing function perfectly, nor are they endowed with unlimited resources. Like anyone else, rational speculators are risk-averse,[2] and the greater their exposed position in a given currency, the greater the size and certainty of gain needed to tempt them to support the currency further. Thus, capital flows cannot necessarily be relied on to respond smoothly to exchange rate movements and to 'fill the gap' while the current account improvement is taking place. A greater exchange rate movement may therefore be necessary to secure a given improvement in the overall payments balance in the short run than will ultimately prove needed in the longer run. An efficient adjustment mechanism may thus still involve some official intervention, even under floating, if the authorities feel they have a more accurate knowledge of the appropriate medium-term exchange rate than emerges from the interplay of private market forces.

The second requirement for efficient adjustment under a floating rate is that the capital and current accounts stand in the proper relationship. A free float naturally ensures that the current and capital accounts will be in overall balance (i.e., will sum to zero) but it does not guarantee that the relationship between the two will be of any particular form. In the long run, the optimum allocation of world resources is achieved when the returns to marginal investment are the same in all countries. This will require capital flows out of those countries where investment opportunities are relatively few, or the savings propensity is relatively high, and into those countries where investment opportunities are relatively abundant and/or the savings propensity is relatively low. However, since capital flows are subject to manipulation by a large number of factors only loosely connected with the marginal productivity of capital, it is quite possible that a market outcome for the current account balance may not represent an efficient allocation of resources. For example, a low interest rate policy adopted by a particular country as a means of encouraging investment will have as a consequence an outflow of funds and a reduction in the exchange rate. This will stimulate a current account surplus which may be entirely unwelcome to the country concerned and to its trading partners.

As noted earlier, however, floating does not remove the need to transfer resources in order to correct potential balance of payments disequilibria. Since the manner in which, and the speed with which, this transfer takes place have important consequences for domestic economic welfare, it is not surprising that countries continue to have objectives in the adjustment field, and intervene in exchange markets in pursuit of these objectives. For example, when rates are free to move in response to market pressures, one of the key objectives for national authorities is to minimize the extent of unnecessary fluctuations in their effective exchange rate. This is because such fluctuations generate reversible movements in the price level of traded goods, and in the level of demand for domestic output. They therefore cause the price mechanism to give confusing signals to producers and consumers, and thus to misallocate resources. Beyond ironing out unnecessary fluctuations, it may be considered desirable to moderate (or conceivably, increase) the speed of adjustment of the exchange rate to a new equilibrium, and to prevent any tendency for the movement to overshoot the equilibrium point. Too rapid a movement in the rate may cause relative prices of traded and nontraded goods to change too suddenly to be accommodated smoothly by a shift of factors of production from one industry to another. Too slow a movement, on the other hand, may unduly prolong the employment of resources in industries which have become basically uncompetitive. Overshooting the equilibrium rate risks setting up an oscillatory movement in exchange rate, which will give the same confusing price signals as the reversible rate fluctuations noted above.

In a managed floating regime, the task of the authorities is to use fiscal and monetary policy to achieve the appropriate level, and desired composition, of domestic demand, and intervention policy to contain the exchange rate within a band which, while securing medium-term adjustment, is consistent with domestic policy objectives. Of course, it is not possible for all countries to intervene simultaneously to achieve a desired exchange rate objective. Among n different countries, there are only $n-1$ exchange rates. Therefore, intervention policy must be coordinated to minimize the extent of conflict.

When the exchange system in operation is without precise rules, intervention to influence the exchange rate becomes a policy variable. This was the situation following the breakdown of the Bretton Woods system, and although the Guidelines for Floating place some limits on countries' freedom to intervene in foreign exchange markets, there remains considerable latitude.

The two extreme possibilities for a country are to refrain from any intervention, and to allow its exchange rate to be determined purely by market forces; and to peg to a single intervention currency in much the same way as when all countries were observing par values. Intermediate solutions are also possible. A country may peg to a weighted average of currencies, rather than to a single major currency. Alternatively, a group of countries which trade extensively with each other (such as the European Common Market countries) may decide to link their currencies to each other, but to allow the group of currencies to float as a bloc against the rest of the world. Finally, countries may wish to avoid any particular obligations in their market intervention, but nevertheless stand ready to intervene to prevent what they consider to be excessive movements in their exchange rate.

As is to be expected, each country's preference depends on the relative importance it assigns to stability of the exchange rate with particular trading partners, vis-à-vis the advantages of continuous adjustment via changes in exchange rates. The choice depends on a number of circumstances, which will naturally differ among countries. Therefore the difference in the adjustment policies that are actually chosen reflects not just variations in preferences among different governments but real differences in economic circumstances.

Countries which trade extensively with a single major country may value stability in the exchange rate with that country particularly highly. If, in addition, a large part of their foreign capital inflow passes through the capital market of that country, this will be an additional reason for favouring a single currency peg. Many countries in the Western Hemisphere feel themselves to be in this kind of position vis-à-vis the United States, and this is probably why so many choose to peg to the United States dollar.

On the other hand, one of the most noteworthy features of

the expansion of world trade in the post-war period has been the diversification of trade flows. It is no longer true, as it was in the colonial era, that most developing countries have a single dominant trading partner. For this reason, a number of countries which continue to desire stability in the exchange rate for their currency have preferred to achieve this by pegging to a basket of currencies.

Another factor influencing the choice of exchange policy is the difficulty of the underlying adjustment problem. Countries which face inflationary pressures substantially greater than those existing amongst their trading partners will be much less able to follow a policy of exchange rate pegging. On the other hand, a group of countries which feel able to achieve adequate policy harmonization, and which in addition have a very high proportion of intra-group trade (conditions which broadly apply to the EEC), may feel able to link their currencies together.[3] In this way, it is hoped, the economic and political advantages of greater integration can be achieved at not too great cost in terms of adjustment difficulties. (It is noteworthy that the European countries which remained outside the snake following generalized floating—Britain, Ireland, Italy and, later, France—were those with the highest inflation rates.)

A reasonably free float depends for its success on an efficient system of financial markets, in which market participants have sufficient knowledge and resources to provide appropriate stabilizing speculation. If such conditions do not exist, exchange rate fluctuations will tend to be excessive, and central bank intervention will be needed to smooth the response of the exchange rate to external shocks.

Finally, there is an important connection between the extent to which alternative ways of financing balance of payments deficits are available, and the extent to which governments have to allow movements in the exchange rates to take the strain. Alternative financing mechanisms include reserves, borrowing facilities, and the freedom and willingness of countries to adjust payments restrictions for balance of payments reasons.

The Exchange Rate Regime and Developing Countries[4]

Most of the issues in connection with adjustment and exchange rate arrangements are usually discussed from the standpoint of the major industrial countries. Perhaps this is only realistic, since these countries account for the bulk of world trade and reserves, and have the power to reach agreements amongst themselves. But it cannot be denied that all countries have a stake in the efficient functioning of the world payments system. Indeed, the poorer countries have in some senses a greater stake, since their economic development plans are in many ways more dependent on the external sector than are the full employment and growth objectives of the industrialized countries. Also, being already poor, the developing countries are that much less able to afford the sacrifices of an inefficient international payments system.

Various characteristics of developing countries have an important bearing upon the costs of alternative exchange rate regimes for this group of countries. In this section, we shall indicate what these characteristics are and what bearing they have on the adjustment process.

The main differentiating characteristics of less developed countries (LDCs) of relevance to their choice of exchange rate regime are their high specialization pattern in production, their inability to affect export or import prices in foreign currency through their own exchange rate policies, the inelastic nature of their demand for imports (and, in the short run, of their supply of exports), the rather rudimentary nature of their financial sector, and the fact that capital flows are probably less responsive to conventional yield considerations.

Most less developed countries have the large majority of their labour force in the primary sector. Production is mainly agricultural, with a high dependence on a few major crops. Some developing countries may, in addition, have a mining sector that contributes a large proportion of total production. Relatively few have a highly developed manufacturing sector, or have more than a trivial volume of exports of manufactures. This contrasts dramatically with more developed countries, where the labour force is concentrated more in the secondary and tertiary sectors and where there is a large diversity of industrial products produced and traded.

Reflecting the highly specialized production structure of developing countries, their foreign sector differs in nature and importance from that of more developed economies. Firstly, since there is very little substitutability between locally produced goods and imported goods, the price elasticity of demand for imported goods is likely to be low. Secondly, since the production of primary products typically involves long gestation periods and since the proportion of most of the major export crops absorbed domestically is limited, the price elasticity of supply of exports is also likely to be rather low in the short run. Thirdly, since primary products are fairly homogeneous and the export share of each less developed country in the international market for its particular export good is in most cases small, most less developed countries are 'price-takers'.

Economic growth in developing countries, as contrasted with that in industrial countries, is significantly more dependent upon the foreign sector for two basic reasons. First, foreign aid and long-term private capital flows into less developed countries play a greater role in supplementing domestic savings and increasing the rate of growth, domestic savings being in many cases not sufficient to enable the country to attain the desired growth target. Second, the fact that capital equipment is mostly manufactured abroad renders developing countries heavily dependent upon imports of capital equipment from developed countries. Thus, domestic savings are insufficient in themselves as a means of capital formation and the availability of foreign exchange plays an important role in channeling domestic savings into productive investment.

In addition, the financial markets in most less developed countries are rudimentary. The process of financial intermediation is still at an early level of development and, hence, very limited; there are only a few banks that provide short-term credit, rationing mainly on the basis of creditworthy and established customers rather than through an interest rate mechanism; the foreign exchange market functions mainly through the central bank with very few, if any, foreign exchange dealers, and a forward market for the country's currency is virtually non-existent.

Related to the level of development of the financial market, capital flows to and from less developed countries are often governed by factors other than interest rate differentials. Official development aid and long-term private capital flows are influenced more by political considerations and expectations of political stability than by pure yield factors. Short-term capital flows, which in the industrial nations respond quickly to changes in interest rate differentials and to expected changes in the exchange rate, may also be less responsive in less developed countries, given the greater uncertainty generated by lack of sufficient information and by the greater probability of change in the political climate.

Although less developed countries may share many of the economic policy objectives of the more developed countries, such as full employment, growth and price stability, adjustment and financing mechanisms will work differently in the developing countries as a result of their differentiating characteristics. The relative changes in the setting of such instruments as the exchange rate, monetary and fiscal policies, and exchange controls may have to be considerably greater than in the more developed countries to attain the same objective for the balance of payments. For example, a deficit in the balance of trade may not be substantially changed, at least in the short run, by a change in the exchange rate, given the inelastic demand for imports, and the inelastic supply of exports. Similarly, a contractionary monetary policy leading to an increase in interest rates may have very little effect on capital flows into the country.

The Options for Developing Countries under Floating

Prior to the breakdown of the Bretton Woods system, nearly all the developing countries maintained a par value by official intervention with prescribed margins against their intervention currencies. The most commonly used intervention currencies were the United States dollar, the French franc, and the pound sterling, though a few other currencies were used in territories which had close links with countries other than the United States, France, and Britain.

When the Bretton Woods system finally collapsed in March 1973, a system of managed floating between most major countries appeared likely to persist for the foreseeable future. Furthermore, early experience with floating indicated that wide swings in the relative value of major currencies (of the order of 20 per cent within a few months) were possible and even likely. In these circumstances, the developing countries clearly had a need to reappraise their exchange rate policy. The three main options available to less developed countries in these circumstances were: (a) to continue to peg to a single intervention currency, (b) to peg to a basket of currencies, or (c) to float independently (with or without official management of the exchange rate).

(1)Pegging to a Single Currency
Pegging to a particular currency may reduce, relative to other alternatives, the fluctuations in the exchange rate between the currency of the less developed country and that of its developed country partner. This facilitates trade between the two countries by reducing the uncertainties associated with changes in relative currency values. For the same reason, capital flows for investment purposes from the developed country may increase. Second, to the extent that the exchange rate of the industrial nation is more stable vis-à-vis the rest of the world than the exchange rate of the less developed country would have been without pegging, trade with and investment from the rest of the world may also be stimulated. Third, a developing country that chooses to peg its currency to an external standard, such as the currency of a major country, gives expression to its intention to align its policies broadly with those of the partner country. If the policies of the partner country are regarded as adequate to the promotion of relatively stable prices, there might be increased *confidence* in the less developed country. Consequently, foreign investment may be stimulated. Furthermore, pegging provides a clear criterion for intervention in the foreign exchange market. Lastly, the disciplinary aspects of pegging can sometimes be viewed as an advantage if a fixed rate acts (in the words of the 1970 Report of the Fund's Executive Directors[5]) as 'a fulcrum for domestic stability'. This report put the argument as follows: ' ... the need to defend a fixed exchange rate against depreciation may promote political willingness to impose unpopular domestic restraints; and where the attempt to defend the parity is ultimately unsuccessful, the psychological

shock of a devaluation may promote broad support for the adoption of the necessary associated measures to curtail domestic demand ... '.

Pegging to a single currency in a world where major currencies are floating does not, however, have the same consequences as adopting a fixed exchange rate in a world of stable parities. Such a policy involves at least three potential disadvantages over a system in which all countries adhere to par values. First, the need for reserves may increase. Movements in the pegged exchange rate of the less developed country will not reflect actual developments in its balance of payments; rather, they will reflect the developments in the balance of payments of the industrial country to which the developing country is pegging. If, as is perhaps likely, the factors affecting the equilibrium exchange rates of the two countries are not closely related, the need for reserves may be greater than under adjustable par values.

A second drawback to a single currency peg is that fluctuations of the exchange rate, since they are exogenous and independent of government policy, may interfere with the pursuit of internal policy objectives.

A third disadvantage is that exchange rates among the currencies of developing countries will be subject to variation, since not all these countries peg to the same major currency. This will be particularly disadvantageous when many of these countries, being small economic units, are trying to attain some of the advantages of market size by promoting intra-regional trade.

(2) Pegging to a Basket
An alternative exchange market policy which attempts to retain the advantages of pegging while minimizing the disadvantages, advocates stabilizing the *effective* exchange rate of a currency, where the effective exchange rate is a suitable average of market exchange rates vis-à-vis the currencies of trading partners. The most comprehensive measure of a country's effective exchange rate would take into account its trade and payments structure, including the price effects generated by exchange rate changes, the price elasticities for different products, the competitive relationships of a country's exports in foreign markets, the pattern of bilateral trade, and the effects on capital flows. Such a computation may be

difficult to make for developing countries, given the poverty of statistics and the strong influence of exogenous developments in the actual pattern of their trade. But for practical purposes, simpler methods of approximating an effective exchange rate may be a sufficient guide for policy-makers.

For countries which wish to retain a system of pegging, but are concerned at the instability which a single currency peg may introduce, a peg to a basket may be an appealing compromise. However, such a policy retains a number of disadvantages. Besides the familiar difficulties of pegging (deriving mainly from the fact that the foreign exchange market is not continuously in equilibrium) there is the problem that, since each developing country would use a different basket, there would be varying cross rates between *all* developing countries using such baskets, while under single currency pegs, there is at least stability amongst those currencies which utilize the same peg. Furthermore, the use of an unfamiliar peg for each developing country's currency might render the countries less attractive outlets for foreign investment. This would be because investors would feel less able to predict the value of each developing country's currency, and might feel that this value was more likely to be manipulated (e.g., through changes in the composition of the basket) than under some alternative regime.

It is to overcome some of these rather intangible drawbacks to the construction of separate baskets for each country, that certain countries have elected to peg on a common numeraire with an already-existing international status—namely, the Special Drawing Right (SDR).[6] A case can be made that if developing countries are going to peg, reducing cross-rate variability between LDCs would be a desirable objective in stimulating their intra-regional trade. Furthermore, pegging to the SDR is 'convenient' from a practical point of view; it has an established value that is determined and published daily on the basis of the exchange rates in major financial markets and is based on trade shares of sixteen major industrial countries. For those developing countries which have a reasonably diversified trade structure, the SDR is not likely to diverge far from the weighted basket of currencies that correctly reflects their 'effective' exchange rate.

(3) Independent Floating
Although pegging to some composite of currencies can help to offset the effect of exchange rate fluctuations among major currencies on the effective exchange rate of developing countries, it does not, of course, do anything to counter other influences on these countries' payments positions. In other words, it does not promote adjustment to exogenous shocks, or ensure an equilibrium in the foreign exchange market.

The question therefore arises whether it might be advisable for developing countries to consider permitting greater flexibility in their exchange rates (i.e., by abandoning any peg) in order to achieve more continuous adjustment to external equilibrium. Here, too, a trade-off operates: the benefits of pegging, noted above, on the one hand, against the advantages of a more continuous adjustment of the external position, on the other. In considering this question it must be noted that flexible exchange rates for developing countries have different implications than for industrial countries, mainly because of the different institutional characteristics of smaller, primary producing countries.

As was noted earlier, for flexible exchange rates to be reasonably stable without government intervention, a well-functioning foreign exchange market with arbitrageurs is needed. Since such a market is virtually non-existent in most less developed countries, there is certainly a danger that, if less developed countries were to float, the private institutional structure might be inadequate to dampen the exchange rate fluctuations.

Another point to be taken into consideration is the possibility of divergence between the long-term equilibrium exchange rate for a country's currency, and the short-term market-clearing rate—a point of considerable importance for less developed countries. The short-term equilibrium rate can be defined as the one that would be established at a point in time by the interplay of market forces. The long-term equilibrium rate can be conceptually defined as the long-term exchange rate of the country when the 'appropriate' structural changes have taken place. For instance, a less developed country may view its balance of payments in a long-term perspective involving a period of sustained deficits while heavy investment is occurring within the country in the context of a development programme. The government may regard the deficit-incurring exchange rate as the appropriate 'long-term' exchange rate that would promote structural changes through sectoral investment that would result in a more diversified production structure. This would, in time, increase and stabilize exports leading eventually to a more balanced position in the external accounts. The short-term equilibrium exchange rate, which would be established under free floating, would then be regarded as an impediment toward the attainment of long-term policy objectives.[7]

Given the commodity structure of the trade of less developed countries, it is uncertain whether the exchange rate alone can be effective in adjusting payments flows. On the one hand, it can be argued that the exchange rate is the instrument which acts most directly on trade and capital flows, and to equilibrate the balance of payments through flexible exchange rates avoids the need for distorting controls on trade and capital flows. It also obviates the additional adjustment costs associated with step-changes in the exchange rate. On the other hand, there may be costs in allowing the exchange rate to play the major role in equilibrating the balance of payments on a more or less continuous basis. In the first place, since the responsiveness of trade flows to exchange rate fluctuations is probably less in developing countries than in industrialized ones, greater movements in rates will be necessary to adjust to external shocks. Given the uncertainties in the adjustment process (relating both to the timing and magnitude of price effects) there is a clear danger that private markets may overshoot the required exchange rate change in order to minimize risks. Furthermore, in so far as foreign investors see exchange rate flexibility as reducing the willingness of a country to follow restrained domestic monetary policies, there may be a harmful effect on capital inflows—at least until the country has established a 'track record' of responsible monetary and fiscal management.

An advantage that is sometimes claimed for floating for developing countries is the economy in reserve holding that such a policy is thought to permit. Given the greater priority accorded to economic growth in developing countries, and the usefulness of foreign exchange in providing funds for the purchase of capital equipment from abroad, any reduction in reserve holdings would be a positive factor in increasing economic growth. Furthermore, to the extent that private holdings of foreign currency are diverted to speculative purposes as a result of the one-way profit possibilities offered by an adjustable par value system, floating may offer the chance to recapture these funds for productive investment.

Too much should not be made of these arguments, however. Given the exchange control system in operation in most developing countries, the possibilities of reducing speculative holdings of foreign exchange through a switch to floating seem limited. And in so far as official reserves are held for the purposes of financing reversible fluctuations in the balance of payments, floating would simply transfer the rate-smoothing function from the authorities to the private sector, without effecting economies in foreign exchange holding to the country as a whole. Furthermore, many developing countries hold reserves also for the purpose of enhancing their credit-worthiness in international capital markets, and the savings in foreign exchange stemming from a reduction in reserves may be offset for them by higher cost, or greater difficulties, in borrowing abroad.

[1] Mundell, R.A., 'The appropriate use of monetary and fiscal policy for internal and external stability', IMF *Staff Papers,* March 1962.
[2] In this connection, it is worth recalling that most speculation is undertaken by institutions such as banks and multi-national corporations for whom it is incidental to their main business activity. For this reason, currency dealing, beyond that required to cover current and forward contracts, is usually subjected to strict prudential limitations.
[3] Though experience with the EEC currency snake indicates how difficult it is to link currencies together, even under relatively favourable conditions when capital movements may take place freely.
[4] The following section draws on material in Crockett, A.D., and Nsouli, S.M., 'Exchange rate policies for developing countries', *Journal of Development Studies,* January 1977.
[5] IMF, *The Role of Exchange Rates in the Adjustment of International Payments,* 1970.
[6] A description of the establishment and the method of valuation of the SDR is provided in Chapter 7.
[7] In theory, private speculators should be able to foresee the long-term improvement in the balance of payments, and thus be willing to finance current deficits through inflows of short-term capital. In practice, this is unlikely to occur where uncertainties are considerable and speculators are risk-averse.

Selected Further Reading

Diaz-Alejandro, C., *Less Developed Countries and the Post-1971 International Financial System,* Princeton Essays in International Finance No. 108, 1975.

Emminger, O., 'Practical aspects of the problem of balance of payments adjustment,' *Journal of Political Economy,* August 1967.

Fleming, J.M., *Guidelines for Balance of Payments Adjustment under the Par Value System,* Princeton Essays in International Finance No. 67, 1968.

Helleiner, G., 'The less-developed countries and the international monetary system', *Journal of Development Studies,* 1975.

Hinshaw, Randall (ed), *The Economics of International Adjustment,* Johns Hopkins, University Press, Baltimore, 1971.

Mundell, R.A., 'The appropriate use of monetary and fiscal policy for internal and external stability', IMF *Staff Papers,* March 1962.

Organization for Economic Cooperation and Development (OECD), *The Balance of Payments Adjustment Process, Report of Working Party 3 of the Fconomic Policy Committee,* Paris, 1966.

Whitman, M.v.N., *Policies for Internal and External Balance,* Princeton Special Papers in Economics No. 9, 1970.

7 *International Liquidity*

International liquidity can be defined as the stock of internationally acceptable assets held by central banks for the purposes of settling balance of payments deficits and defending exchange rates. In many ways, it is not too misleading to think of international liquidity as performing the same function for nations as holdings of money balances do for individuals. Some of the same problems present themselves in analysis, too. For example, it is not always easy to define what should be included in international reserves, just as it is not always easy to arrive at a generally acceptable definition of the domestic money supply. And just as the size and rate of growth of the money supply is a crucial variable for the level of economic activity and prices, so the volume of international liquidity, and its rate of growth, are important elements in the generation and transmission of inflationary and deflationary impulses from country to country. It should be borne in mind, however, that the mechanism by which excess or deficient international liquidity is translated into inflationary or deflationary pressure is rather less direct, and certainly less measurable, than the corresponding mechanism in the domestic economy. There are, of course, other important differences between international liquidity and domestic money which should make one wary of pressing the analogy too far.

There are basically two main categories of question relating to international liquidity. The first concerns the nature of the asset which fulfils the special function of being an international reserve. Since there have been, in practice, several assets which have figured in reserves in recent years, a subsidiary question is whether a multiple reserve standard is desirable, and how the various types of reserve asset can be made to coexist satisfactorily.

The second kind of question, largely separate, relates to the desirable volume of acceptable reserve assets. In order to answer this question, information is needed concerning the factors which give rise to a need to hold reserves, and how these are likely to change over time. In particular, we need to be able to assess the effect of changes in the exchange rate regime, in patterns of trade flows and in the nature of reserve assets, on the desire of countries to hold primary reserve assets. The present chapter will deal with the nature and characteristics of international reserve assets. Chaper 8 considers the factors governing the need to hold liquidity and the mechanisms by which liquidity creation can be controlled.

The Development of Reserve Assets

The nature of the asset which is held in reserves and used in settlement of payments imbalances has long been recognized to be a central feature of any international monetary system. Frequently, this asset has also served as the numeraire of the system, or standard in terms of which the values of national currencies are defined and maintained. Thus, the system that existed before the First World War, and which was revived for a time in the inter-war period, was generally known as the gold standard. When, under the Bretton Woods arrangements, gold was supplemented by gold-convertible foreign exchange, and drawing rights in the International Monetary Fund, the name gold-exchange standard was sometimes used.

In a fixed rate system, reserve assets are needed to make international settlements when private demand and supply for a given currency are not in balance at the fixed exchange rate. Under floating rates, reserves are not strictly necessary since the monetary authorities do not undertake to hold the exchange rate at any particular level; the rate can therefore move to equilibrate supply and demand without any need for official intervention. However, as we have seen in the previous chapter, the fact that governments continue to have objectives in the field of adjustment policies means that they may continue to feel a need for exchange reserves, even though the exchange rate for their currencies is flexible. At the present time, for example, there are three different types of liquidity—gold, SDRs, and reserve currencies, and an even larger number of different assets used in reserves, since each national currency held in reserves should properly be thought of as a different asset.

To understand how different reserve assets can coexist, it is helpful to go back to first principles. International liquidity, like national money, serves at least three potential functions: it is a medium of exchange, a unit of account, and a store of value. As is well known, commodity moneys were used, both domestically and internationally, to provide these functions in the period before the development of deposit banking. Among commodities, precious metals, and particulary gold, acquired pre-eminence, and eventually drove out competitors.[1]

Gold

Deposit banking led to the displacement of commodity money (gold) as a domestic financial asset, not as a planned development, but essentially as the result of a Darwinian process. Gold was difficult to store and expensive to transport, so in conditions of political and financial stability, it was natural to exchange title to gold rather than actual stocks of metal. The initial idea of exchanging title to gold economized only on transactions costs; mining was still necessary if there was to be a physical backing to the gold titles which were exchanged. But why should there by a physical backing? If, as soon became evident to bankers, their customers were rarely interested in taking delivery of metal, why not lend out more than the value of the physical gold that was held? Thus fractional reserve banking developed, and gold was on its way out as a circulating medium.[2]

Why did gold survive as a medium of international settlement long after it had been reduced to insignificance in its purely domestic role? Partly, it may be due to the fact that central banks are less motivated by considerations of profit maximization and cost minimization than are private individuals. But in addition, the alternative to holding gold directly—i.e., holding claims on a financial institution—was not entirely attractive. For one thing, in order for reserves held in this way to constitute a net asset to the country holding them, they would have to be the liabilities of a financial institution in some other country. To the extent that reserves were looked upon as a war-chest of inalienable spending power available in any circumstances, it was obviously less satisfactory to have a claim that was only as good as the willingness and ability of the debtor to pay.

Another factor tending to preserve the central role of gold was the absence of any supranational sovereign power that could enforce the acceptability of an alternative. Therefore, even if one central bank had been willing to hold reserves in the form of financial claims on other countries, these assets would not have been immediately usable in transactions with third countries. Finally, it must be remembered that although bank deposits and paper money were widely used domestically under the gold standard, it was an important feature of such fiduciary money that it continued to be convertible into gold. Indeed, the statutes of many central banks prescribed requirements concerning gold backing for their currency. As a result, central banks were often unwilling to sell their domestic currency except in exchange for gold, thus increasing their liabilities.

Despite the reasons given above, however, the extent to which gold did come to be displaced as the principal monetary instrument for settlements among central banks is noteworthy. Even in the heyday of the gold standard, many monetary authorities, e.g., in the sterling area, held no gold at all and settled their external accounts exclusively by the transfer of balances in London. More recently, the bulk of the growth in international liquidity has been in the form of dollar balances, and most transactions have been through the transfer of these balances rather than by the physical shipment of gold.

The shortcomings of gold as a reserve asset are readily catalogued. Firstly, it is wasteful to use a commodity with a significant positive cost of production to perform a function which could be equally well performed by a financial instrument with a zero cost of production. A second point, related to the first, is that where there is an economic rent attaching to the production of the money commodity (i.e., where its value as money is greater than the cost of production), there will be a transfer of purchasing power to the producers of the money commodity which will not necessarily be regarded as welfare-enhancing. Thirdly, the quantity of the money commodity produced will be determined without reference to the real needs of the world economy for liquidity. Instead of the money supply being managed in relation to changes in the underlying factors governing the demand for money, therefore, it is these underlying factors themselves (economic activity and the price level) which have to move in such a way that the resulting demand for money conforms with the available supply.

These defects are well recognized, though the advocates of gold as an international reserve asset would minimize their importance. They would say that although gold-mining is an unproductive activity in so far as monetary gold does not satisfy intrinsic wants, the proportion of the world's resources currently devoted to gold-mining is trivial—less than one tenth of one per cent. This could be considered an acceptable price to pay if the international economic system were more efficient as a result. Similarly, the arbitrariness of the real income transfer resulting from gold-mining is also recognized; but this objection applies to the exploitation of all raw materials, and in a world where the price of oil (a vastly more important component of world trade) can be quadrupled in a few months, nobody would pay much attention to the income transfer aspects of gold were it not for the political fact that the two principal producers are South Africa and the Soviet Union.

The crux of the case against gold lies in the element of inflexibility it introduces into the control of the world's supply of liquidity. Since the existing flow of gold production is very small in proportion to current monetary stocks, and production is relatively inelastic with respect to price, the physical stock of monetary gold can be regarded as more or less given in the short or medium term. South Africa's annual production, which is about 75 per cent of world output, represents a little over 2 per cent of the world's monetary gold stock.[3] The scope for increasing monetary gold from new production is therefore rather limited. There is somewhat more elasticity in the supply of gold in private hands not currently devoted to monetary use. In principle, some of this hoard could be tempted into official hands, but in practice it has proved difficult or impossible to achieve this. But even if it were possible to attract gold from private hands into monetary uses, it would not really be satisfactory to have liquidity supply arrangements in which liquidity moved in and out of the monetary system in response to largely capricious changes in speculators' demands.

This fixity in the gold stock, in a world of rapid growth in production and trade, meant either that methods had to be devised to operate the system with less liquidity or that the value of gold in terms of goods and services had to go up. This latter result could come about either through a general decline in the price level or through a deliberate increase in the price of gold in terms of currencies. With memories of the Great Depression still fresh at the time of the Bretton Woods Conference, it was widely believed that a gradual adjustment to a shortage of liquidity—through deflationary policies working on output and the price level—was too painful to be lightly contemplated. Therefore the Bretton Woods system was endowed with the mechanism of the 'uniform change in par values'. By this means, an incipient shortage of liquidity could be averted by devaluing all currencies simultaneously and by the same amount, in terms of gold. This would involve no more than each country's writing up the value of its gold reserves by a similar proportion. It would enable the supply of international liquidity to keep pace with demand, without calling on the painful process of a decline in the price level in terms of any national currency.

It would probably have been hard for this mechanism to work well even under propitious circumstances. But given the manner in which the Bretton Woods system actually evolved in the post-war world, it would have been virtually impossible. In any event, the experiment was never tried. In the first place, the emergence of other reserve assets beside gold meant that any proposal to increase the value of gold would have given rise to switches in asset preference, and thus generated disturbing movements in exchange markets. Secondly, the rapidity with which world trade grew, coupled with a fairly continuous rate of inflation, meant that revisions to the gold price would have had to be quite frequent to keep pace with the growing need for liquidity. Since frequent changes would themselves have generated anticipatory speculation, this was another powerful argument against changing the gold price.

Reserve Currencies

Because neither the quantity nor the value of gold could be easily increased, it was natural that monetary authorities should seek alternative types of liquid assets in which to hold their reserves. Holdings of United States dollars were the natural candidates, since the dollar was itself convertible into gold and anyway the dollar was widely demanded as the predominant trading and intervention currency. In the early stages, too, the demand to hold dollars in reserves was also encouraged by the fact that dollar balances attracted interest, while gold did not.

To begin with, the growth in the use of national currencies in reserves provided an important measure of flexibility in the mechanism by which liquidity was provided. Since the reserve currency was in fact easily convertible into the primary reserve asset (gold), Gresham's Law did not come into play, and the mechanism operated smoothly. However, it is clear that the convertibility of a currency into gold can only be guaranteed so long as the guarantor has sufficient gold to maintain confidence in his continued ability to convert. So that the more the flexibility of this arrangement was used to add to the stock of global liquidity, the more the fundamental gold-dollar parity would be called into question. This was in fact what happened, beginning in the 1950s and increasing in intensity during the decade of the 1960s. Table 7–1 shows the declining gold stock and the rising ratio of liabilities to primary reserves of the United States during this period. It is clear that by the end of the 1960s, the United States had lost the ability to guarantee the convertibility of foreign official balances of dollars. The right of convertibility was coming to depend increasingly on its not being exercised.

IMF-based Liquidity

The unsatisfactory nature of a liquidity-creating mechanism based on growing holdings of dollars in reserves was pointed out in an influential book by Professor Robert Triffin as early as 1960.[4] Shortly afterwards, serious discussion began concerning the desirable characteristics of a new reserve asset. It was widely accepted that it should be created by international agreement, and that the quantity of assets so created should be under international control.

Table 7-1 United States Gold Reserves and Official Liabilities
(In billions of US dollars)

	Gold Reserves (1)	Official Liabilities (2)	Ratio 2:1 (3)
1949	24.56	6.94	0.28
1950	22.82	8.89	0.39
1951	22.87	8.85	0.39
1952	23.25	10.43	0.45
1953	22.09	11.36	0.51
1954	21.79	12.45	0.57
1955	21.75	13.52	0.62
1956	22.06	14.90	0.68
1957	22.86	15.83	0.69
1958	20.58	16.85	0.82
1959	19.51	19.43	1.00
1960	17.80	21.03	1.18
1961	16.95	22.94	1.35
1962	16.06	24.27	1.51
1963	15.60	26.39	1.69
1964	15.47	29.36	1.90
1965	14.07	29.57	2.10
1966	13.24	31.02	2.34
1967	12.07	35.67	2.96
1968	10.89	38.47	3.53
1969	11.86	45.91	3.86
1970	11.07	46.96	4.24
1971	11.08	67.81	6.12
1972	10.49	82.88	7.90
1973	11.65	92.37	7.93
1974	11.83	119.10	10.07
1975	11.26	125.98	11.19

Source: *International Financial Statistics*

The main question—leaving aside for the moment whether and how much new liquidity was needed—was whether such liquidity should be created in the form of an unconditional asset or a conditional borrowing right. The difference between the two, of course, depends on the strictness of the conditions attached to borrowing. The knowledge that conditional liquidity is readily available can, in principle, exercise an influence on countries' policies similar to the actual possession of owned reserves. And when such drawing rights come to be used, it can be argued that they are more likely to result in appropriate policies by deficit countries than the use of owned reserves. This is because the conditions on which such drawings are permitted can be designed with a view to encouraging adjustment policies which are appropriate and desirable in the international interest.

Conditional liquidity played an important part in the reserve supply arrangements of the Bretton Woods system, particularly when lending by the Fund began in a large way after the mid-1950s.[5] And the value of such liquidity was acknowledged in a large quota increase in 1959. But, for various reasons, it seemed doubtful that this source of liquidity could completely replace the need for owned reserves. For one thing, countries did not appear to treat the two kinds of liquidity as interchangeable. There is always a degree of uncertainty surrounding the conditions of access to drawing rights that does not apply to owned reserves. Furthermore, borrowing involves repayment according to a schedule that may not turn out to be convenient; whereas the reconstitution of a stock of owned reserves run down to meet a payments deficit is at a country's own discretion.

In the debate on liquidity in the 1960s the distinction between conditional and unconditional liquidity represented an important philosophical difference of viewpoint. Those who argued for unconditional liquidity wanted to free countries from restraints which would be imposed by reserve shortages. Those who favoured creation of conditional drawing rights wanted to back up the natural discipline of the balance of payments by, in effect, making the financing of deficits more subject to international surveillance.

The formula that was eventually agreed in the 1969 revision to the IMF Articles of Agreement was a typically ingenious negotiating compromise. In substance, those who favoured asset status for the new liquidity gained most of their argument. Seventy per cent of any distributions of new reserve assets was to represent unconditional liquidity which could be drawn on with no need to reconstitute. The remaining 30 per cent could be used unconditionally (in case of balance of payments need) but would be subject to specified reconstitution (i.e., repayment) provisions. In form, however, those who favoured liquidity creation through a credit instrument were given a concession in the title of the new instrument—Special *Drawing* Rights.

A further important question was whether the new asset should be viewed as a substitute for existing reserve media or as a supplement to them. It was agreed that SDR allocations should help fill the gap in reserve needs left by the reduced creation of national currencies, expected to result from the elimination of the United States' balance of payments deficit.[6] SDRs were, however, to supplement rather than replace gold, which would remain at the centre of the monetary system. This was an important decision and can be seen to circumscribe closely the nature of the asset that could be created. If countries were to be both willing to hold SDRs in their reserve stocks and at the same time prepared to use them in settlements, the new reserve asset had to be just as attractive as (but not more so than) gold. Alternatively, precise rules governing countries' obligations to accept, hold, and use the new asset would have to be devised.

In the event, a combination of incentives and rules was used. Rules were designed to define countries' obligations to accept and hold SDRs, and to set out the circumstances in which the asset could be used. But in order not to put too much pressure on rules (which, if too onerous, would probably be difficult to enforce) the SDR was to be made as closely comparable to gold as possible. First, the SDR was defined in terms of gold as being worth one thirty-fifth of an ounce at the official price, i.e., equal to 1 United States dollar at the then-prevailing dollar price of gold. Second, it was given a low interest rate of $1\frac{1}{2}$ per cent. This rate was less than that available on reserve currencies, in order to reflect what was thought to be the greater security of capital value of a gold-denominated asset. At the same time, it was greater than the zero yield obtainable on gold, in order to compensate for the restrictions on free use of the asset, and to speed the acceptance of SDRs as a component of reserve holdings. (One and a half per cent was in fact the rate of remuneration payable on creditor positions in the Fund.)

It is very important to recognize that the characteristics of a monetary asset designed to supplement stocks of an existing asset will be different from those of an asset designed to be a primary instrument in its own right. In the former case, the principal requirement is to mirror, as closely as possible, the features of the asset to which the new instrument is to be a supplement. In the latter case, however, more fundamental questions concerning the desired characteristics of monetary assets become relevant.

In retrospect, it is possible to see that a system of international liquidity based on gold with a fixed monetary price, supplemented by gold-linked SDRs, would ultimately have become unworkable, even if an explosion in reserve currency holdings had not occurred. With a fixed gold price and continuing rapid growth in the value of world trade and production, the bulk of additions to world liquidity would have been in the form of SDRs. A growing private demand for gold would make the existing official gold price untenable. If gold was to retain its numeraire function at the official price, this would therefore involve a separation between the value of gold as a monetary asset and the value of gold as a commodity. The monetary value of gold would become tied to the SDR, and not the other way round. With the monetary value of gold below its commodity value, Gresham's Law would come into operation, and bad money (i.e., money of lesser value—SDRs and national currencies) would drive out good (i.e., money of higher value—gold). Gold would sink to the bottom of reserve stockpiles and cease to be used for balance of payments settlements.

The foregoing description represents, in broad terms, what happened over the period following the separation of the private and official gold markets in 1968, and of course the description here owes something to hindsight. But it is important to emphasize that any monetary system which is based on two assets whose relative price does not reflect underlying supply and demand conditions would face the same difficulty.

Following the separation of the private from the official gold market, SDRs continued to be used, on the basis of the official gold price. The exchange rate between SDRs and currencies could be calculated because both SDRs and currencies had an agreed value in terms of gold. However, once floating was introduced, it became increasingly difficult to resort to this method. Different countries had par values in terms of gold which were inconsistent with the market exchange rate between the currencies concerned (this situation was enabled to persist by the fact that after August 1971 no country was prepared to sell gold for its currency at the stated par value).

The problem of inconsistency was relatively easy to overcome. The par value of the United States dollar in terms of gold could be taken to define the dollar value of the SDR; and market exchange rates between the dollar and other currencies could be used to establish the SDR value of all other currencies. In a sense, this technique had been used in valuing the SDR from the outset, since the dollar value of the SDR had been considered fixed, and its value in terms of other currencies had therefore fluctuated within the permitted margins. Under fixed exchange rates, however, the degree to which the value of the SDR could fluctuate in terms of any one currency was limited by the existence of margins (before August 1971, 1 per cent; and after the Smithsonian agreement, $2\frac{1}{4}$ per cent around parity).

New Valuation of the SDR

After generalized floating was adopted in March 1973, the possibility of large changes in the SDR value of currencies became much more real, and at that time the issue of the method of valuation of the SDR became one of more immediate urgency.

The method of using the gold value of the dollar as the 'key' to defining the value of the SDR was unacceptable to many countries for two main reasons. Firstly, it meant that the value of the SDR (and the gold) component of reserves fluctuated with the exchange rate for the dollar. Secondly, it seemed to suggest (although it was clearly only a presentational matter) that the dollar could be regarded as the fixed currency, and the others as floating in relation to it. Since at the time some polemic significance was attached to the assignment of blame for the breakdown of the par value system, this cosmetic argument assumed some importance.

In proposing a method of valuation for an international reserve asset, there were three main approaches which received support:

(1) To define the reserve asset in terms of a basket of commodities entering world trade.

(2) To define the reserve asset in terms of a basket of internationally important trading currencies.

(3) To allow countries to define the value of the asset by declaring par values for their currencies in terms of it. (In this case, the average value of the asset would essentially be reflected in the balance of revaluations and devaluations of national currencies against it.)

A commodity reserve standard is a proposal that has historically had a good deal of support in academic circles, though relatively little official backing. Its attraction is that it would stabilize the real purchasing power of reserves. It would be less subject to fluctuations in value than a reserve asset based on a single commodity (such as gold). And being defined in real assets, it would be insulated from erosion in real value as a result of excess creation of the monetary asset.

The objections are basically twofold. In the first place, the adoption of a commodity-basket standard would amount to the indexation of the world monetary standard. Indexation, it is objected, is a harmful technique since it promotes and perpetuates inflationary tendencies and weakens the resolve of policy-makers to restore price stability. Secondly, in the absence of stockpiles of the assets composing the commodity basket (something which would in itself be wasteful), the continuing convertibility of the commodity reserve unit into equivalent purchasing power could not be unconditionally guaranteed.[7]

An alternative approach, and the one which was in practice adopted, was to define the value of SDRs in terms of currencies. The 'standard basket', as it was eventually established, involved the selection of the sixteen leading currencies,[8] and the assignment of weights to each based on their importance in world trade. These weights then governed the amounts of each currency put in the basket, at the exchange rates ruling on the day the basket valuation was established. The necessary rounding was performed to ensure there was no 'break' on the day when the old dollar-based valuation was discontinued and the new basket-based valuation was introduced. Table 7–2 shows the components of the various currencies in the basket that was established on July 1, 1974.

Table 7–2 Composition of SDR Currency Basket

Currency	Weight (per cent)	Amount (in units of each currency)
U.S. dollar	33	0.40
Deutsche mark	12.5	0.38
Pound sterling	9	0.045
French franc	7.5	0.44
Japanese yen	7.5	26.0
Canadian dollar	6	0.071
Italian lira	6	47.0
Netherlands guilder	4.5	0.14
Belgian franc	3.5	1.60
Swedish krona	2.5	0.13
Australian dollar	1.5	0.012
Danish krone	1.5	0.11
Norwegian krone	1.5	0.099
Spanish peseta	1.5	1.10
Austrian schilling	1	0.22
South African rand	1	0.0082
	100	

The great advantage of the 'standard basket' as a method of valuation is that it can be used under any exchange rate regime. So long as consistent market exchange rates exist among the currencies that make up the basket, there will be an unambiguous and consistent value of the SDR in all currencies. Furthermore, if the coverage of the basket is sufficiently wide, and the weighting system sufficiently reflective of world trade, then the resulting value of the SDR will be very close to an 'average value of currencies'.

The principal concern of those who were less than fully satisfied with this method of valuing the SDR was that an asset which performed with the 'average' of currencies would not be sufficiently attractive to establish itself in an uncertain and inflation-prone world. (This feeling was to some extent reflected in the advocacy of the commodity standard; in a world of high inflation and eroding money, a new asset whose value was being eroded at the average of all others would not command much confidence.) If the SDR could not be made stronger by a commodity link, some other method should be sought of strengthening its currency value.

One means of enhancing the 'effective yield' of the SDR would be to provide for it to bear a sufficiently attractive rate of interest. But because the SDR interest rate is, for legal reasons, tied to the rate of interest the IMF pays to creditors which, in turn, influences the charges levied on debtors, there was likely to be considerable opposition from potential debtor countries. An alternative means of improving the attractiveness of the SDR to holders could be through techniques to strengthen its capital value. One such technique, which was mentioned in the 1974 report on monetary reform, is that of the 'asymmetrical basket'. The asymmetrical basket proposal involved compensating the SDR for any reduction in value caused by the devaluation of a currency included in the basket. Thus, if the United Kingdom devalued by 10 per cent, the amount of British currency included in the basket would be increased by 10 per cent, so as to preserve the value, in terms of other currencies, of the sterling component of the basket. If, on the other hand, a currency revalued (or appreciated), there would not be any corresponding reduction in the number of its currency units included in the basket. There would thus be an 'asymmetrical' treatment of devaluations and revaluations, and the value of the SDR would tend to rise over time against the average of all currencies.

The advantage of the asymmetrical basket was seen to be the added strength imparted to the SDR, which would speed its acceptance as the principal asset of the monetary system. The stronger capital value of the asset would also presumably allow it to carry a lower interest rate, and this was also seen as an advantage. If creditors are more interested in capital value maintenance than in interest, and debtors would prefer to have their debt increased rather than pay a higher rate of interest, it is obviously beneficial to both sides to have a greater component of the yield of the SDR in its capital value.

Against the arrangement of the asymmetrical basket was its artificiality and the fact that the value of the SDR in terms of the average of currencies would become more unpredictable. If there were a number of large, but offsetting, devaluations and revaluations, the value of the SDR might rise substantially. If there were no parity changes, however, the value of the SDR would be unaffected. This uncertainty would obviously complicate the task of planning the orderly growth of world liquidity.

Partly as a means of overcoming these objections to the asymmetrical basket, it was suggested that the SDR's value could be adjusted in response to both downward and upward movements in exchange rates. This would have the effect of making the SDR value of a currency, which did not change in parity, a constant. Thus, it was a major step towards defining currencies in terms of the SDR instead of the other way round. In addition, if devaluations are expected to predominate over revaluations (a state of affairs which had characterized the Bretton Woods system), this method of valuation would still result in an SDR that was stronger than under the standard basket technique. In circumstances where the SDR value is adjusted in response to both downward and upward movements in exchange rates, the concept of a basket loses much of its significance. If all countries fix the value of their currencies in terms of SDRs, and if the value of the SDR is unaffected by individual devaluations or revaluations, there is no need to have a basket to calculate the SDR's value, and no change in the currency composition of the basket could affect the transactions value of the SDR.[9]

In the event, none of the possible means for enhancing the capital value of the SDR was accepted, nor did it prove possible (for reasons noted above) to negotiate a yield that would at least make the asset competitive with reserve currencies. In this the interests of debtor countries were joined with those of the issuers of reserve currencies, and outweighted the interests of the creditor countries. Under the decision establishing the new valuation of the SDR, the yield is to be established every six months by agreement of 75 per cent of the IMF Executive Directors. If a sufficient majority is not available to adopt a new rate by agreement, a formula is used. This formula provides that the SDR rate should be approximately half the weighted average of short-term interest rates in national money markets.[10]

It should be noted that, with the exception of the standard basket technique, the alternative methods of valuing the SDR suggested above all imply the existence of an exchange rate regime in which par values are the rule rather than the exception. If compensation to the basket is to be made for upward and downward movements of currencies, there must be some standard by which to judge that such a movement has taken place and to measure its extent. In a floating world, no such common standard exists.

If the development of an international money is seen as an evolutionary process, there is a logic and even an inevitability about the nature of the SDR that has emerged. It is an international currency that is, as closely as possible, an amalgam of the national currencies which constitute the international monetary system. In many respects, this represents an unsatisfactory compromise, since it could be argued that what is needed is a genuinely new asset providing increased protection against the erosion of purchasing power caused by inflation. This may be true, but it must not be overlooked that in political economy, the best may become the enemy of the good. The establishment of an international money, internationally controlled, is already a substantial step forward.

The Link

Since SDRs bear an interest rate which is well below market rates, their 'cost' (which can be measured as the present discounted value of the stream of future interest payments on them) is much less than their value. The difference between 'cost', thus measured, and value in terms of command over currencies, is sometimes called the 'seigniorage' on the SDR. The term originates in the right of the sovereign to place its stamp on precious metals, thus conferring a value additional to their value as bullion. In advanced monetary systems, where credit money is used, the issuance of money results in an interest-free loan from the holders of the money to the issuers.

The 'Link' proposal involves utilizing the seigniorage which accrues to the issuer of international money for an internationally agreed purpose—in this case, the promotion of development in poorer nations. Until the introduction of SDRs in 1970, there was no international seigniorage to be shared. International liquidity consisted either of gold (where any gap between the cost of production and the value as money accrued to the gold-producing country), or of reserve currencies, where it was the issuer of the reserve currency which reaped the benefit.[11]

At the present time, SDRs are allocated in proportion to IMF quotas. Since IMF quotas, in a rough way, are intended to correspond to the need for international liquidity, such a distribution might be expected to be broadly 'neutral' over time with respect to the distribution of seigniorage benefits. Countries would be expected to hold approximately the quantity of SDRs they were issued without systematically adding to them or reducing them over time. As a result, there would be no net transfer of seigniorage income from one group of countries to another.

The Link proposal involves allocating newly-created SDRs disproportionately to the developing world. (This could be done directly, by using a different key for the allocation of SDRs, or indirectly through using newly-created SDRs to invest in development finance institutions, such as the World Bank and the regional development banks.)

Developing countries which received the additional foreign currency resources would add only a small part to their reserves, and would use the remainder to acquire real goods and services from developed countries. The developed countries would thus 'earn reserves' by running a surplus on current account with the developing countries. The reserves thus earned would, assuming the initial allocation was broadly appropriate in overall size, then be held by the developed countries as part of their normal desired reserve holdings, and would therefore not add to inflationary pressures.

The attraction of such a scheme is that it appears to offer developed countries a relatively painless means by which to increase the volume of aid provided to the developing nations.

Since their need for reserves is growing, they will wish to add to their reserve stock, and will see no objection to doing this by running a balance of payments surplus—which prior to the creation of SDRs was the normal and indeed the only means for a non-gold producer to add to reserves. Provided the overall creation of reserves is in line with the growth in the need for reserves, there need be no undesirable inflationary consequences. The developed countries can be assumed to restrain demand to the extent needed to achieve the desired surplus on the balance of payments, and this will make room for the additional demand generated by the less developed countries' spending of the SDRs that are surplus to their requirements.

Aid provided in this way, since it would be a by-product of liquidity creation, need not be subject to the traditionally parsimonious scrutiny of national legislatures. This is because it would not require budgetary appropriations.

The objections raised to the Link proposal derive from the proposition that liquidity creation and aid provision are two distinct economic objectives, and the desirable amounts of each are only incidentally related. The opponents of the Link fear that decisions on SDR creation are likely to be influenced by the desire to give more (or, conceivably, less) aid, rather than by the liquidity needs SDRs are designed to meet. Furthermore, they doubt whether the net benefit of a link to developing countries would be as great as a simple calculation of the seigniorage would lead one to expect. National legislatures will be well aware that aid is being provided through the Link mechanism, and will move to offset this by reducing the amount of development assistance through normal budgetary channels. Over and above this is a rather more philosophical objection that matters such as the granting of aid should be a parliamentary prerogative, and not circumvented by what could be regarded as sleight-of-hand financial mechanisms.

It is only fair to point out that proponents of the Link scheme recognize these potential objections and attempt to meet them. They acknowledge that overall SDR allocations should be determined by purely monetary considerations, and not influenced by a desire to maximize aid flows. They also recognize that the *net* additional aid they receive is likely to be somewhat less than the gross SDR allocation they would receive under such a scheme. However, they feel that the relatively 'painless' nature of aid provided in this way would not be lost on legislatures in developed countries; and that the reduction in other forms of assistance would be less than proportionate to their additional SDR allocation. Furthermore, they note that an SDR allocation is normally more attractive to them than an equivalent amount of bilateral aid, since the latter is often tied to specific purchases in the donor country.

The discussions in the Committee of 20 on Reform of the International Monetary System were unable to reach agreement on the subject of the Link, and the issue appears likely to remain in abeyance in the immediate future. This is partly because of the opposition of certain major countries to the principle of the scheme, and partly because events have reduced its attractions to the developing countries themselves. The rapid growth of international liquidity in 1972 and 1973, the emergence of inflation as a major problem, and the advent of generalized floating have reduced the likelihood of sizeable allocations of SDRs. Secondly, the effective increase in the interest rate on SDRs has reduced the seigniorage element in reserve creation, and thus the value of whatever allocations the developing countries might expect to receive under such a scheme.

---

[1] Among the characteristics of precious metals which recommended them for monetary use were their high value/weight ratio; convenience to transport and divide into smaller units; and relative stability in price vis-à-vis the generality of other commodities.
[2] A comprehensive and entertaining description of this historical process can be found in Galbraith, J.K., *Money: Whence It Came; Where It Went*, Houghton Mifflin, Boston, Mass., 1975.
[3] This is, of course, a much smaller proportion of the (unknown) total of gold held in all forms.
[4] Triffin, R., *Gold and the Dollar Crisis*, Yale University Press, New Haven, Conn., 1960.
[5] For further discussion of Fund financial activities, see Chapter 12 below.
[6] To recall this expectation is a salutary reminder of the dangers of designing monetary arrangements on the basis of uncertain forecasts of economic developments.
[7] It may be noted in passing that the proponents of commodity-based liquidity do not accept these objections as overriding. Although it would stray too far from the theme of this chapter to go into the arguments in depth, the interested reader is referred to the study of Hart, A.G., Kaldor,

N., and Tinbergen, J., 'The case for an international commodity reserve standard' in UNCTAD, *Proceedings, Volume VIII, Commodity Trade*, 1964.

[8] The number is not very important. The currencies were selected as those of countries whose combined exports and imports during the period 1968-72 amounted to 1 per cent or more of world trade.

[9] This conclusion would be modified to some extent in a situation where currencies are allowed to move in a narrow range around their par values. To the extent that they do move, and if there is no single currency whose SDR parity is deemed to determine the transactions value of the SDR, a basket is needed to ensure equal value in transactions. But this is a second-order consideration, and the usefulness of the basket in this context is simply to eliminate residual discrepancies in valuation within the limited margins of fluctuation allowed.

[10] The relative weights correspond to those used in making up the basket, though only the five major currencies are used because of problems in getting representative short-term rates in some other centres. The formula is actually quite complex, reflecting negotiating compromise rather than any profound economic concept.

[11] The seigniorage in this case was much less than in domestic banking systems. In the first place, these reserves carried interest at market rates. Secondly, they were convertible, directly or indirectly into other assets, which meant that the issuing country itself had to hold a stock of these other assets to enable it to meet the convertibility obligation. Thus it could be, and was, argued that the net benefits from issuing a reserve currency were very low, or even negative.

Selected Further Reading

Gilbert, Milton, *The Gold Dollar System: Conditions of Equilibrium and the Price of Gold,* Princeton Essays in International Finance No. 70, 1968.

Hirsch, Fred, *An SDR Standard: Impetus, Elements and Impediments*, Princeton Essays in International Finance No. 99, 1973.

International Monetary Fund, *International Liquidity—Needs and Availability*, IMF, Washington, D.C., 1970.

Machlup, Fritz, 'Credit facilities or reserve allotments', *Banca Nazionale del Lavoro Quarterly Review,* September 1967.

Polak, J.J., *The Valuation of the SDR*, IMF Pamphlet No. 18, 1974.

Roosa, R.V., *The Dollar and World Liquidity*, Random House, New York, 1967.

Rueff, Jacques, and Hirsch, Fred, *The Rule and the Role of Gold: An Argument*, Princeton Essays in International Finance No. 47, 1965.

Williamson, John, 'International liquidity: a survey', *Economic Journal*, March 1973.

8 The Control of World Liquidity

Quite apart from the form in which it is held and in many ways more important is controlling the *quantity* of global liquidity. Just as domestic prices and economic activity are influenced by the actions of economic agents when the available supply of money gets out of line with the demand to hold it at existing income and interest rate levels, so also international payments are only in equilibrium when the demand to hold reserve assets is equal to the available supply. This presents two main problems in the management of the international monetary system. First, it becomes necessary to ascertain the demand for reserves at the desired level of world output and prices. Secondly, given the rate of growth of reserve needs, a mechanism is required to ensure that the available supply of reserves is sufficient but not excessive.

Too much or too little international liquidity risks setting off inflationary or deflationary tendencies in world trade. A shortage of liquidity will constrain deficit countries to over-rapid measures of economic adjustment and will induce the average country to aim at a balance of payments surplus in order to supplement its reserves. Since not all countries can achieve surpluses at the same time, the result of such a tendency could be competitive external policies having an overall deflationary or restrictive tendency. The three main categories of measure which can be used to secure an improvement in the balance of payments are currency depreciation, domestic demand deflation, and trade and payments restrictions. Any of these measures can be successful in improving the payments of a single country; and provided that the rest of the world is committed to full employment policies, need not seriously affect world economic activity.

However, when there is a generalized tendency for all countries to pursue such measures simultaneously, the results are likely to be self-defeating.

Conversely, the consequence of excess liquidity creation is unwanted inflation. If countries feel they have reserves greater than they need, they will presumably try to convert the 'idle' holdings into either productive capital or current consumption. Even if, as seems likely, the realistic alternatives do not present themselves in quite such a simplified form, countries with high reserves are likely to be more disposed to take risks on the side of stimulating demand too much rather than too little, and therefore on the side of allowing the balance of payments to deteriorate from its planned position, rather than to improve.

Thus, the world will tend to adjust to an excess (shortage) of liquidity by a process which indirectly generates a rise (fall) in the global price level. This shift in the price level of real goods and services will eventually restore equilibrium by shifting the demand to hold reserves to a point where it is once more equal to the available supply.

It is scarcely satisfactory however to rely on the long-run equilibrating tendencies in the price level to restore the correct volume of real liquidity. For one thing, the dynamic process through which equilibrium is restored, i.e., through deficient or excess demand exerting an influence on the price level, will itself be painful, and if at all possible is best avoided. This is particularly true on the side of deflation, where experience suggests that the downward rigidity of wages and prices means that a rather prolonged period of sub-optimal economic activity will be required to secure the desired reduction in prices.

Secondly, since a shortage or excess of international liquidity does not exert any direct effect on final demand for goods and services, but only an indirect effect through its influence on governments' preferences and policies, the process is not likely to work as smoothly as the adjustment of the private sector to a portfolio disequilibrium. Governments which experience a shortage of liquidity do not necessarily act so as to deflate the price level. They may take direct action to limit payments to foreigners (e.g., through trade and payments restrictions, or the imposition of tariffs). Thus, in addition to the effect of too much or too little liquidity in imparting unwanted inflationary or deflationary impulses to the world economy, there may also be harmful side effects in encouraging interference with freedom of international transactions.

In order to avoid these harmful consequences, it is desirable that world liquidity be managed in such a way that the available supply is sufficient to meet demand resulting from non-inflationary growth in world trade. In what follows, we analyze first some of the means by which an estimate of reserve needs can be derived. Then we consider the mechanisms which can be used to control the supply of liquidity.

Assessing Reserve Needs

Since reserves are held to meet the need of countries to have a margin for financing fluctuations in their external payments and receipts, a naïve method of assessing global liquidity needs would be simply to ask countries what volume of reserves they would wish to hold. The resulting figures, when added up, would give the total requirement for global reserves. This does not mean that each country would actually hold the amount of reserves it specified as an optimum level. Some countries would be in a temporarily deficit situation, perhaps because of their relative position in the business cycle, and would have reserves less than their desired long-run average. Others would be in a more favourable cyclical position and would have higher reserves than they wished to hold as an average over the long run. Overall, however, the volume of reserves desired might be considered a reasonable indication of the volume needed.

The method of adding up individual desired reserve holdings to obtain a global need has two main objections. First, the volume of reserves which a country wishes to hold to optimize its own preferences may well differ from the amount it would be desirable for it to hold from the standpoint of the effects of its policies on others. This would be the case if social (i.e., global) costs and benefits did not precisely coincide with private (i.e., one-country) costs and benefits. For example, if a given country considered that trade restrictions were, for it, a relatively painless form of adjustment, it might prefer not to spend real resources (through running a balance of payments surplus) to build up a larger stock of reserves. Instead, it might prefer to rely on the imposition of restrictions to balance its accounts in time of difficulty. In general, it would seem more likely that countries would usually wish to hold fewer reserves that would be desirable from a global perspective. This is because, while the costs of reserve holding accrue largely to the holding country, some of the benefits accrue to its trading partners. Further, when other methods of adjustment are contemplated, their costs may fall mainly on trading partners. On the other hand, one should not overlook the habitually cautious nature of central bankers, something which might lead them to acquire more reserves than their country really needs.

The other argument against simply adding up expressed preferences for reserve holdings is difficulty in getting meaningful answers. Presumably no country would feel able to specify the volume of reserves it wished to hold unless it had information concerning the nature of the payments system expected, the cost (in terms of interest foregone) of holding reserve assets, the degree of freedom of capital movements, and so on. Even if the questioner specified these conditions *a priori*, there would be no guarantee that the responder would not modify his answers to reflect his own perceptions. As if these difficulties were not enough, it is highly unlikely that countries would be prepared to make semi-public statements of their reserve objectives or that they would be prepared to accept global reserve targets based on the stated objectives of others.

A slightly more sophisticated version of the 'preference' approach to reserve needs is to examine, not expressed preferences which would naturally be suspect, but *revealed* preferences. Under this approach, the world's need for reserves would be judged according to whether the policy actions of monetary authorities reflected preponderantly a shortage of liquidity or an excess. For example, in a fixed rate regime, an excess of devaluations over revaluations would be prima facie evidence of a shortage of liquidity. An increase in the number of restrictions on trade and payments might also indicate a shortage of means to finance payments difficulties. (In this connection, it could be noted that the cessation of a trend to liberalization would probably be apparent before the actual imposition of restrictions.) Finally, a relatively greater willingness to resort to deflationary policies to curtail inflation and a willingness to tolerate higher levels of unemployment would also be prima facie evidence of liquidity shortage.

The revealed preference approach to liquidity needs has two main objections, one of principle and one of practice. In principle, it is unsatisfactory to have to wait until an excess or shortage of liquidity has revealed itself in undesirable policy reactions. In practice, it is extremely difficult to disentangle the signals from indicators which will normally be pointing in different directions. For example, if world inflation continues to be high but restrictions on trade and payments are proliferating, does one conclude that liquidity is excessive on account of the continuing inflation or deficient because restrictions are being introduced? Unhappily, the only occasions on which the signals are likely to be relatively consistent are ones on which the needs of the situation will be so obvious that no great sophistication is required to recognize them.

The alternative to the revealed preference approach is to try and assess the underlying determinants of reserve needs and measure how they have changed over time. Reserves are basically held to cover fluctuations in the underlying balance of payments situation. Two different kinds of financing need can be distinguished. Firstly, reserves are needed to cover temporary and reversible balance of payments disequilibria, caused by seasonal factors or random events such as natural disasters. By their very nature, these sources of disturbances should cancel out over time, but reserve holdings ought to be sufficient to cover normal variations in payments needs stemming from this cause. Secondly, reserves are needed to smooth the path of adjustment to an underlying change in a country's position and to avoid the costs of precipitate action to correct disequilibria. A balance of payments deficit may be financed by reserves during the fairly protracted period during which the underlying cause of the deficit is being eliminated. The process will be drawn out for several reasons: firstly, it will take time to distinguish an underlying trend from a chance fluctuation; secondly, more time will be needed to formulate and implement policies needed to secure adjustment, and thirdly, the corrective policies will only have their intended effect on the balance of payments with some delay, if disruptive effects on other objectives of economic policy are to be avoided.

The holding of reserves is, however, a matter of balancing costs and benefits. Reserves which have to be earned have to be paid for in real resources through an export surplus. Even reserves which accrue through the distribution of internationally-created liquidity represent a command over real resources which the holding country could, if it chose, exercise. Those resources which are tied up in reserve holding could be used alternatively to build up a country's stock of real capital or to meet immediate consumption needs. The optimum stock of reserves, therefore, will be that which just balances the costs of reserve holding (which may be measured roughly as the gap between the yield on real capital and the yield on reserve assets) with the implicit return (through the greater freedom of macro-economic policy to pursue balance of payments adjustment in the least disruptive manner).

Because of the difficulties of measuring the demand to hold reserves directly, the more common approach to the problem has been to seek proxies for the systematic factors affecting reserve needs. The choice has usually fallen on some variable which reflects the growth of international payments, the implicit assumption being that payments disequilibria grow broadly in line with gross payments flows.

Such an approach, however, neglects the fact that one of the factors governing reserve needs is the availability of alternative mechanisms of adjustment to balance of payments disequilibrium. One clear change that has come over the monetary system in recent years is the move towards greater flexibility of exchange rates. In principle, this would seem to have introduced an additional degree of freedom in the adjustment process, and thus to have lessened the reliance which needs to be placed on previously existing mechanisms of financing (such as reserve changes). As will be seen later, however, this conclusion can be challenged, and in particular, it is doubtful whether greater flexibility for the major currencies which are floating vis-à-vis each other will reduce the reserve requirements for the minor currencies which choose to peg to one or other of their important trading partners.

It is perhaps easiest to pursue the discussion of global liquidity needs in two stages. First, we will examine the situation under the essentially fixed rate regime which existed up to August 1971, and in a modified form up to February 1973. Then we will consider how the analysis should be modified to take account of the floating regime which has been the rule since then. This distinction is not, of course, all that clear-cut in practice. Several currencies floated at various times prior to the introduction of generalized floating; and some currencies (indeed, most of the smaller currencies) have maintained some sort of peg in the new managed floating regime. Moreover, even in the fixed-rate period flexibility was permitted in the form of movements within the prescribed margins and in the form of step changes in parities that had got out of line. And in the floating period, intervention has taken place which has had the effect of limiting the freedom of movement of currencies in response to market forces. With these caveats, however, it still seems legitimate to regard the pre-August 1971 period as reasonably homogeneous for analytical purposes and distinct from the current floating regime.

Another important institutional change affecting the need countries feel to hold a stock of reserves has been the increased availability of borrowing to finance balance of payments deficits. Countries have tended to become more willing to make use of their drawing rights with the International Monetary Fund, and they have exploited to a greater extent the possibilities of borrowing in international capital markets. These developments may well have reduced their need to hold unconditional liquidity, at any given level of trade.

Reserves Under Fixed Rates

Under the fixed exchange rate regime, an important element in assessing reserve needs was fluctuations in receipts and payments on current account. On the whole, these could be expected to increase with the level of world trade, though it should be noted that one-for-one proportionality is not automatic. Trade growth may be associated with greater synchronization of receipts and payments and thus not give rise to a proportionate increase in reserve needs. Chart 8–1 shows the evolution of the ratio of world reserves to world imports over the post-war period.

Chart 8-1

Ratio of Aggregate Reserves to Aggregate Imports of 60 Countries, 1954−74*

(In per cent)

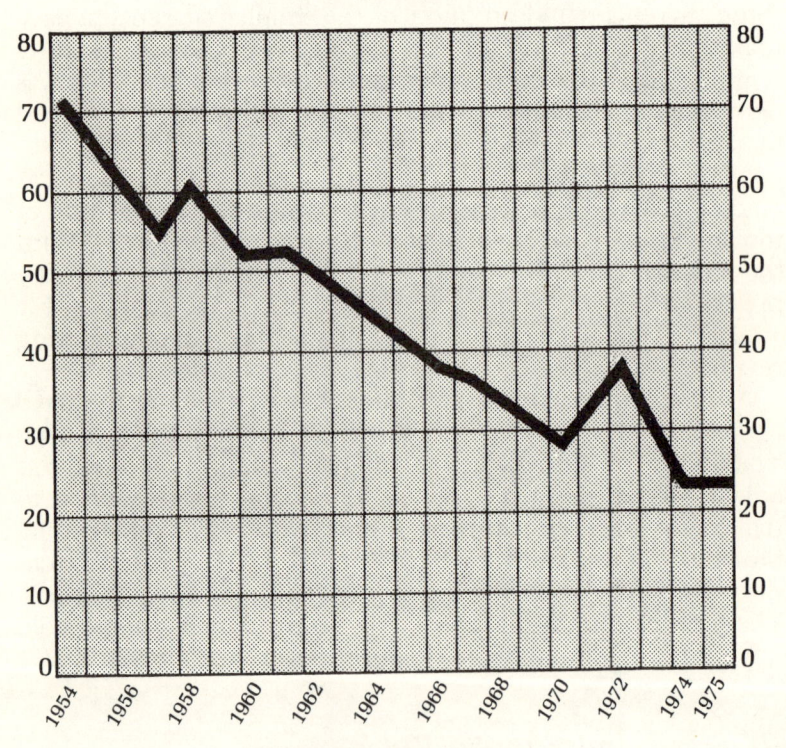

*Reserves are annual averages of monthly data.
The sample of 60 countries includes the United States.

The chief feature of the chart is the steady decline in the ratio. The fact that such a decline was enabled to continue without any serious interruption in the growth of world trade and economic activity clearly indicates that there is no 'right' ratio between reserves and trade that remains stable through time. In part, too, it must be recognized that the ratio was enabled to fall because, in the absence of new reserve creation, alternative financial mechanisms were used to cushion countries against the effects of changes in their payments situation. These included central bank borrowing, both in euro-dollar market and from official sources such as the IMF.

Since reserve changes are the counterpart of the overall balance of payments, fluctuations in invisible transactions and capital movements will affect liquidity as well as those in the trade balance. Taking account of the role of capital movements in generating reserve needs is a difficult conceptual problem. If no attempt is made to manipulate the flows which go to make up the capital account, there may well be fluctuations additional to disturbances occurring in the current account, and these additional fluctuations may therefore give rise to an additional need for reserves. On the other hand, the implication of the Bretton Woods charter is that the authorities should be prepared to control capital flows when these threaten to pose a serious financing problem. Beyond this, it would even be possible to manage capital flows so as to offset fluctuations in the current account, and to this extent reduce reserve needs stemming from variations in receipts and payments on current account.

Experience in the post-war period has been mixed in this regard. In the period up until the mid-1960s, there was a tendency to liberalize capital transactions, and thus capital account needs were becoming, to an increasing extent, additional to those on current account. The clearest example was probably the United Kingdom, where deteriorations in the current account on several occasions provoked a speculative outflow which added to the authorities' financing difficulties. From about the mid-1960s, however, there was a sharp reversal of the liberalizing trend as countries sought to manipulate the capital account as an additional means of financing the current account. To the extent that this reversal of trend was in part due to the inability to absorb capital outflows through reserve changes, it was indicative of increasing stringency.

Any assessment of the adequacy of global liquidity must also take into account the distribution of liquidity. If holdings of reserves are concentrated heavily in a few hands, effective reserve availability is less than if liquidity is more evenly shared. Care needs to be exercised, however, in interpreting the concept of inequality of reserve distribution. Since the function of reserves is to be transferred to meet payments imbalances, it is in their nature to be unequally distributed *at any point in time*. However, if this inequality seems to grow over time, or if some countries hold reserves beyond what could be regarded as a prudent accumulation during a period of temporary surplus, then we may say that 'effective liquidity' is less than implied by global gross reserves. There is some indication that the very substantial accumulation of reserves by oil-exporting countries in the mid-1970s has carried their holdings beyond the point at which they played a role in adding to effective reserve availability.

Although it is traditional to assess reserve adequacy with primary reference to official holdings of unconditional liquidity, it must be recognized that conditional liquidity can also play a part in meeting overall liquidity needs. Furthermore, in a complete analysis, account should perhaps be taken as well of private holdings of international short-term assets.

Official conditional liquidity is available through the International Monetary Fund, whose resources are available to members in balance of payments need.[1] The volume of conditional liquidity depends on the size of member's quotas in the Fund, and on policies concerning rights of access to the Fund in relation to these quotas. Quotas are reviewed every five years. Although they have tended to grow less rapidly than world trade, the willingness of members to borrow from the Fund (and of the Fund to lend) appears to have increased, so that this source of liquidity assumed important proportions in the 1960s.

It is a difficult matter to judge how far conditional liquidity can be regarded as a substitute for the growth of owned reserves. The problem was put in the following way in the 1965 Annual Report of the IMF:

'Ideally, countries' needs for additional liquidity could be met by appropriate increases in conditional liquidity. In practice, however, countries do not appear to treat conditional and unconditional liquidity as interchangeable. For various reasons, countries which have adequate real resources like to have the major portion of their external liquidity at their free disposal. Even if conditional liquidity were expanded on a substantial scale, some countries might attempt—in preference to relying on these facilities—to increase their owned reserves by adopting balance of payments policies which, from a broad international point of view, would have to be regarded as undesirable'.

Because of this, it is difficult to make a quantitative assessment of the contribution of conditional liquidity to overall reserve adequacy. It is also hard to judge the role of privately held international liquidity. For some purposes, it may be appropriate to add such holdings to official reserves to get a measure of 'total international liquidity'. There are, however, serious problems in giving operational content to such a concept. On the one hand, it seems fairly clear that foreign holdings of short-term claims in convertible currencies, whether in domestic money markets or in the euro-currency markets, should qualify as private international liquidity. Perhaps private gold holdings should also be included, though it would be almost impossible to get any worthwhile statistics. However, there is virtually no limit to the volume of assets which could, in one sense or another, be said to represent international spending power. The entire domestic money supply of any country with a convertible currency can be converted on demand into foreign currency to make approved payments abroad.

Although it is not very easy, therefore, to come to an unambiguous definition of what constitutes private international liquidity, the concept should not be overlooked. There are two reasons for believing that privately held international assets may influence reserve ease. The first is that official and private holdings of internationally liquid assets are to some extent substitutes from the point of view of the authorities, since there are often possibilities of mobilizing private assets to help finance a payments deficit. The second is that there is some tendency for private holders to switch between domestic and foreign currency assets, and when this occurs under a system of fixed exchange rates it results in offsetting variations in official reserve holdings that do not reflect underlying imbalances.

The conclusion to be drawn from the foregoing discussion is that it is extremely difficult to make strong statements about the evolution of reserve needs, even when the nature of the international monetary system is taken as given. Presumably there must be some minimum reserves/import ratio below which governments would feel the pressure of reserve shortage; but it is not easy to detect from Chart 8–1 where that level might be. In any event, the basic change in the adjustment mechanism implied by the shift to floating exchange rates must have substantially modified the influence of determining factors on reserve needs.

Reserves under Managed Floating

It is theoretically possible to imagine a situation in which exchange rates were left perfectly free to float and central banks refrained from any intervention in exchange markets. Under such a system, by definition, there would be no need for international reserves. For the foreseeable future, however, it seems unlikely that world monetary arrangements will be characterized by such a situation.

The great majority of member countries of the Fund have chosen to maintain a fixed peg for their currency's exchange rate, either in terms of a single currency, a basket of their own construction, or the SDR. A further group of important industrial countries, participating in the European narrow margins arrangements, maintain fixed rates among their own currencies ('the snake') while allowing the snake as a whole to fluctuate vis-à-vis all other currencies. Even among those countries which allow their currencies to float independently, intervention has at times been heavy to prevent excessive movements in exchange rates. This applies particularly to countries (such as Italy and the United Kingdom) which have experienced substantial disequilibria in their underlying balance of payments.

In the case of countries which continue to peg their exchange rates (the majority of developing countries), the move to floating by the major countries has probably not reduced reserve needs. As was pointed out in Chapter 6, it is unlikely that the adjustment needs of the pegging country will be closely related to those of the country to whose currency it pegs. If they are not, exchange rate fluctuations will be a source of disturbance in the pegging country's balance of payments which does not necessarily offset other disturbances.

Even where countries float independently, it is not absolutely clear that floating will lead to a reduction in reserve use. If par values provided a credible focus for stabilizing speculation under fixed rates, the removal of such a focus might make the foreign exchange market less stable. If that happened, and central banks continued under managed floating to seek to minimize short-run exchange rate fluctuations, it is conceivable that the level of official intervention might even be increased. Such a possibility is perhaps rather unlikely, but it does serve to underline the difficulty of making strong statements about how reserve needs will be affected by floating.

A further problem is that managed floating is not a fixed system. It is evolving through time in a way which may have important effects on the demand to hold reserves. Some countries are moving from pegged rates to floating, while others move in the other direction. Private markets have developed to cope with exchange risks, and market operators have become more accustomed to handling new uncertainties. Certain sources of disturbance can perhaps be expected to decline over time as initial disequilibria are eliminated. Finally, central banks, meeting informally and in international forums, may agree on new methods of cooperation and collaborative management of exchange markets. All these developments have implications for reserve needs and complicate the task of assessing how such needs may be expected to evolve through time. In particular, they suggest that any approach to supplying liquidity which is based on the assumption of a relatively stable demand function for reserves risks producing erroneous results. The problem of assessing liquidity needs and controlling the supply of liquidity is dealt with in the next section.

Controlling Liquidity

In a closed banking system, the monetary authorities are possessed of policy instruments (reserve ratios and open market operations) which permit them to exercise a fairly close control over the stock of domestic liquidity. At the same time, extensive empirical evidence confirms that the demand for money is closely related to a small number of explanatory variables, the most important being the level of nominal income and the opportunity cost of holding money. Both of these conditions are necessary for a policy of controlling the stock of money to be effective.

In the case of the international system, these prerequisites of efficient monetary management do not exist. Different types of reserve asset coexist, and the supply of some of them can be expanded easily on the basis of bilateral transactions, without central decision or control. Turning to the factors governing the demand for reserves, these are, as has been seen, much less well understood than in the case of the demand for domestic money. Furthermore, they can well change through time as a result of changes in payments arrangements or outside disturbances. Also, in contrast to domestic banking systems, a large part of liquid reserves is in the hands of relatively few major holders. This makes them more subject to random shifts as the preferences of individual countries change. Decisions concerning the control of international liquidity must come to grips with the problem of how to cope with these uncertainties.

It can be argued that the unpredictability of shifts in the demand to hold reserves makes strict control of reserve availability undesirable. Consider, for example, the case of an exogenous increase in the demand to hold reserves, due, say to an agreement among central banks or governments to limit more closely fluctuations in market exchange rates. If reserve holdings were previously considered adequate, the shift in demand will produce a shortage of reserves. In the absence of a mechanism to increase reserve availability, such a shortage will result in the deflationary pressures referred to in the earlier section.

It would, of course, be possible to offset these demand shifts by making frequent discretionary changes in the supply of reserves, perhaps through new allocations (or cancellations) of SDRs. But the process of reaching agreement on reserve needs is cumbersome, and anyway it will usually be very difficult to judge with precision the quantitative implications for reserve needs of changes in monetary arrangements. Thus, it could be argued that, when reserve needs are subject to volatile shifts, it is better for the supply of reserves to expand or contract flexibly in response to changes in demand. This has been broadly the situation, at least as far as the reserves of the major industrial countries are concerned, in the later years of the Bretton Woods system and the early years of floating. Reserves can be relatively easily acquired through borrowing on international capital markets. And provided such reserves are held in currencies and not converted into primary reserve assets, the accumulation of liquidity by one country need not deprive any other of reserves.

While the flexibility of reserve supply arrangements is useful in situations where external conditions are disturbed and reserve needs are changing rapidly, several observers consider that this flexibility may have been a contributory factor in the inflation of the 1970s.[2] The fact that deficit countries face a reduced reserve discipline—because in effect they can finance deficits by issuing liabilities—means, it is argued, that they are less willing to adopt needed anti-inflationary domestic policies. This line of reasoning leads to the conclusion that there is an optimum quantity of world liquidity which would result in a proper balance between deflationary pressures on deficit countries and inflationary pressures on surplus countries.

If this optimum quantity can be determined—something that is much easier, of course, when underlying economic conditions are reasonably stable—then it is clearly a desirable objective of international economic policy to achieve this optimum quantity of reserves. This would require some reduction in the flexibility of arrangements which permit reserves, for creditworthy countries, to be largely demand-determined.

One way of achieving control over the quantity of international liquidity would be to provide that all reserve assets should be centrally created and could be held only by central banks. These criteria are met by SDRs, but not by gold or reserve currencies. The quantity of gold in the system can be changed by sales to or from the private sector, as well as by the accrual of newly-mined gold, and reserve currency balances can be generated through credit operations financing payments imbalances.

The lesser of the two problems is that of gold. Since no country is prepared to convert its currency into gold on demand, the risk of massive uncontrolled movements of gold out of central bank reserves is small. Similarly, few countries are willing to buy unlimited quantities of gold, and the likelihood of large amounts coming onto the market are also small, so that monetary gold stocks are unlikely to increase substantially. Price changes, of course, can have a sizeable effect on the *value* of gold holdings, but central banks and governments are probably not likely to change their policies as a result of fluctuations (which may well be reversible) in the private market price of gold.

The more difficult problem is that of reserve currencies. If there is no restriction on the expansion of reserve currencies in reserves, then there is effectively no control over liquidity. To reassert central control over the quantity of reserve assets, countries must accept some limitation of their freedom to hold reserve currencies and use them in official settlements.

The problem is complicated by the fact that there are substantial holdings of national currencies presently in official reserves, which cannot easily be rapidly reduced. A reduction in a reserve country's liquid liabilities to foreign central banks must be financed, either by running down its reserves or by a surplus elsewhere in the balance of payments. Since officially-held liquid liabilities in sterling and dollars are large relative to the primary reserves of the United Kingdom and the United States, the repayment of short-term liabilities by these countries might involve a substantial exchange rate movement to enable them to earn the necessary balance of payments surplus. One way of avoiding this result would be to consolidate the outstanding liabilities of the reserve centres into an account of the IMF, which would then issue SDRs against them.[3] Having in that way removed national currencies from reserves, it could be provided that all future settlements of payments imbalances should be by the transfer of primary reserves (a so-called 'asset settlement' scheme).

Alternatively, national currencies could remain in reserves, but countries could accept a limitation on the amounts they could hold. This might operate in a similar manner to reserve ratio arrangements in a domestic banking system. The IMF would provide for a minimum ratio of primary reserve assets (SDRs and perhaps gold) to be held in reserves, and this ratio, combined with control over the stock of primary reserve assets, would enable control to be exercised over total liquidity.

However, the more basic objection remains whether it is desirable to constrain countries' financing options in the manner implied by control over liquidity. Reserve-holding countries for the most part prefer to hold high-yielding reserve currencies rather than lower-yielding primary reserve assets. And countries which foresee the possibility of being in deficit are not always willing to sacrifice the flexibility of financing through the issue of liabilities in order to achieve the somewhat intangible advantages of a better operation of the system as a whole. Opponents of stricter liquidity control would probably argue that appropriate harmonization of countries' policies could better come about through direct international collaboration rather than through the anonymous and inflexible mechanism of the demand and supply of reserve assets.

[1] For a more complete discussion of the conditions on which Fund assistance is available, see Chapter 12.
[2] See for example Heller, H.R., 'International reserves and worldwide inflation', IMF *Staff Papers*, March 1976.
[3] The reserve centres would then provide the resources for interest service, and would amortize the debt according to some agreed, long-term schedule.

Selected Further Reading

Flanders, M. June, *The Demand for International Reserves*, Princeton Studies in International Finance No. 27, 1971.
Fleming, J.M., *Towards Assessing the Need for International Reserves*, Princeton Essays in International Finance No. 58, February 1967.
Grubel, Herbert, 'The demand for international reserves: a critical review of the literature', *Journal of Economic Literature*, December 1971.
International Monetary Fund, *International Reserves: Needs and Availability*, IMF, Washington, D.C., 1970.
International Monetary Fund, *International Monetary Reform: Documents of the Committee of Twenty*, IMF, Washington, D.C., 1974.
Machlup, Fritz, 'The need for monetary reserves', *Banca Nazionale del Lavoro Quarterly Review*, September 1966.
Williamson, John, 'International liquidity: a survey', *Economic Journal*, March 1973.
Witteveen, H.J., 'The control of international liquidity', IMF *Survey*, October 28, 1975, pp. 313–7.

9 The Control of Capital Movements

The Argument for Liberalization

It is widely recognized that an ideal world economic order would permit all international transactions to be undertaken without arbitrary interference by governments. Thus the argument for free trade in goods can be applied, with little modification in theory, to the case of transactions of a financial character also. In a world of uncertainty, however, with separate governments having different economic objectives, perfect freedom for private agents to make international transactions will not necessarily result in the best attainable allocation of resources. For example, capital movements generated by political or economic uncertainties may give rise to exchange rate movements which inhibit trade transactions that might contribute to economic welfare. Thus a choice has to be made as to whether the benefits of allowing certain kinds of transactions outweigh the potential costs. In practice, freedom for capital movements has usually been accorded a lower priority in the hierarchy of international economic objectives than the removal of restrictions on current account transactions. Balance of payments theory has usually concentrated on the benefits of an international exchange of goods and services and has somewhat neglected the benefits of freedom of capital flows.

Within the group of transactions which make up the capital account, there is a further class distinction between those flows which rather clearly improve the global allocation of resources, and those whose contribution to economic efficiency is more indirect. For example, the benefits of a flow of real resources from economies where capital is abundant (and therefore has a relatively low marginal productivity) to economies where it is scarce and its marginal productivity is high, are widely accepted. This is the economic rationale for promoting the transfer of real resources from developed to developing countries—though it may be noted in passing that just because capital is scarce in developing countries does not mean that its marginal productivity is automatically greater than in a more advanced country. This will depend also on the quality and quantity of labour available to operate the capital equipment, the level of technology, entrepreneurial skills, access to raw materials, etc. As a general matter, however, there is clearly advantage in permitting savings to be channeled from those countries where the desire to save runs ahead of available investment opportunities to those where there is more scope for productive investment than can be satisfied by domestic saving.

Direct investment, even when it is between developed economies and no net transfer of real resources takes place, is also usually recognized as beneficial. Direct investment is frequently the vehicle for a transfer of technological knowledge and managerial skills, whose spread can contribute to an increase in world output.

The Argument for Control

Short-term financial flows between developed countries have much less obvious economic advantages, however. It is not clear that a net flow of resources between economies at a similar stage of development will on balance benefit total world output, unless there is some special factor at work, such as the need to exploit a particular natural resource (e.g., oil in the North Sea). Given the many factors such as tax positions, expected currency changes and so on which may distort the economically efficient allocation of resources, short-term capital flows may easily not correspond with underlying economic forces. In addition, it needs to be borne in mind that short-term capital flows, at least in a fixed-exchange-rate system, are substantially generated by interest rate differentials. These differentials are caused mainly by short-run changes in the stance of monetary policy, and bear very little relation to the basic productivity of investment.

The principal advantage of short-term capital movements is that they can be manipulated so as to smooth an adjustment when the other components of the balance of payments get out of equilibrium. Under the gold standard mechanism, a deficit on current and long-term capital account signalled an increase in interest rates, which attracted sufficient liquid funds to balance the external position in the short run, while at the same time dampening domestic demand and contributing to an improvement in the underlying competitive position of the economy.

In a floating exchange rate regime, short-term capital fulfils the function of preventing the exchange rate from diverging too far from its medium-term equilibrium. If current and long-term capital transactions drive the rate too far in one direction, owners of short-term funds, expecting a reversal, will perceive a profit opportunity and will acquire the currency they expect to appreciate. In this way, they will prevent the original movement in the exchange rate from going very far.

Under the adjustable peg system (and to some extent also under managed floating), private speculation need not, however, play the beneficent role assigned to it by theory. Since the authorities of a country in disequilibrium have two main options for improving their balance of payments (domestic deflation or an exchange rate change[1]), holders of short-term funds have to take a view on which option the authorities will choose. If a deficit country chooses to hold its rate and apply restrictive measures internally, there will be a benefit to continuing to hold its currency, since holders will get the advantage of the higher interest rate which will be part of the deflationary measures. If, on the other hand, the authorities decide to correct a deficit by devaluation, the advantage will be on the side of switching into holdings of a foreign currency.

The risks and returns, however, as perceived from a short-term speculative viewpoint, are not symmetrical. The higher interest rate available in a deficit country is, when it is a question of holding the currency only for a few days, small when compared with the capital gain that would be realized if the country were to devalue. This means that it could be in speculators' interest to move out of a currency even though they thought devaluation unlikely: a 10 per cent probability of a capital gain of 10 per cent represents an expected yield of 1 per cent. A 5 per cent interest differential would have to be sustained for ten weeks to compensate for this.

A further point which adds to the destabilizing potential of short-term capital movements under the adjustable peg system is the limited resources which governments are known to possess for the defence of exchange rates. Thus, when a holder of short-term funds observes a speculative run on a currency, he may believe the currency's value to be appropriate, and even believe the issuing country's desire to maintain that value, but still switch out. What the speculator has to take a view on is not the underlying value of the currency, but its value next week.

In the early years of the Bretton Woods system—say until the early 1960s—short-term capital movements were not seen as a particularly threatening problem. They were in any event restricted by exchange controls until the advent of convertibility (in 1958) by the major European countries. Subsequently, it was felt that a well-functioning adjustment process, which corrected incipient payments disequilibrium through largely domestic measures, would induce capital movements to play the stabilizing role they were thought to have had under the gold standard. The permitted bands around par (one per cent either side) coupled with a use of interest rate policy to protect the balance of payments, would provide sufficient incentive to attract short-term funds to countries temporarily in deficit.

The mechanism worked in roughly the desired manner so long as the underlying disequilibria were not too great, and official expressions of intent to preserve the existing exchange rate were believed. Thus, following the Suez crisis of 1956, a sharp increase in bank rate was enough to attract funds to the United Kingdom. Similarly, the United Kingdom in 1961, Italy in 1963 and Japan in 1967 were able to protect their reserves by using interest rate policy to attract short-term capital. These apparently successful examples of official management of short-term capital flows resulted in an attempt to generalize these experiences into a theory of wider relevance. Mundell[2] proposed an assignment of economic instruments whereby fiscal policy would bear the main burden of stabilizing the domestic economy, while monetary policy could be used to manage the balance of payments. A further refinement of the approach can be seen in 'Operation Twist', where the United States authorities attempted to twist the yield curve so that lower long-term interest rates would stimulate domestic capital investment, while higher short-term rates would protect the balance of payments by attracting an inflow of liquid funds from abroad.

Later in the 1960s, however, it became clear that short-term capital flows could not be relied upon to operate in the textbook stabilizing manner. The disequilibria to be corrected became larger, and the possibilities of correcting them without a change in the exchange rate were recognized to be more limited. Thus devaluation (and revaluation) became more talked about as policy options, with the result that holders of short-term funds presumably revised the basis on which they formulated their expectations. This probably happened even before the devaluation of sterling in 1967; but with this and other exchange rate changes in fairly quick succession,[3] it became clear that central banks would not resist speculative pressures to extremes.

Methods of Control

Faced with the problem that short-term capital flows hampered their ability to manage an adjustable peg system, officials sought means to neutralize the disruptive consequences of these flows. The measures which were advocated can be grouped under several headings:

(1) Harmonization of domestic policies (especially monetary policies) so as to avoid unintended incentives for international capital flows.

(2) Creation of liquidity so as to provide central banks with the means to finance speculative flows.

(3) Forward exchange market intervention to generate offsetting arbitrage flows.

(4) Administrative controls and prohibitions over certain types of transactions.

(5) Separation of certain transactions into a different market to which a different (usually a floating) exchange rate would apply.

These different types of response each presented their own advantages and problems, and it will be convenient to deal with them in turn.

(1) Harmonization of Domestic Policies

One of the factors which is most likely to initiate a capital flow is an interest rate differential between major financial centres. An interest induced flow can be troublesome in itself, but in conditions where confidence is weak and traders are nervous, the major danger is that a speculative run of larger proportions may be generated. By coordinating monetary policies between countries, it is hoped that interest rates can be prevented from getting so out of line that they become a major incentive for capital flows. Harmonization of domestic monetary policies is, of course, part of the wider objective of coordinating all policies affecting the balance of payments with the aim of spreading the burden of adjustment to disequilibrium.

The desire for policy harmonization receives much lip service, and institutional arrangements have been established to try to promote it. For example, Working Party 3 of the OECD was originally established in 1961 to permit major countries to meet regularly and informally to discuss adjustment needs and policies. Similarly, the regular meetings of central bank governors in Basle are intended to facilitate the harmonization of monetary policies. Unfortunately, however, the effectiveness in practice of harmonization falls far short of what is claimed for it in principle. There are two main reasons.

First, policy harmonization implies that individual countries will be willing to concede part of their freedom to frame policies to meet domestic goals, in order to avoid creating problems for others. In practice, countries are rarely willing to give up domestic goals in order to meet some ill-defined purpose of harmonizing their policies with countries whose problems and objectives may be quite different. This has become particularly true in recent years with the revival of emphasis on monetary policy as a means of controlling the domestic economy. In the post-Keynesian period in which monetary policy was thought to be relatively unimportant in the manipulation of domestic demand, it was fairly costless to use interest rates as a means of protecting the balance of payments, while relying on fiscal policy as the main domestic stabilizer. Now that policy authorities use monetary policy more actively for domestic stabilization purposes, they are increasingly reluctant to be constrained by external considerations—particularly when the external consideration is to ease the problems of a partner country which is thought to be pursuing inappropriate policies anyway.

The second reason why policy harmonization has proved ineffective is that the forces causing capital movements in the later years of the par value system became too strong to be contained by acceptable manipulation of interest rate differentials. This was partly due to the growing size of the disequilibria in international payments, and partly due to a realization that exchange rate adjustment had become increasingly acceptable as a means of restoring payments balance. Thus, the size of interest rate differential required to produce a given capital flow probably increased, at a time when the willingness of policy authorities to accept balance of payments discipline on their policy freedom had diminished.

Under floating exchange rates, policy harmonization is not necessary to prevent speculative capital flows, since a movement in the exchange rate can perform the function of equilibrating the supply of and demand for currencies. However, if potentially disruptive fluctuations in exchange rates are to be avoided, it remains desirable for the domestic policies of individual countries not to get too far out of line. This, indeed, is the thrust of the exchange rate obligations of IMF members under the amended Articles. Countries are expected to pursue 'orderly' domestic economic and financial policies, and this is expected to result in a 'stable' international monetary system.

(2) Liquidity Creation
An alternative to adjusting policies to influence capital flows is to create sufficient international liquidity so that such flows can be financed. The financing of capital flows does not deny the need for eventual adjustment where there is an underlying

imbalance. It does, however, avoid the need to adjust to factors of a temporary and reversible nature, and it permits a more gradual and planned adjustment to basic disequilibria.

In the early 1960s, when the resources available to speculators appeared to be modest, the creation of additional liquidity appeared to be one of the most promising avenues for avoiding the disruptive consequences of short-term capital flows. Initially, the new liquidity was mainly of a conditional (i.e., repayable) nature. The resources of the International Monetary Fund were used in a major way for the first time following the speculative crisis caused by the Suez adventure in 1956. In recognition of the potential usefulness of this source of balance of payments finance, IMF quotas were increased by an average of some 50 per cent following the quota review of 1959.

IMF drawings were appropriate to protect a country's reserves in conditions where there was an underlying disequilibrium which would take some time to correct. However, some types of speculative disturbances arose more quickly, and in a manner which made recourse to the IMF not practicable. It was to meet these needs that an inter-central bank swap network was established, beginning in the early 1960s. In essence, a swap is extremely simple. It involves the exchange of national currencies between central banks at a point of time, coupled with a contract to reverse the transaction, at the same exchange rate, at a fixed future date (usually after three months). The Federal Reserve Bank of New York initiated the first swap network at a time when there was pressure on the dollar following the revaluation of the Deutsche mark and Dutch guilder. Subsequently, the Bank of England negotiated a similar network of agreements to protect sterling.

Generally speaking, the swap networks (which were added to over time) were sufficient to cope with very short term movements of 'hot money'. There remained, however, the problem of how to deal with rather more sustained speculative pressure as international financial markets developed and became more integrated. Although quota increases provided the IMF with additional resources, there were difficulties in making adequate resources available to members. The problem was twofold. Firstly, it was not clear that the IMF would have a sufficient stock of usable (i.e. convertible) currencies to meet the demands on its resources that would be made in a drawing by a major country. Secondly, international liquidity was not growing as fast as the potential need for it, and IMF policies limited the amount a member could draw from the Fund according to its quota.

The first problem was solved through the negotiation of the General Arrangements to Borrow, an agreement among ten of the largest industrial country members of the Fund. Under the GAB, the Group of 10 (as the participants in the GAB quickly became known) undertook to lend to the Fund to protect its liquidity should this be threatened as a result of a drawing by a member of the group. The second problem—a shortage of global reserves—was not so easily solved and, indeed, was not universally recognized as a problem. For if certain countries felt a shortage of liquidity, this, it was argued, would be the necessary spur to ensure that adjustment measures were undertaken. It was therefore not until the latter half of the 1960s that the international community began to study seriously the question of creating new sources of medium-term liquidity. (A discussion of the issues involved in the negotiations leading up to the creation of the SDR is provided in Chapter 7.)

(3) Forward Exchange Market Intervention
One means of economizing on reserves, while supporting the exchange rate against speculative pressure, is for the authorities to intervene in the forward market. Because the possible spread in the relationship between the spot exchange rate and the forward rate is limited by the activities of arbitrageurs (discussed below), forward intervention can achieve similar results to direct intervention in the spot exchange market. At the same time, because it does not involve immediate use of foreign exchange, it is not limited by the availability of reserves.

The forward exchange market is simply a market in which contracts to deliver currencies at some fixed future date are exchanged. If the forward rate is different from the spot rate, a capital gain can be made by buying now the currency whose forward rate is at a premium, and contracting to sell it forward at the higher price. This situation can only be sustained if the interest rate on the currency which is at a forward discount is higher by a margin which will just compensate holders for their capital loss. Whenever the forward exchange rate does not just equal the spot rate plus the interest rate differential, there will be a guaranteed profit in 'arbitraging' between the spot and forward market.

Forward intervention can help support the spot rate of a weak currency in the following way. Suppose relative interest rates remain the same, and the authorities enter into contracts to buy their own currency forward in a volume sufficient to raise the forward exchange rate by, say, 1 per cent. This movement in the forward exchange rate will make it now more attractive to hold the weak currency spot, and contract to sell it forward, because it is now possible to obtain the same running yield, yet sell the currency at a better price when the forward contract matures. The induced demand to buy the weak currency spot will tend to push up the spot exchange rate. In fact, if there is no change in interest rates, and arbitrage works smoothly, the spot exchange rate will have to go up by roughly the same amount as the forward rate.

The great attraction of forward intervention is that it economizes on reserves; for this reason the technique was used quite intensively by the Bank of England when sterling was under attack in the 1964–67 period. Of course, when forward contracts mature, settlement has to be made from the reserves, so that reserve economies are only achieved if forward contracts are 'rolled-over' on maturity. The danger here is that if no action is taken to improve the underlying balance of payments, speculation may continue so that the outstanding volume of forward commitments grows continuously. This growth will be evident both to speculators and to policy authorities. The former may see this growth as further evidence of disequilibrium and step up speculation; while the latter may conclude that the spot rate cannot be indefinitely defended and devalue, thus validating speculators' expectations.

(4) Direct Controls on Capital Transactions
Direct controls over certain types of capital flow have always played a role in the post-war adjustment process, though precisely what that role should be has never been clearly defined. The original Articles of the Fund[4] state that members cannot borrow from the Fund in the credit tranches to meet 'a large or sustained outflow of capital', and that the Fund may

in some circumstances request a member to impose capital controls. The use of Fund resources is, however, permitted for capital transactions of 'reasonable amount'. This formulation clearly leaves the issue of control for later interpretation.

It is alien to the spirit of a liberal international economic system to place restrictions on transactions unless there are good grounds. Thus, as the European countries proceeded with reconstruction, and their external situation regained strength, the tendency was to dismantle barriers to international capital flows. To some extent, this trend was encouraged by the move towards economic integration in Europe. It was thought that a well-functioning adjustment process would be able to use the freedom of short-term capital flows to promote adjustment and help to finance short-term disequilibria. However, for the reasons noted earlier in this chapter and elsewhere, the adjustment process was not able to work in the textbook manner. Thus, if fixed exchange rates were to be preserved, along with a reasonable measure of freedom over domestic monetary policy, some interference with capital movements would have to take place.

Generally speaking, such interference involves restricting the freedom of residents to acquire claims on non-residents, although sometimes the freedom of non-residents to acquire claims on the domestic economy is restricted. The major countries in recent years have been unwilling to restrict the freedom of non-residents to withdraw funds. The reason is quite clear: any interference with the repatriation of funds is likely to dry up the original investment flow. Aside from considerations of equity, such a move is likely to be counterproductive in its medium-run effect on net investment flows.

In designing exchange controls, policy authorities face the extremely difficult task of defining controls tightly enough to secure a worthwhile benefit to the balance of payments, while nevertheless permitting investment flows which are likely to be internationally beneficial. Longer-term direct investment is generally treated more freely than short-term and financial investment. This is because it is recognized that such investment promotes the international division of labour, and serves as a vehicle for the international dissemination of technological and managerial information. In addition, direct investment is usually undertaken for its return in the longer term, and is not particularly sensitive to exchange rate factors and speculative expectations. It is not likely, therefore, to be a major cause of sudden unforeseen disturbances in the balance of payments.

There are temptations, however, to restrict even longer-term direct investment when the balance of payments is weak. This has been particularly the case for the two countries which were traditionally the largest capital exporters: the United States and the United Kingdom. The argument against direct investment is perhaps strongest when a country has large net overflows of direct investment. A substantial part of the benefit of direct investment abroad accrues to the receiving countries (e.g., through taxes on profits earned, and exposure to technical progress).

With domestic capital formation, on the other hand, taxes and other spinoff benefits from investment remain within the domestic economy. So long as the *gross* yield from domestic investment is greater than the *net* yield from foreign investment, it can be argued that the former is preferable from the national point of view, quite apart from any balance of payments benefits. (It needs to be recognized, however, that simply curtailing foreign investment will not necessarily lead to an equivalent amount of domestic capital formation.)

Controls over financial transactions are usually implemented by administrative prohibition, or by some price mechanism which discourages undesired flows. The advantage of the administrative prohibition is that it is more predictable in its impact on the balance of payments. However, it introduces a greater degree of allocative distortion than reliance on the price mechanism, since all transactions of a particular category are prevented, regardless of their return. Another problem with administrative prohibition is that since there will normally be exceptions to the rule, an administrative machinery has to be set up to review applications on a case-by-case basis.

An example of use of the market mechanism is the Interest Equalization Tax, introduced by the United States in 1964. This taxed receipts of interest from abroad, thus discouraging Americans from acquiring foreign securities unless the yield was high enough to compensate for the tax. The tax had the effect of drying up foreign bond floatations on the New York capital market. An example of use of the market mechanism in the opposite direction (i.e., to discourage inflows) is the Bardepot system in Germany. This scheme, which has analogues in a number of other countries, involves very high reserve requirements on bank deposits by non-residents. These requirements can be varied in response to the balance of payments situation, and can be applied discriminatorily to the *increment* in deposits. Some countries have even placed a charge on non-resident deposits, so that overseas depositors effectively received a negative rate of interest. However, market-related instruments which are designed to have their effect on the *interest yield* of different classes of asset are usually not sufficient to offset strongly held expectations of a capital gain from a change in the exchange rate.

(5) Dual Markets
An alternative mechanism for neutralizing pressures on the official exchange rate from capital movements is to separate the foreign exchange market for current transactions from that for capital transactions. Usually, this is done by prescribing a category of transactions which must pass through a 'financial market'. The exchange rate in the financial market is left free to move in response to supply and demand pressures, while that in the market for exchange arising from current account transactions is pegged at an 'official' rate. Exchange rate movements in the free, or financial, market create two different types of incentive for equilibrating capital flows. First, since the yield on capital, as a current account item, is repatriated at the official exchange rate, movements in the financial exchange rate will alter the *rate of return* on foreign investment. This is because investment will be undertaken at one exchange rate, while the yield on that investment will be converted back into domestic currency at a different exchange rate. Secondly, the further an exchange rate moves in one direction, with given underlying economic conditions, the stronger will be expectations of a reversal and the greater the capital gain incentive to hold the temporarily weak currency.

By allowing disturbances affecting capital flows to be felt in exchange rate changes rather than reserve movements, the authorities of a country can keep their reserves to finance an excess demand for (or supply of) foreign exchange in the official market. This makes it easier to preserve a pegged exchange rate for current account transactions—which is an advantage if these transactions are considered to benefit from exchange rate stability. The great advantage of a dual market system over administrative controls is that it preserves the possibility for transactions within the capital account to take place freely so long as they meet the test of profitability at the exchange rate prevailing in the financial market. Thus a dual market promotes an efficient use of foreign exchange and reduces incentives for the evasion of controls.

In their management of a dual market system, the authorities normally refrain from any intervention in the financial market, and intervene as necessary to preserve a target rate in the official market. This is not the only possible intervention rule, however. If importance was attached to stabilizing the level of reserves, it could be provided that any foreign exchange acquired or lost by the authorities in stabilizing the rate in the official market could be offset by equivalent sales (or purchases) in the financial market. Or if it was desired to promote capital inflows or discourage outflows, the authorities could systematically buy foreign exchange in the financial market. (This is, in effect, what the Bank of England achieves by providing that only 75 per cent of repatriated capital can be sold in the investment currency market, while the remaining 25 per cent must be surrendered to the reserves at the official rate.)

Although the incentive to evade controls may be somewhat less under a dual market than under a system of administrative authorization, it still exists, and becomes a serious problem when the spread between exchange rates in the two markets becomes significant. Some of the means by which transactions can be switched between the two markets will be noted below, but this possibility means that policy authorities must always be careful not to allow the rate in the financial market to depart too far from the official rate. Effectively, this has the consequence that the authorities have to intervene in the financial market, and therefore cannot totally protect their reserves from capital flows. In the case of the dual market systems of France, Belgium and Italy, it seems that a spread of about 5 per cent between rates in the two markets was the maximum sustainable.[5]

The reason why rates cannot diverge by very much is, as noted above, that there is substantial scope for switching between the two markets. For example, the purchase of foreign currency by tourists, which is a current account item and should therefore be permitted in the official market, can be used as a vehicle for capital exports. More important, however, is the ability of traders to use the official market for speculative purposes through 'leads and lags' in international payments. 'Leads and lags' arise when traders make advance payments in currencies which are expected to appreciate and slow down payments in currencies expected to depreciate, hoping in both cases to take advantage of a more favourable exchange rate at a later date. Leads and lags are one of the most potent sources of speculative capital flow, and one of the least susceptible to official management. Since industrial countries' reserves are on average now less than about two months' trade (imports and exports), it can be seen that a movement in the timing of payments for international transactions of only a few days can have a very significant impact on the reserve position of the country concerned.

Capital Movements and Monetary Reform

As was noted in Chapter 2, capital flows were the proximate cause of most exchange crises under par values; and it was speculation that caused the rupture of the Bretton Woods system at the particular time it occurred.

Because of the importance of the whole question of capital flows to the functioning of the adjustment process, the ministerial committee formed to study the reform of the international monetary system (the Committee of 20) established a technical group to report on the matter, with the following terms of reference:

'To define and analyze the sources of disequilibrating capital flows, and the technical problems involved in the use of measures to influence them, whether applied nationally or to euro-currency markets, and of measures to finance or offset them'.

The group was unable to reach any strong conclusions, but did express the opinion that the factors which had given rise to troublesome capital flows under fixed exchange rates could continue to operate in a floating regime. They expressed the hope that a better functioning of the adjustment process would diminish incentives for capital flows, but thought that countries should be able to use a variety of measures, including controls, to combat disequilibrating movements. No specific measures were proposed, and the report was agnostic in its judgment on whether controls would in fact work. As regards the specific question of the euro-currency market, discussed in more detail in the next chapter, opinion was sharply divided. Some members of the group thought the euro-currency market had added significantly to the volume of capital flows, and favoured collaborative action to restrict the growth of the market. Others saw the market as merely facilitating transactions which would have taken place anyway through another channel. For this reason, they believed controls over the euro-currency markets were likely to be largely ineffective.

The one area in which the technical group was able to reach a reasonable measure of agreement was in the analysis of movements of official funds. Transactions by central banks and other official agencies had in the later years of the Bretton Woods system contributed to payments instability in two main ways. Firstly, a number of countries had attempted to diversify their portfolio of reserve assets by moving out of such traditional (and generally weak) reserve currencies as the dollar and sterling. Secondly, a number of countries had switched their holdings of dollars out of traditional instruments such as treasury bills and into euro-dollar deposits.

The potential for such switches on the part of official bodies, particularly central banks holding large reserves, to create problems for reserve currency countries, was widely recognized. Indeed, well before the C-20 had been established, the major central banks represented in the Bank for International Settlements had agreed (in June 1971) not to place any additional funds in the euro-currency market, and to withdraw funds when such action might be prudent in the light of market conditions. Other countries were reluctant to enter into any similar commitments, pointing out the particular needs which the euro-currency market served in their cases. They were also unwilling to accept any limitation on their freedom to switch reserves between different currencies, pointing out that they were not likely to abuse such freedom as currency fluctuations would not be in their own interests.

[1] As noted in Chapter 3, these are not exactly exclusive alternatives, since an exchange rate change, to be effective, will also require some restraint of domestic demand to free resources for the external sector.
[2] Mundell, R.A., 'The appropriate use of monetary and fiscal policy for internal and external stability', IMF *Staff Papers*, March 1962.
[3] The more important of these being the termination of free convertibility of the dollar into gold in 1968, the devaluation of the French franc in 1969, the revaluation of the mark and guilder in the same year and the floating of the Canadian dollar in 1970.
[4] Article VI.
[5] Lanyi, Anthony, 'Separate exchange markets for capital and current transactions', IMF *Staff Papers*, November 1975.

Selected Further Reading

Barattieri, V., and Ragazzi, G., 'An analysis of the two-tier foreign exchange market', *Banca Nazionale del Lavoro Quarterly Review*, December 1971, pp. 354–72.
Fleming, J. Marcus, 'Dual exchange markets and other remedies for disruptive capital flows', IMF *Staff Papers*, March 1974, pp. 1–27.
Hodgman, D.R., *National Monetary Policies and International Monetary Cooperation*, Little Brown, Boston, 1974.
International Monetary Fund, *International Monetary Reform: Documents of the Committee of Twenty*, IMF, Washington, D.C., 1974.
Lanyi, Anthony, 'Separate exchange markets for capital and current transactions', IMF *Staff Papers*, November 1975, pp. 714–49.
Makin, John, *Capital Flows and Exchange Rate Flexibility in the Post-Bretton Woods Era*, Princeton Essays in International Finance No. 103, 1974.
Williamson, John, 'Payments objectives and economic welfare', IMF *Staff Papers*, November 1973, pp. 573–90.

10 The Euro-currency Market

From its beginnings in the early 1960s, the euro-currency market has grown to become the largest international market in funds in the world. Indeed, the total of deposits held in the market is, according to some measures,[1] greater than the money supply of any country other than the United States. The market began in United States dollars, and the dollar is still the principal currency traded, but all major currencies are borrowed and lent, and the relative position of the dollar is declining compared with that of the strong European currencies such as the Deutsche mark and Swiss franc.

The rapid growth of the euro-currency market, which is shown in Chart 10–1, has presented a number of questions to policy authorities. In the first place, it has been contended that this new financial system, outside the control of any national monetary authority, represents an additional source of liquidity which complicates the task of national governments in controlling aggregate demand. Specifically, the euro-currency market has been blamed for part at least of the inflationary upsurge of the late 1960s and early 1970s. Secondly, it has been suggested that the existence of the euro-currency markets has facilitated the international movement of short-term funds, and thus contributed to the downfall of the par value system. Thirdly, with the failure of a number of banks involved in the market, and heavy losses on the part of others, the question has been raised as to whether there exists a satisfactory regulatory authority over activities in the market.

Chart 10-1

Size of the Euro-currency Market
(Foreign liability positions of banks in reporting countries)

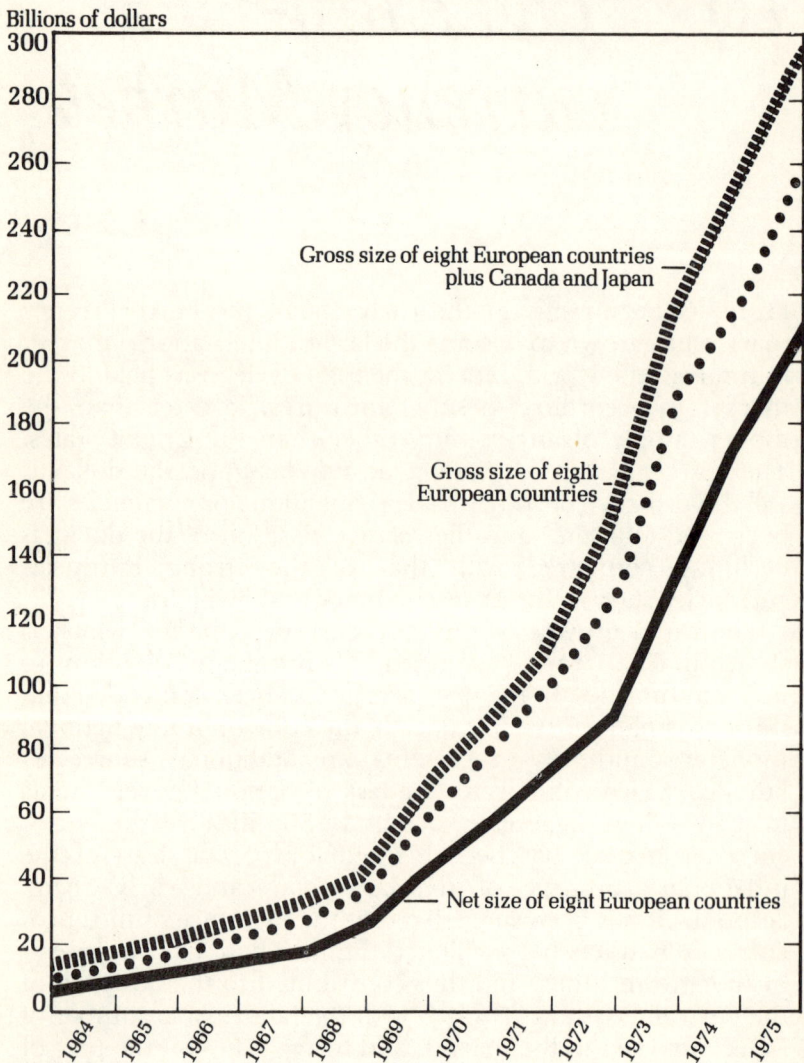

Billions of dollars

Gross size of eight European countries plus Canada and Japan

Gross size of eight European countries

Net size of eight European countries

Source: Bank for International Settlements, Annual Reports.

Each of these questions deals with a different aspect of the working of the euro-currency market, and each deserves to be dealt with separately. First, however, it is useful to review the development of the market, since the reasons for its recent growth are central to an understanding of how to influence its future development.

The Growth of the Euro-currency market

A euro-currency deposit is simply a deposit with a bank in a currency other than that of the country in which the bank is located. The market began by the taking of deposits in dollars by banks in Europe (mostly in London)—hence the original name of euro-dollar market. Now however, the term is used loosely to describe transactions in all expatriate funds, and in centres as far apart as Singapore and the Caribbean.

The euro-currency market received its initial impetus in the late 1950s when the introduction of convertibility in major European countries facilitated the international transfer of funds, and thus the holding of balances in foreign centres. Other factors which contributed to the early growth of the euro-currency (and particularly the euro-dollar) market were the increasing size of operations of multinational corporations, especially American firms in Europe; the United States deficit, which beginning in 1958 was placing increasing quantities of dollars in European hands; and the desire of certain East European countries to hold balances in convertible currencies outside the United States.

Other factors, too, were tending to limit the capacity of the New York capital market to meet international needs, and thus to reducing the need to hold balances in New York. The Interest Equalization Tax, introduced in 1964 as a measure to protect the United States balance of payments, effectively closed the New York capital market to foreign borrowers. Later on, the voluntary programme of foreign investment restraint prevented American banks from financing the overseas investment of American corporations, and thus forced these companies to have increasing resort to the euro-dollar and euro-bond markets.

In large degree the market is a wholesale, interbank market. The usual denomination of transactions is $1 million or more, and the bulk of lending is between banks. Indeed the average deposit from outside the market passes through several banks before being lent to a non-bank borrower. This adds flexibility to the operation of the market, but it also tends to obscure the nature of the basic credit on which the market's expansion rests. The active participation of large numbers of banks in the market ensures that credit will be smoothly directed to the borrower who is able to pay the highest rate. And the wholesale nature of the market means that the margin added at each transaction (the 'cut' of the intermediating bank) is small. However, the pyramiding of interbank lending means that no single bank can be sure of where the credit it extends will end up.

Most euro-dollar deposits are for short-term maturities. This reflects the use to which banks and large corporations put the market in actively managing their short-term cash position. Chart 10–2 provides an analysis of the maturity structure of euro-banks' assets and liabilities. It may be seen that over 90 per cent of euro-banks' assets are for maturities less than 1 year, with some 60 per cent being for three months or less. Assets and liabilities are fairly closely matched in each

Chart 10–2

Asset to Liability Ratios of Euro-currency Banks (London)

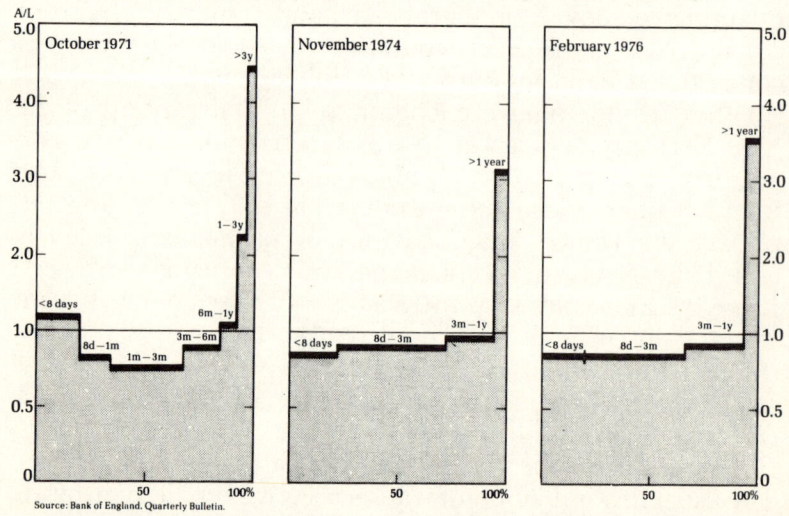

Source: Bank of England. Quarterly Bulletin.

maturity, with only a limited amount of maturity transformation. The euro-currency market may have a comparative advantage in competing for very short-term deposits if there are regulations in domestic markets (as there are in the United States) constraining the interest rates which banks may pay on such deposits.

Although the interbank market in euro-currencies serves a valuable function in enabling individual banks to improve their portfolio allocation, it also provides important services to the non-bank private sector. The euro-currency market attracts funds because it offers higher rates of interest, greater flexibility of maturities, and a wider range of investment qualities than other short-term capital markets; and the market is able to attract borrowers because it lends funds at relatively low rates of interest. It is enabled to be competitive in the interest rates it charges and receives, both because of the economies of scale afforded by concentrating on wholesale transactions, and because banks in the euro-market are not subject to the regulations which tend to raise costs in domestic banking.

Among the main participants in the market, aside from commercial banks, are multinational corporations. The fact that such corporations typically hold substantial balances in the market facilitates, *inter alia*, their operations in hedging against exchange rate changes. Since 'hedging' to a private firm is 'speculation' to a central bank, it may be claimed that the existence of the euro-currency market has exacerbated the problem of disruptive capital flows. However, it should be noted that the market itself does not generate the tendency for such flows; it merely provides an improved mechanism by which they can take place.

Central banks have also participated in the euro-dollar market, and heavily at times. Such participation has been recognized to undermine the control of international liquidity, and since 1971 the major central banks have agreed to refrain from it. However, the central banks of developing countries continue to use the euro-currency markets extensively, both as borrowers and as lenders. Access to borrowing in the euro-markets has increased developing countries' capital inflows and allowed them to step up their development efforts, while placements in the euro-currency markets are generally more flexible and bear a higher rate of interest than holding temporarily surplus funds in other types of reserves.

The effect of the euro-currency market on international liquidity comes about as follows: when private markets have a surplus of dollars (the consequence of a United States balance of payments deficit) they present their excess holdings of dollars to their central bank for conversion into domestic currency. If that central bank then immediately reinvests these dollars in private euro-currency markets, the excess supply is reconstituted, and the process begins again. Indeed the process can be even more direct, where some central banks are lenders in the market and others are borrowers. In this case, the expansion of liquidity is direct when the surplus country acquires liquid assets backed, directly or indirectly, by the liabilities of the deficit country. The assets add to the reserves of the surplus country, while the borrowing of the deficit country is not considered to adversely affect its reserve position.

Ultimate borrowers in the euro-market tend to be traders, and a large proportion of short-term loans to non-bank borrowers is to finance the international shipment of goods. Longer-term borrowers (who usually borrow in the euro-bond market) are usually large corporations financing capital projects. However, developing countries are also important borrowers, as are local authorities and para-statal entities in the developed countries.

Analyzing the Euro-markets

The first source of confusion in any analysis of the euro-currency market is a reflection of the age-old controversy in monetary economics as to whether banks create money, or merely act as brokers between lenders and borrowers. The answer to this question is clear; banks operating in the euro-currency market can create money in the same way (though not subject to the same types of constraint) as banks operating in national money markets. This can be easily seen by looking at the basic mechanics of a euro-currency transaction.

Originally, euro-dollars are created when the owner of a deposit with an American bank transfers the title to that deposit to a bank based, say, in London. He then has a dollar claim on the London bank, and the London bank has a dollar claim on a New York bank. At this stage, a euro-dollar is simply an indirect way of holding a deposit with an American bank. When the London bank starts lending its euro-dollar assets, however, the situation changes. If the dollars lent by the London bank are re-deposited in London, then euro-dollar liabilities in London will no longer be fully matched by claims in New York. By making loans, and taking deposits, banks in London can create euro-dollars in excess of the extent to which they hold deposits in New York. *Somewhere* in the system, there must be deposits in New York, for it is by shifting the title to funds in New York that transfers of funds are made. But these deposits need not be very large for the market to function efficiently.

From the correct interpretation that euro-currency banks can create credit, some observers have jumped to the faulty conclusion that the credit-creating facility of euro-banks may be analyzed using the same credit-multiplier analysis as is often applied in national banking systems.

A number of studies of the multiplier variety have been undertaken, and their conclusions have ranged from a finding of an extremely large power of credit multiplication, to one that credit will actually expand by less than the initial injection of funds from outside the market. The attempt to discover a useful multiplier relationship in the euro-currency market, however, rests on a false interpretation of the basic relationships at work.

Multiplier analysis is essentially a tool for examining credit-creation in a closed-economy framework. The more open an economy is, the more misleading it can become. In the case of the euro-currency market, an explanation running in terms of the multiplier is more likely to obscure than to clarify the basic forces at work. To see this, it is helpful to review briefly the logic of the multiplier in a closed economy framework.

If a central bank makes available assets (currency or central bank deposits) which carry a zero yield, commercial banks will try to minimize the proportion of these assets they hold, above basic working balance requirements. If the central bank sets a minimum holding level for these assets (a reserve requirement) one can say with reasonable certainty that commerical banks will act so as to bring their actual holdings of such assets into line with the prescribed proportion. If, in a closed economy, the commercial banking system finds itself with excess reserve assets, it can get rid of them by purchasing assets from the non-bank public. These assets can be either securities or loans; in the present context it does not matter very much which. In either event, the deposits of the non-bank public will rise to the extent of the purchases of assets by the banks. But since the purchase of assets by banks (or the making of loans) results in additional deposits there will be no leakage of funds from the banking system. Thus the stock of reserve assets held by banks will remain unchanged—although the proportion this stock bears to deposits will decline. Clearly, there will be an equilibrium point at which the ratio of reserve assets to deposit liabilities will be at the prescribed level. In this new equilibrium, interest rates on all assets (except money, which has an assumed zero rate)[2] will have changed in such a way as to restore an overall portfolio equilibrium in which the new supply of money is willingly held. The authorities are therefore able to control the money supply by making use of this fixed ratio between the creation of central bank money (high-powered money) and the total money stock. The existence of a fixed ratio however depends on two basic factors:

(1) That the central bank is the sole creator of reserve assets, and there is no way in which reserve assets, once created, can leak out of the system.

(2) That there is a reasonably precise and predictable relationship between reserve asset holding and total deposits.

The fact that in the case of the euro-currency market neither of these conditions holds means that no more than a very partial explanation of the growth of euro-currency deposits can be obtained by looking at the factors determining the stock of reserve assets.

There is no threshold volume of reserves which banks are required, by law or custom, to hold. Furthermore, euro-banks hold their liquidity in the form of short-term inter-bank deposits or money market assets earning a competitive rate of interest. Consequently, any change in relative interest rates on reserves and other assets will require a shift in portfolio composition (and thus in reserve ratios) if portfolio equilibrium is to be preserved.

The practical significance of shifts in reserve holding for variations in the multiplier (which is the reciprocal of the reserve ratio) is enhanced by the fact that reserves are likely to be extremely low anyway. To a large extent, euro-banks match deposits and liabilities and thus have very little need to hold liquid reserves to meet unforeseen withdrawals of funds. Furthermore, the market for deposits is sufficiently well organized that banks can usually meet their needs by buying deposits at short notice. Finally, banks can maintain a readiness to meet a run off reserves by maintaining stand-by facilities with correspondent banks, as well as by holding owned assets.

Not only are reserve ratios subject to substantial variation, but the stock of reserve assets available to the euro-banking system is, for all intents and purposes, almost indefinitely expandable. A reserve asset to an off-shore banking system such as the euro-currency market is a deposit in the national money market of the country of issue. So long as loans yield more than deposits, euro-banks can expand their balance sheet and meet their need for reserves by placing additional deposits with the banking system of the currency of denomination. The total volume of deposits in a domestic banking system is, of course, limited, but since this stock is very large relative to the potential reserve needs of the euro-markets, an absolute shortage of reserves will not be the factor limiting the expansion of business.

The means by which portfolio equilibrium is maintained when both the stock of reserve assets and reserve ratios are subject to variation can be traced quite simply. Suppose there is an increase in the demand for euro-dollar loans by private borrowers. This will raise the marginal return to banks from their lending activities and thus create a disequilibrium in their portfolios. The higher yield on euro-dollar investments will encourage individual banks to seek additional deposits, and to switch out of reserves and into the higher yielding investments. Because the liquidity services provided by reserves may be presumed to be a diminishing function of the amount of reserves held, marginal reserves now have a higher liquidity value. At the same time, the expansion of loans may result in banks accepting loans with lower returns (either with a lower coupon, or with a greater discount for riskiness). Both these tendencies will continue until a new equilibrium is struck.

The growth of the euro-currency market cannot therefore be explained in terms of the traditional analysis of the expansion of bank reserve assets. The difference is that in the domestic monetary system, the authorities can exercise close control over the banking system's willingness to lend (and therefore over the supply of money) by creating a fixed quantity of zero-earning base money and prescribing minimum reserve ratios. The minimum ratio sets an upper limit to banks' willingness to accept deposits, while the zero yielding nature of reserve assets ensures that banks will not willingly hold excess reserves. However, the mechanism by which the demand for bank deposits is accommodated to the fixed supply is one of *price,* and in this sense does not differ from the mechanism which operates in an unregulated market, such as the euro-currency market. But looking at price, rather than a mechanical multiplier, as determining the size of a particular financial market focuses attention immediately on the factors underlying the demand and supply curves for the instruments traded in the market.

To the depositor, of course, a dollar is a dollar whether it is inside or outside the United States; and similarly for other currencies. The depositor's sole concern is with the yield his deposit offers—in terms of interest convenience, liquidity, etc. To a bank, however, the location where the deposit is taken may make a considerable difference to its attractiveness, because different legal and administrative regulations will apply. Banks operating in the United States, for example, are subject to regulations and controls that make it more expensive to raise lendable resources through taking deposits in the United States than in money markets outside the United States. The same applies to the taking of deposits in most other currencies in the countries of issue. Since the euro-dollar market is the dominant international financial market, however, we concentrate here on banking regulations in the United States. Perhaps the most obvious of these cost-increasing controls is the reserve requirement obligation. To the individual bank, this does not appear as a quantitative restriction on its ability to attract deposits and make loans, since it can always bid for additional deposits in the market. It does, however, act as a tax, raising the margin which a profit-maximizing bank must impose between lending and deposit rates. Even the relatively small addition to this margin implied by a reserve requirement of the size applied can be a significant factor in large transactions where competition is highly developed. Thus, there is a tendency for such business to be encouraged to move to offshore[3] locations where such a tax does not apply.

Another restriction, of a somewhat different type, which boosted the growth of the euro-market in times of credit stringency in the United States, is Federal Reserve Regulation Q. Regulation Q prescribes maximum interest rates which may be paid on different categories of deposits. So long as the Regulation Q limits are above market determined interest rates, the Regulation is of course ineffective. But in times of monetary tightness the Regulation has been used to protect the inflow of funds to Savings and Loan Associations from competition by banks. In such circumstances banks, seeing a run-off of their deposits which they are powerless to prevent by bidding more for deposits, have turned to the euro-market to provide them with the funds which will enable them to continue to satisfy the demands of borrowers. In the two credit 'crunches' of 1966 and 1969, there was a very sharp expansion of euro-dollar deposits, fuelled by borrowing by branches of American banks for on-lending to their head offices in the United States.

The fact that the growth of the euro-dollar market during periods of credit stringency in the United States was not subsequently reversed demonstrates that its function is not simply that of a vehicle to avoid domestic controls. Participants in the market have found considerable convenience in dealing with banks located in important trading centres outside the United States. For example, multilateral corporations operating in Europe need banking facilities in foreign currencies, particularly in dollars, and they need an outlet for temporarily surplus balances. These services might be provided by banks in New York, but there would be obvious expense and inconvenience in the distances and time-differentials involved. It is, in fact, no more surprising that companies with plants and offices in Europe should want a European bank to provide financial services than that a firm based in Liverpool should prefer to use the Liverpool branch of a bank rather than the London head office for most of its transactions.

It is sometimes asserted that the United States balance of payments deficit is the primary reason for the rapid growth of the euro-dollar market during the 1960s and early 1970s.[4] The reason given is that the United States deficit placed dollars in the hands of Europeans, dollars which were deposited with euro-banks and then gave rise to multiple credit expansion. In its simplest form, this argument can be refuted both by theoretical reasoning and by empirical evidence. When a European company receives dollars as a result of exports to the United States, there is no need for it to retain the dollars unless its own requirements, or interest rate factors, make it attractive to do so. If it does not wish to hold dollars, it can sell them to the central bank. The central bank may, of course, choose to hold the dollars in the euro-market, and up until 1971 the major European banks were adding to their euro-dollar holdings quite substantially. This again, however, is purely a matter of choice and interest rates. There is absolutely nothing to prevent a central bank which receives dollars as a result of its country's payments surplus with the United States from investing those dollars directly in United States liabilities.

In point of fact, the vast bulk of the assets of banks operating in the euro-dollar market consists of claims on non-United States residents, contrary to what would be the case if the United States balance of payments deficit had simply been generating a market for instruments to finance it. And the change in dollar liabilities of European banks does not seem to bear any positive relationship to the position of the United States balance of payments—if anything, the relationship is negative, as may be seen from Chart 10-3.

Thus, it must be concluded that the rapid growth of the euro-dollar market in recent years is mainly accounted for by the convenience value of the market, and by the differential treatment of national and 'offshore' banking operations. In addition to the factors already mentioned, other measures which hampered the capacity of American domestic banks to compete for international business included the introduction of the Interest Equalization Tax in 1964; the voluntary programme of restraint on non-resident lending by banks and other financial institutions, tightened in 1965; and controls over United States direct investment abroad, which limited the

Chart 10-3
United States Balance of Payments and the Growth of the Euro-dollar Market

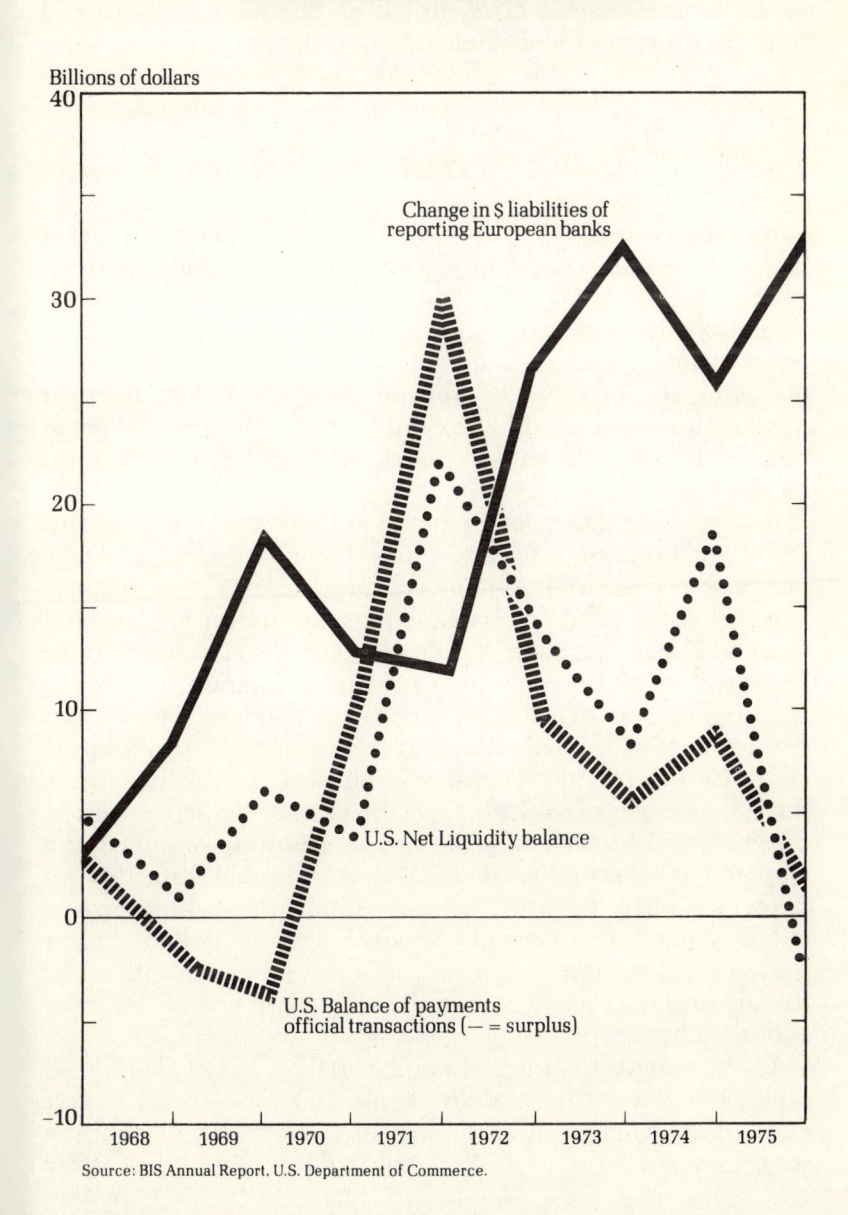

Billions of dollars

Change in $ liabilities of reporting European banks

U.S. Net Liquidity balance

U.S. Balance of payments official transactions (— = surplus)

Source: BIS Annual Report. U.S. Department of Commerce.

use of American bank credit to finance new or additional direct investments abroad.

Having reviewed some of the factors making for the secular growth of the market, we are now in a position to consider the role the market has played in contributing to the three problems mentioned above: inflation; disequilibrating capital flow, and international financial instability.

The Euro-currency Market and Inflation

Some observers have claimed that the euro-currency market had added to the inflationary potential in the world economy, because credit creation in it is not controlled by any central authority. Because euro-banks are not required to hold reserves in the central bank of issue of their euro-currency liabilities, the existence of the euro-dollar market makes it possible for world credit to expand more rapidly with a given base of commerical bank reserves held on deposit in central banks.

It is possible, however, that the authorities could take this credit creation into account in their formulation of monetary policy objectives, and tighten other instruments in such a way as to offset the effects of credit expansion in offshore banking markets. Such a response would be analogous to the action of a central bank in moving to offset a change in reserve requirements or an inflow of capital from abroad. Two factors make the task difficult of judging how much to allow for credit-creation in the euro-dollar market. In the first place there is a dearth of statistics, and the lack of any firm criterion on the basis of which to avoid double-counting of inter-bank transactions. Secondly, there is a conceptual difficulty of knowing to which country's money supply to attribute a euro-dollar deposit. If a German resident deposits dollars with a London bank, there is a prima facie case for saying that the money supply (or more generally liquidity) in any of the three countries has increased.

To the extent that the euro-dollar market has made it more difficult to identify and measure one source of credit expansion, it may well have hampered the ability of national monetary authorities to offset, in a timely way, inflationary disturbances in their domestic economies. Nevertheless, it must be noted that to the extent demand management has been over-expansionary in recent years, there has usually been no shortage of more direct explanations. One must conclude that on the whole, countries have got the level of demand that their own policies determined, and that the role of the euro-dollar market in this connection has been marginal at most.

Broadly the same conclusion applies when the role of euro-dollars in destabilizing capital flows is considered. Destabilizing capital flows are caused by expectations of a change in parity, expectations which arise regardless of specific institutional arrangements in financial markets. It is true that the existence of a well-functioning market facilitates transfers of funds, and therefore may even make them greater over some short run, but the underlying motive for the flows is independent of the euro-dollar market. Any attempt to control the growth of the market would therefore attack a symptom, rather than a cause of the problem.

Regulation of the Euro-currency Market

The failure in 1974 of a number of individual banks which were heavy participants in the market revived interest in the question of whether there existed a satisfactory regulatory authority over the market. Two questions were at issue: first, who should be responsible for the good order and conduct of participating institutions, and for protecting depositors against loss and the system against panic? Second, whether and how the overall growth of the system should be regulated in the interests of monetary control?

With regard to the first issue, the problem is much more complicated than in the case of national monetary systems, since at least three countries are involved. The host country in which a bank operates has the clearest legal authority over the banks' operations within its boundaries. However, the country of issue of the currency in which the bank deals also has an important interest in transactions conducted in its currency. And the country in which the bank's head office is located bears a responsibility for the good conduct and solvency of its branch or subsidiary abroad.

The problems involved in sorting out these relative responsibilities are complex, and it would stray too far from the theme of this chapter to pursue them. It is sufficient to note that control over banks involves obligations as well as rights, since in the last analysis central banking theory expects the regulatory authority to protect the system by acting as lender of last resort to a bank in difficulties. There is as yet no agreement concerning a fair sharing of these rights and responsibilities.

The division of responsibility for monetary control is no easier either. If controls are not comprehensive (in a geographical sense), their main consequence will be to drive business to centres without monetary controls, which are also likely to be the centres where legal and other regulatory restraints are most lax. Furthermore, as was noted in the theoretical discussion at the beginning of this section, conventional instruments of monetary control are likely to be less effective or less desirable if applied to the euro-dollar market.

---

[1] The 'net' figure of deposits given in Chart 10-1 excludes interbank deposits within the reporting area (the eight major countries of Western Europe), but includes deposits by banks from outside the reporting area.

[2] Of course, as money becomes more scarce its utility—which to a bank is the security it provides against falling below the minimum reserve requirement—increases, thus raising the non-financial yield.

[3] 'Offshore' markets in a given currency simply mean a market located outside the country of issue.

[4] See, for example, Clendenning, E.W., *The Eurodollar Market*, O.U.P., London, 1970.

Selected Further Reading

Bell, G.L., *The Euro-dollar Market and the International Financial System*, Macmillan, New York 1973.

Crockett, A.D., 'The euro-currency market: an attempt to clarify some basic issues', IMF *Staff Papers* July 1976.

Friedman, Milton, 'The euro-dollar market: some first principles', *Federal Reserve Bank of St. Louis, Monthly Review*, July 1971, pp. 16–24.

Hewson, John and Sakakibara, Eisuke, *The Euro-currency Markets and their Implications: A New View of International Monetary Problems and Monetary Reform*, D.C. Heath, Lexington, Mass., 1975.

Machlup, Fritz, 'Euro-dollar creation: a mystery story', *Banca Nazionale del Lavoro Quarterly Review*, September 1970.

McMahon, C.W., 'Controlling the euro-markets', *Bank of England Quarterly Bulletin*, March 1976.

Mayer, Helmut W., *Some Theoretical Problems Relating to the Euro-dollar Market*, Princeton Essays in International Finance No. 79, 1970.

Niehans, Jurg, and Hewson, John; 'The euro-dollar market and monetary theory', *Journal of Money, Credit and Banking*, February 1976.

11 Inflation and the International Monetary System[1]

The nature of the international monetary system has an important influence on the ways in which economic disturbances are transmitted from country to country. In the nineteenth century, the international business cycle became a recognizable phenomenon, with the London capital market forming the link by which booms and slumps originating in one country spread to the rest of the world. More recently, concern has been expressed about the apparent tendency of flexible exchange rates to permit, or at least to fail to resist, inflationary tendencies.

Actually, there are two ways in which the international monetary system influences inflation, which deserve to be distinguished in analysis. In the first place, monetary arrangements can affect the way in which a given inflationary disturbance is *shared,* without necessarily changing the overall size of the disturbance. Secondly, monetary arrangements, by influencing the extent to which disturbances can affect exchange rates and therefore prices, may change the behavioural response of individuals and governments to such disturbances. Where this happens, it is possible that the particular international monetary system in existence may have implications for the global rate of inflation.

In what follows it will be convenient to compare the effects on inflation of, respectively, a predominantly fixed exchange rate system and a predominantly floating system.

The Transmission Mechanism

The mechanisms by which inflationary impulses originating in an individual country are transmitted across national boundaries under a system of fixed exchange rates can be divided into three main types (which are not mutually exclusive). These are:

(1) effects on the price of traded goods, which have implications for the volume and distribution of expenditure;

(2) monetary effects, operating through money supply changes, caused by disequilibria in the overall balance of payments; and

(3) reserve discipline effects, operating through policy measures undertaken by governments in the light of external objectives.

Each of these effects may be reviewed in turn, although it should be clear that in practice they are likely to be mutually reinforcing.

(1) Traded Goods Price Effects
An inflationary impulse in one country will put upward pressure on the price level of its trading partners in a number of ways. To the extent that the exports of the inflating country enter into the price level of its trading partners (either directly in final consumption, or indirectly as production inputs), the inflationary impact is immediate. Beyond this, however, the loss of price competitiveness in the country experiencing the initial inflationary impulse will tend to restrain its exports and increase its imports. This will increase the net demand for the products of other countries, which will of course have a fairly direct effect on their price levels. Furthermore, the higher income and profit levels which result from the higher net exports of these countries will have a multiplier effect on demand there. Lastly, in so far as traded goods of different provenance may be considered substitutes, a change in the price of goods coming from one source is, due to competitive forces, likely to introduce a sympathetic movement in the price of competing goods.

To the extent that some of the inflationary consequences of a disturbance originating in one country are transmitted to partner countries, the impact of the disturbance in the country where it occurs will be moderated. Competitive forces will prevent cost increases in one country from being translated fully into price adjustments; this is because net imports will absorb part of an increase in demand, without allowing it to increase the pressure on domestic resources. And to the extent that imports are an important component of the price index, domestic costs increases will result in a less than proportionate rise in the price level of final output.

It is relatively easy to see that, if countries start from balance of payments equilibrium at full employment and stable prices, if there are no offsetting government policies and if the original disturbance does not influence the structure of demand within countries, then an inflationary impulse in one country, transmitted through the trade accounts, will eventually lead to a similar rise in the price of tradeable goods in all countries. This is because, so long as a price disparity remains, some countries will have surpluses and others deficits in their trade accounts. This will produce excess demand and thus rising (relative) prices in the surplus countries and unemployment with falling (relative) prices in the deficit countries.

Under flexible exchange rates, on the other hand, the upward pressure caused by additional domestic spending will, if capital flows are ignored or assumed constant, cause the exchange rate for the currency of the country where the disturbance originated to deteriorate just sufficiently to maintain domestic absorption equal to domestic real output. And since exports and imports can be assumed to depend on relative prices, it is to be expected that the exchange rate will decline by exactly the amount that domestic prices have increased. If this happens there will be no leakage of real demand and, assuming output was previously at the full employment level, the entire inflationary impulse will be exhausted in price increases in the country of the original disturbance.

(2) Monetary Effects
A further mechanism through which the exchange rate regime influences the transmission of inflationary impulses is

through the effect of balance of payments deficits and surpluses on the money supply of various countries. An overall balance of payments disequilibrium gives rise to a monetary flow which, under a fixed exchange rate regime, will tend to equalize inflationary pressures across countries. This mechanism, which was described in Chapter 3 above, was first set forth by Hume,[2] later expounded by Smith, Ricardo, and Mill and developed in its most complete form as the price-specie-flow mechanism of adjustment of the gold standard.

This view of the transmission mechanism lost adherents at a time when Keynesian theories were applied to balance of payments analysis; but in the context of a general reappraisal of the importance of monetary factors, it has recently regained considerable popularity as the basis of the monetary approach to the balance of payments. The essence of the monetary transmission mechanism can be simply described: consider a case in which equilibrium in the global pattern of payments is disturbed by a monetary expansion in one country. The excess supply of money in this country will tend to push up prices, which will lead to a deterioration in the balance of payments. The balance of payments deficit will, under a fixed exchange rate, result in a transfer of reserves to trading partners which, in the absence of sterilization, will cause an expansion of their money supply. This monetary expansion will then generate in turn an increase in prices in these countries[3]. Since there is considered to be a stable relationship between the demand for money and the level of nominal income in all countries, payments equilibrium under a fixed exchange rate system will be restored when the money stock (and the price level) in all countries has increased in an equal proportion. In a flexible exchange rate world, on the other hand, the fact the monetary authorities neither acquire nor provide domestic currencies through their exchange market operations means there is by definition no leakage of reserves abroad, and so pure monetary effects on inflation remain 'bottled up' in the domestic economy.

The foregoing analysis has described a monetary transmission effect working through the current account (i.e., capital flows have been assumed unaffected). It is just as possible, and perhaps in modern circumstances more likely, for the relevant transmission to be effected through the capital account. An increase in the money supply in a given country will lead to a decline in interest rates and an outflow of capital to its trading partners. These countries will therefore find their money supply increasing and interest rates declining until there is no further incentive for capital flows. At that point, the money supplies of all countries will have increased in equal proportions, even though the effect of the increase may not yet have worked its way through to the price level.

The primacy of monetary effects in the transmission of inflationary disturbances is sometimes advanced as a reason why free flexibility of the exchange rate is a necessary and sufficient condition for a country to insulate itself from disturbances arising from developments abroad. While it is true that floating prevents unwanted changes in the domestic money supply, this would only insulate an economy from foreign influences if there was a unique relationship between the money supply and the level of money income. In fact, as is well known and accepted, interest rates also play an important role in determining the demand for money (at least in the short run in which real interest rates can be induced by policy to depart from their long-run equilibrium value). Provided, therefore, that capital flows are responsive to interest rate differentials, monetary disturbances in one country can influence the rate of inflation in its trading partners, even when flexible exchange rates ensure that the quantity of money in the trading partners' economies is unchanged. This mechanism can be traced through in a little more detail.

An increase in the money supply requires a decline in the level of interest rates in the short run, if the demand for money is to remain in equilibrium in a situation where the level of nominal income has not changed. With capital mobility, there will therefore be a tendency for capital to flow out of the country where the monetary expansion occurred and towards countries which now have an interest differential in their favour. This will tend to push up the exchange rate of the capital-receiving countries, which will both moderate the initial capital flow and cause a deterioration in their current account. (The new short-run equilibrium exchange rate will be determined at the point where the current account deterioration just matches the capital flow.) This exchange rate appreciation, which is caused by a capital inflow, will turn the terms of trade in favour of the capital-receiving countries, and will therefore have a downward impact on their price level. Thus the transmission mechanism for monetary disturbances under a flexible rate system can actually cause perverse consequences for trading partners, at least in the short run.[4]

(3) Reserve Discipline Effects
Although the combination of traded goods price effects and monetary effects should be sufficient, by themselves, to equalize inflationary pressures across all countries on a fixed exchange rate standard, they may in practice be relatively slow acting, or may even be offset by conscious policy decisions. For this reason it is important to take into account the implicit policy response required by adherence to the fixed exchange rate system. It is usually argued that the rules of the game dictated by a fixed exchange rate system imply a policy response to disequilibrium that reinforces the automatic influences of the two mechanisms just discussed.

The basis of the policy reaction mechanism is the notion that the monetary authorities have a fixed external objective, which may be thought of in terms of a target holding of international reserves (though it is conceivable that the target may relate to other components of the balance of payments as well). The desire of the authorities to achieve this external target influences inflation by systematically modifying the chosen trade-off between inflation and unemployment. For example, in a fixed exchange rate regime, a country which is losing reserves will give relatively more weight in its policy choice to restraining inflation and relatively less to promoting employment. Similarly, a country with a strong balance of payments will be less concerned about developments which tend to increase prices and more concerned about developments which tend to increase unemployment. If relative prices are the main determinant of balance of payments positions, the net result will be for demand management policies to be conducted so as to equalize price developments across countries.

Under floating exchange rates, on the other hand, the overall balance of payments is by definition always in equilibrium, and therefore there is no factor which modifies the choice of trade-off. There is, therefore, nothing to prevent a country which perceives a domestic advantage from having an inflation rate different from that of its trading partners from following this policy.

This brief review of transmission mechanisms makes it clear that the salient characteristic of inflation under a fixed exchange rate regime is that all countries, if they are not to alter their exchange rates or impose new restrictions on capital flows, must accept a common rate of inflation over the long term. However, as Milton Friedman notes, 'the only discipline is to keep in step with the rest of the world, not to march in the right direction'.[5] And there is no presumption that this common (world) rate of inflation should be low, high, moderate, or even positive.

Of course, the strength of the tendency towards coordination of inflationary pressures depends on how fixed, fixed rates really are. In a rigidly fixed exchange rate system, such as that of the gold standard, there is no escaping the discipline of conformity with world price trends. Even in such a case, however, pressures to coordinate price levels can be withstood for a significant period of time—money flows can be sterilized; indicated policy responses can be ignored, and imported price effects on real demand can be offset by fiscal policy. If, in addition to neutralizing transmitted inflationary effects in the short run, countries are willing to cancel them out over the longer term through periodic exchange rate adjustments, the mechanism by which inflationary influences are transmitted will be much weakened. However, it will remain true in a qualitative sense that a regime where the exchange rate is less free to fluctuate will tend to transmit cost and demand influences on price to a greater extent than one in which the impact of such influences is softened by exchange rate changes.

All of the transmission mechanisms noted above are essentially neutral with respect to their effect on the world average rate of inflation. Their effect is to *generalize* a given disturbance under fixed rates, but there is no *a priori* reason to suppose that the disturbance would thereby be magnified or reduced. In order for international monetary arrangements to have a systematic effect on inflation, therefore, it is necessary for behavioural reactions in some countries to be different from those in others, or for them to change systematically in response to a change in monetary environment.

For example, whether or not 'bottling up' a monetary effect will have a net effect on global inflation depends on whether a given expansion in the money supply has a greater effect on prices in the country where the monetary disturbance originates or in the rest of the world. Similarly, whether a transfer of real demand from one country to another will affect inflation depends essentially on the amount of spare capacity available in the respective countries. Over time, however, it appears unlikely that there would be a systematic tendency for inflationary disturbances to be concentrated in one group of countries rather than another.

It is perhaps more likely that the way in which disturbances are transmitted would modify the behavioural response of individuals and governments. For example, greater openness to price changes originating abroad (the result of a fluctuating exchange rate) might, under certain assumptions, strengthen cost-inflationary pressures. This in turn could modify the unemployment/inflation trade-off and cause governments to select a different target inflation rate.

Effects of Exchange Regimes on the Price Level

The exchange rate regime will have an effect on the price *level* if it causes an upward movement in either costs of production or levels of demand. In so far as any upward movements in these curves are validated by government policies and repeated, they may result in a longer-run shift in the rate of inflation. The question of whether governments' policy responses will be *systematically* influenced by the exchange rate regime, however, is one which bears on the rate of inflation rather than the price level, and is dealt with later in the chapter.

Since the production of export goods normally yields, in the first instance, foreign exchange, any uncertainties and transaction expenses involved in converting foreign currency receipts into domestic currency available for the payment of factors of production must be included as a cost of production. In cases where it is possible to buy protection against these uncertainty costs, e.g., where forward exchange markets are developed for the relevant maturities, such costs can be simply added to the costs of production and distribution. Where such insurance protection is not available, the increase in uncertainty will still give rise to *quantity* adjustments, i.e. the volume of international transactions will decrease.

Although the argument from uncertainty is conceptually easy to grasp, for flexible exchange rates to cause an increase in effective costs requires two additional assumptions. Firstly, it must be assumed that exchange rates will be more variable under flexible rates than under fixed rates. Secondly, it must be the case that exchange rate variability captures all the relevant uncertainties faced by international traders.

Friedman, among many others, has pointed out that the fact that exchange rates are free to move under flexible rates does not imply that they will in fact be unstable. Provided economic conditions and underlying costs of production in different countries are reasonably stable, there is no reason to expect sudden shifts in the demand for and supply of traded goods, and thus no reason for exchange rate changes to be needed to equilibrate supply and demand in the foreign exchange market.

Even if it is accepted that, because of the resistance it offers to random or speculative disturbances, a par value system diminishes the degree of exchange rate uncertainty, it could still be argued that this type of uncertainty is no worse than the other uncertainty involved in trying to maintain a fixed pattern of rates. As Friedman puts it, 'if floating rates are highly unstable it will be because the internal monetary policies of the countries or some other aspects of their economy are highly unstable. But in that case, the uncertainty is there and the only question is what form it takes'.[6]

Recognizing that exchange rate stability may be purchased at the cost of some additional uncertainty with respect to the alternative policies which may have to be used for external adjustment, it needs to be asked how large or costly the uncertainty generated by flexible exchange rates might be. In principle, the cost of uncertainty can be measured by the price of purchasing insurance against it. In the case of exchange rate uncertainty, the cost to traders can be measured by the spread between the bid and asked price for forward exchange.

Even a cursory examination of the evidence shows that the qualitative importance of cost increases due to the need for forward cover is likely to be insignificant relative to other factors affecting (influencing) costs and inflation rates. In markets for major currencies, the spread between bid and asked prices for forward foreign exchange are virtually never greater than one-tenth of 1 per cent of the transaction price. If it is borne in mind that the expected future spot price is the mean of the spread, the cost added to trade in each direction is therefore rarely greater than one-twentieth of 1 per cent. Furthermore, since any increase in costs will be once for all, it will therefore have a virtually negligible impact on the continuing rate of inflation.

Forward markets, however, generally exist for maturities not exceeding one year, while certain decisions involving international trade and investment may cover much longer time spans. For example, the decision to serve a world market from a single low cost source, or to establish subsidiaries in each export market, could well be influenced by exchange variability (among, of course, many other considerations). Thus it may be the case that long-term exchange variability militates against international specialization, thus eventually reducing the level of world trade and increasing unit prices. Unfortunately, given the long-term nature of this hypothesis it is not yet possible to gather evidence from actual experience that would convincingly support or reject it.

On the whole, it seems likely that the impact of uncertainty on trade volumes and on the price levels of traded goods is so small that any contribution to inflationary pressures that a flexible exchange rate regime might produce can probably be ignored. At any event, they should only be taken into account if the other advantages and disadvantages of the alternative regimes are very finely balanced.

In addition to possibly raising the cost curve for world output, the nature of the exchange rate regime may also have an effect on the demand side. Since the exchange rate regime affects the rate at which one currency can be converted into another, and the degree of confidence with which such transactions can be made at some future time period, it is clearly possible for the nature of the exchange rate system to influence demand to hold balances in a given currency. Furthermore, since the demand for money is the opposite side of the coin to the demand for other assets, it is clear that a shift in the demand for money function, with a given world money supply, implies changes in the level of demand for goods and other financial assets also.

Both the private sector and national monetary authorities may be affected in their portfolio decisions by a change in exchange rate regime. The private sector may choose to hold more or fewer money balances because of the lower degree of certainty with which balances in one currency can be converted into another currency under a flexible exchange rate system. Similarly, governments may find a reduced need for currency reserves in a floating system where adjustment to balance of payments disequilibrium can take place through changes in the exchange rate.

An increase in the variability of exchange rates means that the range of transactions for which balances held in a given national currency are an optimum store of value is curtailed. For this reason, one might expect that a move to floating would lead to a reduction in the desire of private wealth holders to hold the traditional vehicle currencies. However, it should be noted that the decline in the usefulness of a single vehicle currency probably has as its counterpart an increase in the incentive to hold a diversified portfolio of currencies. If a private asset holder (e.g., a multinational corporation) has to hold balances in several currencies to meet fluctuations in payments and receipts in each currency separately, then it is likely that its total combined holdings will be greater than if all such balances were centralized in a single account.

If the foregoing argument is accepted, it would seem more likely that a move to flexible exchange rates would cause an upward shift in the demand for money, i.e., a decrease in the real demand for goods and services at a given level of the world money supply. But it is probably virtually impossible to disentangle whether such an influence was at work following the move to greater exchange rate flexibility in the early 1970s. For one thing, the existence of an active euro-currency market, in which most banks and non-financial corporations with a substantial international business participated, meant that the system as a whole had plenty of flexibility to adapt to the kind of demand shifts to which changes in exchange rate regime might give rise. Secondly, the possibility for monetary authorities to allow the supply of money to accommodate to shifts in the demand are substantial, particularly in a world where most monetary authorities have at least half an eye to interest rate targets.

In addition to demand effects stemming from shifts in the private sector's demand function for money, it is possible for a change in exchange rate regime to have an impact on inflation through monetary authorities' demand for international liquidity. The extreme version of this argument runs as follows: since under flexible exchange rates the supply and demand for foreign currencies will always be in equilibrium, there is no need for government authorities to hold foreign exchange reserves. As a result, governments which hold such reserves will seek to run down this unproductive investment of the national patrimony by having overall deficits in their balance of payments. Since one country's deficit is another's surplus there will be an inconsistency in policy objectives and the general attempt to have imports greater than exports will result only in inflation.

More realistically, the argument recognizes that governments will continue to feel some need for reserves, either to sustain a fixed exchange rate on a bilateral or regional basis, or to intervene to moderate fluctuations in a floating rate, but will nevertheless experience economies in reserve needs as a result in the greater flexibility of exchange rates.

Accepting that there is a likelihood that flexible exchange rates may result in some reduction in reserve needs, to what extent would this contribute to inflation? For several reasons this contribution is probably less serious in its effects than in the case of excess monetary creation in a closed banking system. First of all, monetary authorities having reserve holdings excess to needs are unlikely to attempt to run them down quickly, if only because they cannot easily direct additional demand to the foreign sector, and they will be fearful of setting in train a domestic inflationary spiral. Secondly, since the greater portion of world reserves are the liabilities of another country, holdings that are excess to demand can be run down without necessarily giving rise to expenditures on real goods and services. Lastly, the fact that the adoption of widespread floating in 1973 was quickly succeeded by a largely exogenous increase in payments disequilibria (due to the increase in oil prices) meant that any excess liquidity that might have been generated by the move to flexibility was quickly absorbed in the growth of general reserve needs.

For all of these reasons, it seems unlikely that the direct effect of reserve ease on inflation, resulting from the change in exchange rate regime, was very significant. And since it was earlier concluded that any uncertainty costs attributable to exchange rate variability must have been quantitatively very small, it seems reasonable to conclude that the net direct effects of the exchange rate regime on the price *level* is ambiguous as to direction, and small as to amount. However, while countries may not have reacted to floating by deliberately trying to run down their reserve holdings, there could well be an indirect effect on inflation if greater exchange rate flexibility led to changes in policy decisions about the appropriate rate of demand expansion.

Effects on Inflation

In principle, as has been noted, once-for-all shifts in cost or demand curves can affect only the price *level*, not the rate of inflation. However, to the extent that cost or demand shifts are subsequently validated by policy measures, they can affect the continuing inflation rate. Since the exchange rate regime has an effect on the way in which cost and demand influences impinge on national economies, it can thereby affect the relative strength of cost push and demand pull in inflation, and so the trade-off between inflation and unemployment.

The concept of a 'trade-off' between unemployment and inflation was first introduced into the literature by Phillips[7] and has since been subject to an enormous amount of theoretical and empirical study. To begin with, there was considerable acceptance of the Phillips curve as an empirical phenomenon which had important implications for policy choice. More recently, however, there has been a substantial body of opinion, first put forward by Professors Friedman[8] and Phelps[9] and now known as the accelerationist or expectations view, that denies the existence of such a trade-off, at least in the long run. This school of thought argues that a perfectly foreseen rate of inflation will affect only nominal rates of interest and will not have any lasting effect on the allocation of output or factor imputs.

If this monetarist view of the Phillips curve is correct, then there is no reason for governments' choice of the appropriate rate of expansion to aggregate demand to be affected by the nature of the exchange rate regime. For in the long run, real output is given, and changes in money supply affect only the price level. There is no cost to having a perfectly stable price level.

However, since the potential impact of a change in exchange rate regime depends not only on a shift in the Phillips curve itself but on the point on the curve selected as optimal by the policy authorities, all that matters is that governments *think* that there is a trade-off between unemployment and inflation in the short run. If they do, then a shift in the policy options which they perceive to be available may result in a change in the rate of inflation even though, as monetarists would have it, this shift is without long-run consequence for the level of real output.

Effects on the Phillips Curve

Since the nature of the exchange rate regime affects the size and frequency with which inflationary disturbances are transmitted across national boundaries, it will affect national price levels if price-increasing disturbances are relatively stronger or more quick-acting than price-reducing disturbances under the other. This can be referred to as the 'ratchet and asymmetries argument'. As it is generally put, this argument holds that flexible exchange rates are more inflationary than fixed exchange rates because they give rise to more and larger exchange rate changes. Although if prices were perfectly flexible in both directions, greater fluctuations in exchange rates would be neutral as regards the overall price level, it is argued that prices respond more, or more rapidly, to shifts in costs or in demand that put upward pressure on prices than to those which put downward pressure. As in the case of price *level* effects the ratchet argument can be divided into effects that work from the cost side and those that work from the demand side.

One version of the ratchet argument employs the familiar Keynesian assumption of downward price inflexibility to infer that flexible rates will be more inflationary than fixed rates. This argument may be briefly recapitulated as follows. Competition and the 'law of one price' ensure that the real price of traded commodities must be the same in all markets. Thus, when one country devalues its exchange rate, restoration of price equality requires either that nominal prices go up in the devaluing country or else that they go down in the appreciating country. Under conditions of downward price inflexibility, however, domestic prices would not fall in the appreciating country. Consequently, nominal prices would have to increase, to the full amount of the devaluation, in the devaluing country. Allowing that complete price inflexibility is perhaps an extreme case, an inflationary impact from exchange rate flexibility can still be inferred from less restrictive assumptions. So long as prices are less flexible in the downward than in the upward direction, similar qualitative conclusions follow though the actual consequences will be less strong.

A ratchet effect may also operate on the demand side. Because the nature of the exchange rate regime affects the transmission of economic disturbances across national boundaries, it will influence where a given increase in demand ends up both in terms of countries and product markets. If it could be shown that a movement from fixed exchange rates to flexible rates, or vice versa, systematically resulted in a movement of effective demand away from areas where it had a relatively small impact on prices to areas where it had a relatively large impact on prices, then it could be said that the change in exchange rate regime had an inflationary impact on the Phillips curve trade-off, i.e., for a given level of world demand, upward pressure on prices would be greater in one regime than in the other. For example, a departure from full employment demand in the upward direction would, in a closed economy, be expended mainly in a price increase; whereas a departure in a downward direction would be reflected much more in a drop in the volume of output. The point at which output effects are overtaken by price effects is not, of course, a precise one. But it can clearly make an important difference whether a given inflationary disturbance is contained within an economy or spread evenly throughout the world economy. If it is assumed that all countries aim at full employment and that, on the average through time, they achieve this objective, then deviations from the target level will result in price changes which depend on both the direction *and* the size of the deviation. If a given inflationary disturbance is shared among a group of countries, the effect on the *average* rate of inflation will be less than if it is concentrated in a single country.

The foregoing has referred to shifts in aggregate demand across national frontiers. However, exchange rate fluctuations also lead to demand shifts within national economies, i.e., from traded to non-traded goods or vice versa. Shifts in purchasing patterns brought about by exchange rate changes, or even the expectation of such shifts, may tend to raise prices in the countries of depreciating currencies without effecting a corresponding price reduction in the countries of appreciating currencies. The inflationary effects of demand shifts can result both from the real resource costs of switching factors of production from one employment to another and from greater pressure on prices stemming from the uneven distribution of a given change in aggregate demand.

Such demand shifts are likely to be induced by changes in relative costs between trading partners. This would seem, at the superficial level, to be more likely to occur under flexible than under fixed exchange rates. However, it must be remembered that relative costs are affected by the combination of changes in domestic currency costs and changes in exchange rates; and in a situation where domestic costs in local currencies are changing rapidly, it may be necessary for exchange rates to adjust also in order to maintain equality of cost levels. Thus there is certainly no overwhelming theoretical reason to expect that flexible exchange rates will give rise to additional inflationary pressures through demand shifts.

Furthermore, it must also be noted that, so long as the policy authorities keep the money supply constant, and thus do not permit a permanent increase in nominal expenditure, ratchet effects can only push up prices by lowering real demand. The lowering of real demand will change the unemployment inflation trade-off in such a way that the additional *upward* price pressure from the ratchet effect is offset by the additional *downward* price pressure resulting from the higher level of unemployment. Thus, so long as the authorities do not try to offset the increase in unemployment by easing monetary policy, the operation of the ratchet effect can increase only temporarily the underlying rate of inflation.

Any inflationary effects stemming from the ratchet effect would, of course, be magnified by the presence of a wage-price spiral. Indeed, it is sometimes argued that deficit countries can by this mechanism find themselves in a vicious circle of deficit and inflation. An initial deficit causes a depreciation in the exchange rate, which pushes up domestic prices, thus provoking wage claims which accelerate the process of inflation. Although certain countries have faced serious problems resulting from the wage-price spiral effect, it would be incorrect to say that this factor, by itself, imparts an inflationary bias to a flexible rate regime. The nature of the regime will affect the size of inflationary disturbances, not the extent by which they are subsequently magnified. Unless floating can be shown to have an inflationary impact for reasons other than the existence of a wage-price spiral, the argument is without importance in judging inflationary potential of different exchange rate regimes. However, the existence of a wage-price spiral does need to be taken into account in assessing the ultimate effects of whatever external inflationary impulses may occur (though it should be noted that neither theoretical reasoning nor empirical evidence suggest that the spiral is likely to become explosive).

Effects on Policy Choice

In addition to influencing the nature of the trade-off between inflation and unemployment, it is also possible for the exchange rate regime to cause a shift in the combination of the two objectives which authorities select. This is because additional objectives may enter into the government's welfare function under a fixed exchange rate regime. This additional objective is the need to maintain balance of payments equilibrium, and the way in which it enters into the welfare function is through so-called 'reserve discipline'. It is sometimes argued that the removal of the discipline imposed by limited international reserves will make a flexible system inherently more inflationary than fixed rates.

A simple statement of the discipline argument would run as follows: under fixed exchange rates, a country which inflates at a rate higher than that of its trading partners will, *ceteris paribus,* suffer a deterioration in its balance of payments and a loss of international reserves. If there is an inhibition about using the exchange rate to restore equilibrium in the foreign exchange market, the high inflation country will ultimately have to discipline itself by restraining aggregate demand so as to bring its inflation rate into line with that of its trading partners. Even when an exchange rate alteration is possible, as under the Bretton Woods system, it can be argued that 'the need to defend a fixed exchange rate against depreciation may promote political willingness to impose unpopular domestic restraints; and where the attempt to defend the parity is ultimately unsuccessful, the psychological shock of devaluation may promote broad support for the adoption of the necessary associated measures to curtail domestic demand'.[10] In contrast, no such discipline is said to exist in a world of flexible exchange rates, since in such a case the immediate consequences of a relatively high inflation rate is a depreciation of the exchange rate of the high inflation country.

For the foregoing argument to imply a net increase in the average rate of world inflation under flexible rates, it needs to be demonstrated that discipline applied to a country which would otherwise be above the world average inflation rate is greater than the discipline on a country which would otherwise be below the world average rate. For the salient characteristic of inflation under a fixed exchange rate regime is that all countries, if they are not to alter their exchange rates or engage in new restrictions on trade and capital flows, will ultimately be tied to a common rate of inflation. In principle, it is quite possible for the discipline on surplus countries to inflate to offset the discipline on deficit countries to restrain demand. So although discipline would certainly apply to each country taken individually, and although it would reduce the dispersion of world inflation rates about the mean, there is no theoretical reason for such a system to lead to a higher world average rate of inflation.

There are, however, certain institutional characteristics of a fixed rate system that can be adduced to explain why such a system would probably work to restrain inflation, on balance. Firstly, the nature of the adjustment mechanism, as it actually operated under the Bretton Woods system, placed a greater burden on deficit than on surplus countries. This was due to the fact that deficit countries were limited in their ability to resist adjustment because their reserve holdings were finite; surplus countries, on the other hand, could continue to accumulate reserves without sanctions other than those of moral reprobation. Secondly, there is a tendency in political discussion of payments questions to extrapolate from

Micawberesque economics, and to equate surpluses with virtue and deficits with financial turpitude. The pressure to adjust, therefore, frequently falls more heavily on the countries which are suffering from more rapid inflation rates.

Although the reserve discipline argument, in conjunction with the discrepancies in adjustment pressures applying to surplus and deficit countries, respectively, would seem to indicate that a flexible system would be more inflation prone, arguments can be advanced on the other side. In the first place, it may be noted that the deflationary features of reserve discipline under par values all spring from deficiencies and asymmetries in the working of the adjustment process in the Bretton Woods system. Since these deficits are well recognized and would presumably be rectified in any return to a par value system, they should not be regarded as features *generally* attributable to a fixed exchange rate system.

Secondly, the discipline argument can be turned around. Under a par value system, a country with sufficient reserves can choose to expand demand excessively and hold back domestic prices by running a payments deficit. Under a flexible rate system, however, a country which inflates at a rate exceeding that of its trading partners will witness a depreciation in its exchange rate. This results in an immediate increase in domestic prices in the inflating countries. Thus the cost of running a higher inflation rate cannot be concealed from the general public by a decline in reserves but immediately becomes apparent in the declining purchasing power of domestic incomes over foreign goods. Assuming that inflation is unpopular and that the government is responsive to popular opinion, the foregoing implies that inflationary policies will be more quickly reversed under flexible exchange rates than when there is the possibility of financing them by running down reserves.

Conclusions and Welfare Implications

It has been suggested above that the transmission mechanism *by itself* is neutral with respect to the question of the net inflationary impact of different exchange rate regimes. However, differences in the transmission mechanism may result both in changes in private spending decisions which affect prices, and in changes in governmental policy decisions which affect the rate of demand expansion and thus the long-run rate of inflation. Whether the net impact of these factors is inflationary or deflationary, on balance, depends on the relative importance which is ascribed to each. Yet despite the numerous arguments and counter-arguments about the effects of moving from one exchange rate system to another and despite the importance attached to this issue in discussions concerning international monetary reform, it is hard to escape the conclusion that the type of exchange rate system has relatively little influence on the average rate of world inflation. Put in other words, there does not seem to be any argument of convincing general applicability that would prompt one to select either fixed or flexible rates on grounds of expected anti-inflationary behaviour.

There is perhaps a suggestion that, because of downward price inflexibility, ratchet effects will operate more strongly in a flexible exchange rate regime, and that such a system may be somewhat more prone to inflation. However, even if it were true that there was a slightly more inflationary bias in a flexible system, this would not necessarily imply that there would be a welfare advantage in selecting such a regime. There are basically two reasons for this.

In the first place, the exchange rate regime has implications not only for the world average rate of inflation but for the *dispersion* of individual countries' inflation rates about this mean. If there are considered to be advantages in permitting countries to follow their own preferences concerning the inflation/unemployment trade-off, then there are clearly costs involved in constraining countries towards a common inflation rate, as a fixed exchange rate regime implies. Secondly, it should be noted that many of the costs associated with inflation, for example, misallocation of resources, redistribution of income, etc., relate primarily to *unanticipated* inflation. The basis of this argument is that a perfectly foreseen inflation will be discounted in all contracts relating to the future, and the only welfare loss will be that associated with the induced reduction in holdings of real money balances.

The conclusion suggested by the arguments in this chapter is an agnostic one. Although the exchange rate regime has clear implications for the distribution of individual countries' inflation rates about the world average, it is much more difficult to be confident that it has any systematic effect on this average. And even if it did, it is debatable whether welfare would be improved by choosing an exchange regime on the grounds of anti-inflationary characteristics.

---

[1] Much of the material in this chapter is drawn from a study prepared by the present author and Morris Goldstein (See below: Selected Further Reading.)
[2] David Hume, *On the Balance of Trade,* (1756).
[3] It should perhaps be noted that the monetary approach to the balance of payments views the link between monetary expansion and a balance of payments deficit as being direct; in view of the lags which are known to operate, however, it seems clearer to follow the effects through sequentially, as done here.
[4] For completeness, however, it should be noted that such a situation does not represent a long-run equilibrium. Lower interest rates in the countries which experienced the initial monetary expansion coupled with the current account surplus will generate an expansion of demand. This will eventually lead to rising incomes and a higher level of prices which, with no further change in the money supply, will push up the interest rate which is consistent with equilibrium in the money market. When this happens, the international capital flow will dry up, and the exchange rate of the country which experienced the monetary expansion will have depreciated by just the amount of the increase in its domestic price level. Thus, it remains true that, in the long run, countries can insulate themselves from external monetary effects on their domestic price level by a policy of free floating.
[5] Friedman, M., and Roosa, R.V., *The Balance of Payments: Free vs Fixed Exchange Rates,* American Enterprise Institute, 1967.
[6] Friedman, M., 'The case for flexible exchange rates' in *Essays in Positive Economics,* University of Chicago Press, Chicago, 1953.
[7] Phillips, A.W., 'The relationship between unemployment and the rate of change of money wage rates in the U.K., 1861–1957', *Economica,* vol. 25, pp. 283–99.
[8] Friedman, M., 'The role of monetary policy', *American Economic Review,* March 1968.
[9] Phelps, E., 'Money wage dynamics and labor market equilibrium', *Journal of Political Economy,* July/August 1968.
[10] *The Role of Exchange Rates in the Adjustment of International Payments,* Report by the Executive Directors of the IMF, 1970, page 32.

Selected Further Reading

Crockett, A.D., and Goldstein, M., 'Inflation under fixed and flexible exchange rates', IMF *Staff Papers*, November 1976.

Heller, H.R., 'International reserves and worldwide inflation', IMF *Staff Papers*, March 1976.

Hirsch, F., and Higham, D., 'Floating rates—expectations and experience', *Three Banks Review*, June 1974.

Laffer, A.B., and Meiselman, D. (eds), *The Phenomenon of Worldwide Inflation*, American Enterprise Institute, Washington, D.C., 1975.

Michaely, M., *The Responsiveness of Demand Policies to Balance of Payments: Postwar Patterns,* New York, Columbia University Press and National Bureau of Economic Research, 1971.

Phaup, E., 'Reserve changes and the discipline argument,' *Quarterly Review of Economics and Business,* 1975.

Teigen, R.L., 'Interpreting recent world inflation,' *American Economic Review*, May 1975.

Witteveen, H.J., 'Inflation and the international monetary system', *American Economic Review,* May 1975.

12 The International Monetary Fund

The International Monetary Fund is the central institution in the international monetary system. As such, its role is implicit in many of the arrangements and proposals that have been discussed in earlier chapters. The purpose of this chapter is to consider in somewhat more detail the form and functions of the IMF, and how, by interpretation and amendment of the Articles of Agreement, they have evolved through time.

Origins

The International Monetary Fund had its origins in the desire of members of the international community to avoid the economic mistakes of the 1920s and 1930s. After the First World War, many countries had attempted to return to the old gold standard system, without realizing that the conditions under which the gold standard flourished had disappeared. The old version of 'normalcy' was no longer attainable. When the worldwide financial crash forced first Britain and later other countries off the gold standard, there was a general retreat into purely nationalistic policies. Faced with enormous problems of depression and unemployment, nearly all governments set about erecting trade barriers to protect their domestic industries, and trying to force down their exchange rates to give themselves a competitive edge in export markets. The result was the exacerbation of an already catastrophic decline in world trade, and an extension and prolongation of the depression.

It was against this background of historical experience that representatives of the Allied Nations met at Bretton Woods, towards the end of the Second World War, to lay plans for a post-war monetary order. It was natural that the concern uppermost in their minds was to construct a framework which would help to prevent a repetition of the 1930s. Lack of cooperation in matters of trade and payments was seen as the main problem to be tackled in the field of international economic policy. Accordingly, the first purpose of the International Monetary Fund, set out in Article 1 of the Articles of Agreement is 'to promote international monetary cooperation through a permanent institution which provides the machinery for consultation and collaboration in international monetary problems'.

Of course, simply to provide a forum for collaboration would be an empty achievement if there were not also some agreement on the objectives such collaboration was intended to promote. Since one of the major failings of the exchange system in the inter-war period had been currency instability and competitive exchange rate practices, another of the purposes of the Fund is stated to be 'to promote exchange stability, to maintain orderly exchange arrangements among members and to avoid competitive exchange depreciation'.

Beyond currency instability, however, international economic relations had been bedevilled in the inter-war period by the proliferation of restrictions on trade and payments, preferential trading arrangements, bilateralism and autarky. In an attempt to eliminate these practices, which could benefit the countries which resorted to them only by placing additional burdens on their trading partners, a further purpose of the Fund is stated to be 'to assist in the establishment of a multilateral system of payments in respect of current transactions between members, and in the elimination of foreign exchange restrictions which hamper the growth in world trade'.

These purposes define, in general terms, the broad outlines of a desirable international monetary system. It is also a purpose of the Fund to help countries to live up to these objectives when they are in financial difficulties, 'by making the Fund's resources temporarily available to them under adequate safeguards, thus providing them with opportunity to correct maladjustments in their balance of payments without resorting to measures destructive of national or international prosperity'.

Taken together the purposes just described stake out a broad regulatory and financial role for the Fund. The remaining Articles of Agreement, agreed in 1944, are rather more specific in giving operational content to these broad purposes. The purposes of Article 1 remain valid to the present day, though the institutional mechanisms to put them into practice have changed. For example, the promotion of exchange stability remains desirable, but whereas the original articles envisaged that this would best be achieved through a par value system, it is now recognized that stability of exchange rates depends on the stability of underlying economic conditions, and cannot be imposed by a particular set of exchange arrangements.

Structure

At the end of 1975, the Fund had 128 member countries. The only important countries which were not members were the socialist countries of Eastern Europe (though Romania and Yugoslavia were members), North Korea, North Vietnam, Cuba and Switzerland. China continued to be represented by Taiwan.

Like many international organizations, the Fund is run by a conference comprising all its members; a more restricted executive body, responsible for most of the operational decisions, and an international staff. In addition, there has been in existence since 1972 a Committee of Governors (i.e., Ministers) which initially had an advisory function, but which will probably eventually be given formal powers under the title Council of Governors.

Rights and obligations in the Fund are based on a system of quotas. Quotas are decided by vote of the board of governors, and roughly reflect the importance of members in the world economy. Quotas are reviewed every five years, and increase when necessary to enable the Fund to meet the need for additional international liquidity of a conditional nature. To calculate individual quotas a formula is used which takes into account the volume of a country's international trade, its importance in relation to the domestic economy, fluctuations in its balance of payments, and sometimes also its level of international reserves. The results of the formula (or formulae, for there are several) are subject to modification where it can be shown that there are other relevant factors which have not been taken into account. A quota review needs to be approved by an 80 per cent majority before it can be put into effect, and each country has a veto over changes in its own quota.

Quotas determine subscriptions and borrowing rights, which will be described in more detail later on. They also determine, in large measure, voting power. Each member country has a basic allocation of 250 votes, plus one vote for each SDR 100,000 of quota. For most decisions, a straightforward majority is sufficient, but for certain important decisions higher majorities are required. In the newly amended Articles (agreed in 1976) there has been a tendency to subject more decisions to the requirement of a weighted majority, and in a number of cases to increase majority requirements.

The highest decision-making body of the institution is the board of governors, in which all members are represented, and which meets once a year, invariably at the same time and place as the governors of its sister institution, the World Bank (International Bank for Reconstruction and Development). Governors are, with a few minor exceptions, ministers of finance or central bank governors. The chief importance of the annual meetings lies less in the formal speeches and decisions, than in the bringing together of many of the world's financial leaders and in the discussions that take place informally. Very few decision-making powers continue to be reserved to the board of governors.[1] Most of them have been delegated to the board of executive directors, including all decisions on access by members to the Fund's resources, decisions on charges and remuneration, and the review of consultations between the Fund and its members.

It may be readily seen that the executive board has substantial powers, and it is therefore of interest to consider its composition and functioning in a little more detail. At the end of 1975, the executive board had twenty members—this number having increased in steps from the original twelve (the minimum number prescribed in the Articles). Five executive directors are appointed by the members having the five largest quotas. The other fifteen are elected by the remaining members, which normally form constituencies on a roughly geographical basis for the purpose. Elections take place every two years, and constituencies usually remain fairly stable, though it is not unknown for countries to move from one constituency to another. There is a provision for three of the elective seats to be reserved for the American republics other than the United States, and an informal agreement that the sub-Saharan African countries should be represented by two directors.

The managing director of the Fund, who is an international civil servant, is the non-voting chairman of the executive board. The managing director is, according to the Articles, elected by the executive directors, but the position is regarded as an important appointment, and in practice governments have usually involved themselves closely in the choice. There has been an informal understanding that the managing director of the Fund should be a prominent European official or politician (while the president of the World Bank has traditionally been American.)

There are, perhaps, two main characteristics that distinguish the Fund from other international organizations, with the exception of the World Bank. The first is that the executive directors function in continuous session and meet not periodically, but as often as Fund business requires. (In the period 1972-75, for example, there were an average of over 100 board meetings a year). Through the executive board, governments exercise a closer control over the day-to-day activities of the Fund than is generally the case with international organizations—with one or two exceptions such as the Organization for Economic Cooperation and Development (OECD).

The second distinguishing characteristic is the system of weighted voting. The voting strength wielded by each governor or executive director is based essentially on the quotas or financial subscriptions of the member or members which appointed or elected him. In fact, the great majority of the decisions of the executive board is taken by consensus, without a formal vote, but the nature of the consensus arrived at is inevitably influenced to some extent by voting strength. Thanks to this feature, the Fund is able to avoid both the lack of realism that sometimes characterizes bodies of worldwide membership based on the one-country, one-vote principle, and the tendency, sometimes visible in bodies whose membership is confined to the principal powers, to take too little account of the interests of less-developed countries.

The original Articles of Agreement established a division of decision-making powers between the board of governors and the executive directors. This was workable when most of the decisions to be taken were of a technical nature, relating to the implementation of rules to manage a system which was, in its main lines, accepted and enshrined in the Articles. However, when it became clear that the basic features of the monetary system would have to be changed, and perhaps would have to continue to change in an evolutionary manner, the bipartite division of powers was no longer satisfactory. The board of governors was too unwieldy to conduct negotiations on intricate matters of monetary reform, while the executive board was not at a high enough political level to negotiate and take decisions on matters affecting important economic interests.

This was the reason for the establishment of a committee of governors which, it is envisaged, will have decision-making powers in the management and adaptation of the monetary system, including the surveillance of adjustment policies and the review of liquidity arrangements. The genesis of the present committee was the Committee of 20, established in 1972 to negotiate international monetary reform (see next chapter). During the course of these negotiations, however, it became clear that a new set of rules which would be as precise and as durable as those set up at Bretton Woods, could not be established. The monetary system would have to be flexible enough to change in response to evolving circumstances, and the committee therefore decided to recommend the perpetuation of its existence, with slightly different and broader terms of reference.

The membership of the committee reflects that of the executive board. Each country or group of countries that is represented by an executive director has the right to appoint a member of the committee of governors. This member can be accompanied to meetings of the committee by up to seven advisers. Representatives of other important international organizations (such as UNCTAD, the World Bank and the BIS) are also invited to attend.

Although it is perhaps too early to be certain at the time of writing, it seems likely that this committee of governors will become the most important decision-making organ in the Fund. It is expected to meet three or four times a year—frequently enough to undertake reasonably continuous surveillance of adjustment policies. Recommendations concerning amendments to the Articles of Agreement will pass through it, and agreement by the committee will in most cases be tantamount to agreement by the board of governors.

The Fund as Custodian of Monetary Order

The Fund is sometimes referred to as the guardian of a code of good conduct in the payments sphere, but that code has become increasingly difficult to define precisely. Certain mandatory provisions were set out in the Bretton Woods Articles of Agreement and remain widely accepted to the present time. It is the Fund's duty to monitor the observance of these provisions by member countries. Other provisions of the original Articles (those relating to exchange rates, for example) have become outmoded by events, and for a while the Fund devised working arrangements to take their place. Under the newly amended Articles of Agreement, most obligations are of a looser character, establishing principles of conduct rather than precise rules of behaviour.

Exchange rate policies and practices are, however, only one way in which the economic actions of a country can impinge on the welfare of its trading partners. Monetary policies, exchange controls, tariff policies, indeed the whole range of economic policy instruments, have an effect on other countries, and so should be harmonized if inconsistent policies are to be avoided. For this reason, the Fund has a legitimate interest in the means which countries use to achieve and maintain balance of payments equilibrium.

Lastly, since it is accepted that monetary arrangements should be able to adapt flexibly to changes in world economic conditions, the Fund must provide the mechanism by which such institutional changes can be discussed, planned and implemented. It must also have a coherent long-term framework so that the *ad hoc* changes that emerge from an evolutionary process are mutually consistent, and serve to move the system towards a planned ultimate objective.

The Fund was conceived at Bretton Woods as only one of a pair of twin institutions which together would act as guarantors of a code of behaviour governing international transactions as a whole. The other twin was the International Trade Organization, which never succeeded in being born as a fully-fledged international institution but has nevertheless led a separate life as an executive agreement, the General Agreement on Tariffs and Trade (GATT). The Fund is broadly concerned with the payments side of international transactions, while the GATT is concerned with the goods and services side. Since the two are opposite sides of the same coin, this division of functions is one not of logic but of convention, based partly on the fact that, within national governments, payments questions are dealt with by central banks and treasuries, whereas trade questions are dealt with separately by ministries of commerce.

Under the Bretton Woods statutes, the regulatory functions of the Fund could be grouped into two main categories according as they dealt with, respectively, (i) exchange rate practices or (ii) restrictions on international payments. The code of behaviour of which the Fund and the GATT are guardians is essentially a liberal one. It seeks to reduce tariffs and other barriers to trade if imposed on the transactions themselves, and to eliminate them altogether if imposed on payments. It also seeks to eliminate discrimination and restrictions on multilateral settlement, however imposed. In order that this objective might be achieved, it was envisaged that all members, after a transitional period of varying duration, would accept certain obligations set out in Article VIII of the Fund's charter. This Article provided that no member might, without the approval of the Fund, impose restrictions on the making of payments or transfers for current international transactions, or engage in discriminatory currency arrangements or multiple currency practices. These provisions retain their acceptability to the present day, and although not all countries have yet managed to live up to them, they are generally acknowledged as a desirable objective.

Turning to those aspects of the Fund's role which deal with exchange rate arrangements, the Bretton Woods system was based on par values. Various provisions were included in the Articles to govern the means by which par values could be established and changed, and the obligations countries had in relation to maintaining par values. Since 1971, most of these provisions have no longer been operative, and under amended Articles agreed in 1976 they will be replaced with more permissive obligations. Although the new system does not involve par value obligations,[2] the Fund is called upon to establish principles for the guidance of members' exchange rate policies, and these principles will form the basis of its surveillance activities.

Although the Fund does not have specific jurisdiction over countries' choice of adjustment policies, the surveillance of the adjustment mechanism bulks very large in its work. Surveillance of adjustment policies takes place with all members about once a year, or perhaps a little less frequently. A team of four or five economists from Fund headquarters visits the national capital to gather unpublished statistics, hear at first hand the motivation for recent policy changes, and the authorities' interpretation of recent trends, and to discuss policy objectives with the competent authorities in the finance ministry, central bank, and other agencies responsible for economic matters. The fruits of this consultation mission are incorporated in a lengthy background study and a shorter, more policy-oriented report on the discussions. The two resultant papers are then discussed at the executive board, where comments and advice are expressed, to be relayed to the authorities of the country concerned.

Naturally, the regular consultations have only a limited impact on policy formation. Of more significance from this point of view are the staff missions and consultations surrounding drawings by members on the resources of the Fund. Policies applied by the Fund in authorizing the use of its financial resources are dealt with in more detail later in this chapter, but we may note here that drawings are not approved by the executive board unless the country requesting assistance meets certain criteria regarding need, and unless the programme of economic stabilization which it proposes is considered adequate to overcome its fundamental economic problems.

The multilateral aspects of the adjustment process have become considerably more important in recent years. A number of factors have contributed to an increasing emphasis on multilateral surveillance. First, the growth of trade has increased the scope for economic developments in one country to affect its trading partners. Second, the integration of international capital markets, and the liberalization of payments arrangements has caused a parallel, though even greater, expansion in capital flows. Third, the growing equality in the economic strength of major countries has meant that it is no longer sufficient to look at a single exchange rate (that with the United States dollar) in gauging the appropriateness of a country's external policies. Fourth, and related, the advent of widespread floating means that there is no such thing as *the* rate of exchange for a country; there are separate rates against each independently floating currency. This means that global equilibrium can only be achieved and maintained by all countries acting together.

The Fund's Financial Role

Besides its regulatory and consultative function, the Fund is an important financial institution with subscriptions, in 1975, of some SDR 30 billion (or $36 billion). These resources are available to member countries to assist them in meeting balance of payments deficits without resorting to measures that would be unduly wasteful of domestic resources or unnecessarily harmful to international interests. These resources are made available under different facilities to cover balance of payments needs arising from a variety of different causes. A common characteristic of all Fund lending is that it is to meet general balance of payments requirements (and not to provide finance for specific development or reconstruction projects). This feature has received considerable emphasis over the years, and is regarded as one of the main characteristics distinguishing the Fund from its sister institution, the World Bank.

It is, however, a distinction that is easier to make in principle than in practice. Money is fungible, and although a World Bank loan may be earmarked for, and related to, a particular project, it represents a net addition to the overall import capacity of the country concerned, in just the same way as does assistance from the Fund. Perhaps a more significant characteristic of Fund lending is that it is short or medium-term, whereas the World Bank and other development agencies typically lend at longer term. To some extent this distinction is becoming blurred at the edges (as will be seen later) but it still remains essentially true.

Fund lending differs also in its conditionality. Since Fund assistance is intended to help countries overcome balance of payments difficulties, and since repayment ultimately has to be made out of strengthening reserves, the conditions imposed usually relate to the macro-economic management of the economy. In this, the Fund's position as a potentially large creditor undoubtedly strengthens its hand in encouraging policies that promote domestic stabilization, without damaging the interests of trading partners.

The overwhelming bulk of the Fund's resources comes from capital subscriptions by member countries. Under the original Articles, each member was required to furnish its subscription, 25 per cent in gold, and 75 per cent in its national currency. The national currency component is in non-interest-bearing form and thus, so long as it is not drawn for the purpose of making payments, is costless to the subscribing member. When it is drawn by another member and presented in exchange for goods and services, or another currency, a cost does, of course, fall on the subscribing member.

There are two other means by which the Fund can acquire currencies for use in its lending operations, besides using the subscription of its members. One is through the sale of gold to members to 'replenish' currency holdings. The other is by borrowing. The Fund's powers in this respect are quite wide, and the executive board may enter agreements with governments, central banks or private institutions at mutually satisfactory terms. The lender does not even have to be resident in a Fund member country.

Apart from a sale of gold in replenishment, transactions between the Fund and its members take the form of an *exchange* of currencies for currencies, or currencies for SDR of gold. Such a transaction is identical, from an economic point of view (though not legally) to an act of borrowing by the drawing member. It involves a change in the Fund's holding of the member's currency; if this holding rises above the 75 per cent initial subscription, a 'repurchase obligation' is created. When a member makes a repurchase it purchases its own currency from the Fund in exchange for gold or some currency acceptable to the Fund. Such a transaction is identical to repayment, in that the repurchasing member's net position vis-à-vis the Fund improves.

It will be seen that transactions will always affect the Fund's holdings, not only of the currency of the drawing or repurchasing member, but also of the currencies of other members as well. As noted above, the critical number for the Fund's holdings of a member's currency is 75 per cent of quota.[3]

Because of the significance of 75 per cent as the dividing line between creditor and debtor status, the Fund's policies with respect to use of currencies are aimed at getting countries back towards the 75 per cent mark. When a member draws or repurchases, it will normally ask the Fund's advice on which currencies to use, and it is this which affords the Fund the chance to manage its portfolio of currencies.

The Fund now has a variety of facilities under which its resources are made available to members. An early interpretation of the Articles of Agreement made it clear that the resources of the Fund are to be used to give temporary assistance to members in financing balance of payments on current account,[4] and this was understood to include assistance in connection with seasonal, cyclical and emergency fluctuations in the balance of payments.

Lending Facilities

What are now known as the Fund's regular facilities, to distinguish them from the special facilities which have been evolved in recent years, were in fact the only facilities under which members could draw for much of the Fund's existence, and they still constitute the most important permanent element of its financial operations. The Articles of Agreement are rather vague concerning the terms and conditions of drawings. The Fund is required 'to adopt policies on the use of its resources that will assist members to solve their balance of payments problems in a manner consistent with the purposes of the Fund and that will establish adequate safeguards for the temporary use of its resources'.[5] Exactly what the policies should be, however, was left for later decision by the executive board.

In 1952, the executive board decided that a member could count on receiving the overwhelming benefit of any doubt respecting drawings within the 'gold tranche'.[6] A gold tranche drawing is one which leaves the Fund's holding of the member's currency below 100 per cent of quota, and is termed the 'gold tranche' in recognition of the fact that a drawing of this amount simply matches the gold that the member had originally paid as a subscription.[7] The gold tranche may be drawn on automatically, upon representation by the member that it is in a situation of balance of payments need. There are no interest charges for drawings in the gold tranche, though such drawings are subject to repayment in the normal three-to-five year period. Drawings below 75 per cent, i.e., drawings which do not cause the Fund's holdings of a member's currency to rise above the initially subscribed amount are termed 'super-gold' tranche. Members are expected to have a balance of payments need for these, as for any other drawing, but they are different in that no repayment is required (because the 'drawing' amounts to the reduction of a credit, rather than the increase of a debt).

Because of the ease, cheapness, and lack of conditions attached to drawings in the gold tranche and super-gold tranche, these credit positions are considered part of a member's reserves, and are so included in statistics on international liquidity. Thus Fund operations which affect members' positions in the gold and super-gold tranches have an effect on world liquidity, since drawings beyond the gold tranche are not considered to affect adversely the liquidity of the drawing member.

In 1955 and 1957, the Fund added definitions of its drawing policies in the so-called credit tranches, i.e., for drawings which carry the Fund's holdings of a member's currency beyond the 100 per cent point, and up to the normal prescribed maximum of 200 per cent of quota. The Fund's attitude to requests for drawings within the first (25%) credit tranche is a liberal one, provided the member is making reasonable efforts to solve its problems. Requests for drawings beyond 125 per cent require substantial justification. They are likely to be favourably received where the drawings in question are intended to support a sound programme aimed at establishing or maintaining the exchange stability of the member's currency at a realistic rate of exchange. What constitutes a satisfactory programme, warranting the provision of Fund resources, is in the last analysis a matter for the judgment of the executive board. However, a country contemplating a drawing usually invites a mission from the Fund staff to visit the country for consultations, and this mission will negotiate the terms of a drawing, *ad referendum* to the executive board. The staff mission will know what kind of programme the Fund's management will be prepared to recommend to the board, and the management in turn will have a fairly good idea of what the board will accept. Thus a member who is considering a drawing has the opportunity to negotiate frankly and confidentially with the Fund's staff before submitting an application to the Executive Board. If the staff is prepared to endorse the programme the member proposes, an application for a drawing can be made with little fear of rebuff.

The bulk of the Fund's financial assistance is provided under stand-by arrangements, whereby a member receives assurance that, during a fixed period of time, requests for drawings up to a specified amount will be allowed on the member's representation as to need. Such arrangements are usually granted for a period of twelve months, but they are renewable. In considering a request for a stand-by arrangement, the Fund applies the same policies, varying according to tranche, as are applied to requests for immediate drawings.

Drawings on the Fund under the regular tranche policies apply the same criteria to all member countries. However, since not all countries face the same economic circumstances, this resulted in criticism that the Fund's policies were unduly rigid. Developing countries, in particular, faced problems that were more difficult, and in some respects more intractable, than those confronted by the industrialized countries. For example, their export receipts were more at the mercy of fluctuations in world commodity prices. These fluctuations resulted in much more severe disturbances to their balance of payments positions than those experienced by developed countries. It could be argued that it was unfair to make a country conform to ordinary tranche criteria when it was suffering the effects of external, though temporary, adverse factors. It could also be argued that the economic structure of developing countries was such that they could not respond as quickly to changes in policy instruments as could industrial countries.

For these reasons, the Fund has developed a number of special facilities, designed with particular types of balance of payments need in mind. For the most part, these facilities benefit developing countries, though like all the Fund's operations, criteria are applied without discrimination to all members.

Under the *compensatory financing facility* originally adopted in February 1963 and liberalized in 1975, it is provided that members can draw to meet payments difficulties arising out of temporary export shortfalls, providing that the shortfall is largely attributable to circumstances beyond the control of the member (e.g., a change in world market prices); and provided that the member is willing to cooperate with the Fund in seeking appropriate solutions for its balance of payments difficulties, where such solutions are called for. This second provision is less strict than the policy conditions generally required for drawings beyond the first credit tranche.

The extent of an export shortfall is defined as the amount by which its actual exports during a given year fall short of its average over a five-year period centred on the shortfall year.[8] Members are allowed to draw up to 50 per cent of quota in any year, and subject to a maximum of 75 per cent. Drawings under the compensatory facility are not counted against a member's entitlement to draw in the regular facilities.

In connection with the Fund's increased attention to the subject of commodity stabilization and to the policies of member countries in the commodity field, the executive directors adopted a decision in June 1969 establishing a *buffer stock facility* to assist members in financing contributions to international buffer stocks, provided that members have a balance of payments need, and that the relevant commodity agreement meets appropriate criteria. (The criteria are essentially that the agreement is cooperatively established between producers and consumers to stabilize prices, rather than adopted by one party unilaterally to try and influence the average level of prices in one direction or the other.)

Drawings for the purpose of financing buffer stocks in connection with international commodity agreements may be made in amounts equivalent to 50 per cent of quota. As with the compensatory financing facility, drawings under the buffer stock facility do not count against the ceiling of 200 per cent of quota for the Fund's holdings of a member's currency.

The oil facility, established in 1974, was different in a number of respects from the other facilities within the general account. In the first place, being established to meet the needs of a particular situation (the consequences of the 1973–4 increase in crude oil prices) it was limited in time. Drawings were permitted for deficits, attributable to the rise in the price of oil, incurred in 1974 and 1975. Thereafter, if a member still had a balance of payments need, and wished to draw on the Fund, it had to make its application either under the regular facilities, or under the 'extended facility', described below.

Secondly, although drawings and repurchases under the oil facility pass through the general account, like all the Fund's other lending operations, they are kept substantially separate from other operations with different sources of finance, terms and conditions of lending, and charges. Under the oil facility, resources made available to members are supplementary to any assistance that members might obtain under other policies on the use of the Fund's resources.

Another point of difference from other types of drawings is that drawings under the oil facility were entirely financed by borrowing by the Fund. The rationale for this lay in the purpose of the facility to promote recycling of funds from surplus to deficit countries. Since many of the countries which had large surpluses as a result of the increase in oil prices had small quotas in the Fund, and frequently also had currencies that were not fully convertible and therefore not usable in the Fund's operations, the scope for promoting recycling by using the Fund's existing resources was limited. Accordingly, it was decided that the Fund should borrow from countries in strong surplus. In the first year of operation of the facility, the bulk of lending came from oil-exporting countries, but for the second year there were much more substantial loans from those industrial countries that still enjoyed balance of payments surpluses.

The most recent development in policies related to the use of the Fund's resources was the decision by the executive board to establish an *extended facility*, adopted in September 1974. A number of countries, especially developing countries, had felt that the size of their drawing rights in the Fund was not sufficient, nor was the length of time for which they were available long enough, to justify the major policy reorientation which would be needed to secure structural changes in an economy. Yet in many cases it was recognized that the balance of payments could not be put on an enduringly sound basis unless these structural changes were brought about. There was in fact a noticeable 'gap' in the range of financing facilities available through international institutions. The longest finance available through the Fund was 3–5 years, whereas the shortest available through the World Bank was over 10 years. Furthermore World Bank finance was normally project-related although some steps had been made in the direction of 'programme loans' (i.e., loans related to a general programme and not a specific project). Very little was available to meet what was felt to be a growing need for balance of payments support over the medium-term (5–10-year) period.

Under the extended facility, the Fund will provide, in certain circumstances, assistance to members to meet their balance of payments deficits for longer periods and in amounts larger in relation to quotas than is the practice under normal credit tranche policies. For example, a member might apply for assistance under the facility if it has been suffering serious payments imbalance relating to structural maladjustments in production, trade and prices, and it is prepared to implement a comprehensive set of corrective policies covering a period of two to three years. Alternatively, an appropriate situation for use of the facility might occur when an economy suffers from slow growth and an inherently weak balance of payments position that prevents pursuit of an active development policy. This situation is typical of many less-developed countries, whose economies are characterized by dependence on one or two export commodities and that are inadequately equipped to mobilize and efficiently allocate domestic savings. Such countries need longer-term assistance to carry out an economic programme including, *inter alia,* a strengthening of monetary and fiscal instruments and appropriate trade and exchange policies.

Since the number of facilities has grown quite large, and some of them are overlapping, it may be helpful to tabulate the resources that could theoretically be made available to members, as percentages of quota. This is done in Table 12-1.

Table 12-1 Financial Facilities of the Fund and Their Conditionality[9]

Type of Facility	Per Cent Of Quota Available	Cumulative Per Cent Of Quota Available
Tranche policies		
Gold tranche Without conditions	25[10]	25
First credit tranche Programme representing reasonable efforts to overcome balance of payments difficulties; performance criteria and instalments not used	25[11]	50
Higher credit tranches Programme giving substantial justification of member's efforts to overcome balance of payments difficulties; resources normally provided in the form of stand-by arrangements which include performance criteria and drawings in instalments	75[11]	125
Extended facility Medium-term programme for up to three years to overcome structural balance of payments maladjustments; detailed statement of policies and measures for first and subsequent 12-month periods; resources provided in the form of extended arrangements which include performance criteria and drawings in instalments	140	190[12]

Compensatory financing facility Existence of temporary export shortfall for reasons beyond the member's control; member cooperates with Fund in an effort to find appropriate solutions for any balance of payments difficulties	75[13]	265
Buffer stock financing facility Existence of an international buffer stock accepted as suitable by Fund; member expected to cooperate with Fund as in the case of compensatory financing	50	315[14]
Oil facility 1974	Up to 75	— [15]
Oil facility 1975 For 1975: As under purchases in the first credit tranche; member expected to follow trade and payments policies consistent with the Rome Communique of the Committee of Twenty	Up to 125	— [15]

---

[1] These included proposals for amendment to the Articles (where ratification by legislatures is also required), changes in quotas, and the admission of new members. Voting on these issues can take place at the annual meeting, but more normally is performed by mail.

[2] Except in the unlikely event that an 85 per cent majority of countries vote for a return to a par value system.

[3] Under the newly amended Articles (1976), the 25 per cent gold portion of quota subscriptions will no longer be payable in respect of quota increases. As a result, the critical number, or 'norm', for Fund holdings of members' currencies will rise above 75 per cent. But the rest of the description here holds, *mutatis mutandis*.

[4] Executive Board Decision No. 71, 2 September 1946.

[5] Article V Section 3 (c), original Articles. The amended Articles are formulated slightly differently, though the substance is similar.

[6] Under the Articles agreed in 1976, th gold tranche will be termed the 'reserve tranche' (see also footnote 3 above).

[7] Though the terminology should not be construed as implying that the member has any legal right to the gold after its subscription is paid.

[8] For this purpose, forecasts of exports have to be made for export receipts in future years.

[9] Members are not expected, and may not qualify, to use all of the available facilities at the same time. In addition, use of the maximum available resources under a particular facility, namely, tranche policies, is usually made in a period of years and not in one year.

[10] The gold tranche will become less than 25 per cent following the ratification of amendments.

[11] Credit tranches are 'stretched' to 36¹/₄ per cent pending the increase in quotas.
[12] The combined use of the extended facility and the regular credit tranches may not be above 165 per cent of quota.
[13] Normally, not more than 50 per cent of quota in any 12-month period.
[14] A member with gold tranche drawing rights which purchases under the buffer stock financing facility would lose its gold tranche drawing rights *pro tanto*.
[15] The oil facility was set up on a temporary basis for 1974 and 1975 only.

Selected Further Reading

Deane, R.S., *International Monetary Reform: Content and Perspective*, Reserve Bank of New Zealand.
Fleming, J.M., *The International Monetary Fund: Its Form and Functions*, IMF, Washington, D.C., 1964.
Harrod, R.F., *The International Monetary Fund, Yesterday, Today and Tomorrow*, Kiel, 1966.
Horie, Shigeo, *The International Monetary Fund: Retrospect and Prospect*, London, Macmillan, 1964.
International Monetary Fund, *The International Monetary Fund 1945–75*, IMF, Washington, D.C., 1969
Kafka, Alexandre, *The IMF: The Second Coming?* Princeton Essays in International Finance No. 94, 1972.
Schweitzer, P.P., *The Role of the International Monetary Fund*, Stamp Memorial Lecture 1971, University of London Press, 1971.

13 *Reform*

When President Nixon announced the end of dollar convertibility in August 1971, it was clear to all observers that this was more than an ordinary crisis in the system. It was a crisis of the system itself, which could only be satisfactorily resolved by the establishment of a new set of ground rules for international monetary cooperation.

New ground rules implied, in effect, a rewriting of the Bretton Woods charter, an endeavour that required international collaboration of a very high order. The first question that presented itself to the member countries of the International Monetary Fund was the nature of the forum in which such a new agreement should be worked out. There were two conflicting considerations which came into play. On the one hand, it was desirable to have as broad a participation as possible, so that all the countries that would have to live under the monetary system should have a voice in its construction. On the other hand, the evident need for negotiation and compromise argued for a small group in which meaningful discussions and bargaining could most easily take place.

There was also a dichotomy between the desire to have a discussion at the highest possible level of technical expertise, and the need for effective political decision-making. The former consideration argued for a group of expert officials, such as the IMF executive board, the latter for a ministerial body. When the problem was put concretely to the annual meeting of the Fund's governors in September 1971, they elected to ask the executive board of the Fund (a group of twenty middle-level financial officials) to prepare a detailed report on reform, while giving consideration to the nature of the body which would eventually be charged with making detailed recommendations on the shape of the new system.

Meanwhile, world monetary relationships continued with no basic guiding rules. This did not immediately lead to difficulties as the major industrial nations tacitly adjusted their policies to make them consistent (this consisted mainly of the United States accepting intervention by European countries to stem the rise in their currencies, and the European countries accepting the resulting accruals to their external reserves). However, the potential for discord in such a system was evident, and it was recognized that it would be dangerous for the long-drawn-out process of a thoroughgoing reform of the system to take place against a backdrop of uncertainty in monetary relationships.

In recognition of these dangers, the Group of Ten countries initiated exploratory contacts among each other to see whether a pattern of exchange rates could be mutually agreed as a temporary *modus vivendi* pending a more lasting agreement. These contacts culminated in a full-scale ministerial meeting in Washington in December 1971, at which a new set of exchange rates was agreed. Under the Smithsonian agreement two currencies (sterling and the French franc) retained their exchange rates unchanged in terms of SDR, one continued to float (the Canadian dollar) and the other currencies were divided between devaluations and revaluations.

The re-establishment of agreed exchange rates was not a full-scale return to Bretton Woods, however. For one thing, no country accepted any formal convertibility obligations. This meant, in particular, that the United States did not undertake to provide gold in exchange for dollars if the latter were presented for settlement. Since the United States did not have any substantial holdings of foreign exchange, this essentially meant that resistance to any further speculative pressure against the dollar could only come from other central banks intervening to acquire the American currency. Another point of difference from the Bretton Woods system was in the acceptance of wider margins within which foreign exchange transactions would be permitted. While under the Bretton Woods rules, foreign exchange transactions had to take place within one per cent of the established par value, under the Smithsonian arrangements transactions could be at rates up to $2\frac{1}{4}$ per cent either side of the agreed 'central rate'.

A number of other features of the Smithsonian agreement were worthy of note. Perhaps most important was the fact that, for the first time, ministers from the major countries had agreed on a *multilateral* realignment of exchange rates. Secondly, this realignment was based, it is not too misleading to say, on sophisticated calculations of adjustment needs. Thirdly, the principle was established that the dollar had the same possibilities for changing its exchange value as other currencies. And finally, the exchange rate changes were expressed in terms of the SDR,[1] thus enhancing the status of the new international asset.

The executive directors met to discuss reform frequently during the winter of 1971–2 and into the summer of the following year, finally producing their report in September 1972, just in time for the Fund annual meeting of that year. The report represented the highest common factor of agreement, which meant that on most of the difficult issues it was couched in terms of generalities. Nevertheless, it represented an important step, for it reflected the agreed aspirations for the reform, the negotiation of which was about to get under way.

The executive directors' report identified a number of areas in which the functioning of the Bretton Woods system was deficient. In the first place, it was noted that the existing institutional mechanism was not able to ensure 'timely and adequate changes in exchange rates', and in particular that the United States had in practice less freedom to adjust its exchange rate than did other countries. Second, it noted that the volume of global reserve creation was not under adequate international control. While the agreement on SDR creation provided a means to supplement inadequate reserve growth, there was no effective mechanism to curtail excess liquidity caused by the accumulations of reserve balances in national currencies. Third, the report mentioned a number of factors which had tended to increase the imbalances which the system had to finance. These included higher and more varied rates of inflation, differences in the timing of business cycles, and a growing unwillingness to use domestic monetary policies for purposes of achieving external balance. Fourth, the growth in size and volatility of externally owned balances had meant that short-term capital flows posed an increasing threat to the stability of the system.

Although the executive directors' report did not make specific recommendations in dealing in detail with the points just mentioned, a number of directions in which they hoped the reformed system would move became apparent. On the exchange rate system, the report accepted as a basis for its recommendations that there would continue to be a system under which relative exchange rates were centrally agreed, and maintained within prescribed margins. However, the report did represent a step back from the rather positive endorsement of the par value system that characterized the 1970 report.[2]

The report suggested that the international rules governing par value changes should be made more 'symmetrical'. By that, it was understood that not only should countries refrain from making par value changes when they were *not* in 'fundamental disequilibrium'; they should also have some kind of obligation to adjust when they *were* in 'fundamental disequilibrium'. Making this change in the rules of the game would amount to putting 'competitive non-appreciation' on the same plane as 'competitive depreciation'. But the recommendations of the report went somewhat further than this. Additional changes would have to be made to significantly improve the working of the system. In the first place, the volatility of the capital movements made it necessary for needed par value adjustments to take place promptly, before a speculative run would have a chance to develop. This implied smaller and more frequent par value changes which it was believed would make the system more resilient by preventing the build-up of large disequilibria. Secondly, it was noted that countries would have to be more willing than under the Bretton Woods system to concert the measures to be used for controlling capital flows.

An idea which had received a certain amount of support in the period leading up to the publication of the 1972 report was that there should be 'objective indicators' that could signal adjustment needs in a non-arbitrary manner. The United States, in particular, was attracted to this proposal, since it seemed one way of sharing the burden of adjustment more systematically than under the old system. However, although the idea was an appealing one in principle, it foundered on practical grounds. Although there are a number of indicators which are broadly correlated with external strength, no one of these indicators is uniquely correlated with the underlying balance of payments. The executive directors therefore sidestepped this difficult issue with the comfortable bromide 'the search for effective and acceptable objective indicators should be pursued with vigour and imagination'.

The report saw a somewhat greater role for the international community, acting through the Fund, to initiate, as well as merely to approve, par value changes. It also underlined the by-then accepted proposition that surplus and deficit countries shared an equal obligation to adjust. On the issues of how the international community should make its view felt, and what sanctions it might employ against offending members, views were naturally more divided, and the report reached no conclusions.

In regard to floating, the 1972 report took a significantly more liberal attitude than previous official documents. It recognized that situations might arise in which individual countries would be forced to float, and felt that the Fund's rules ought to take account of this. Only thus could the international community exercise the requisite amount of surveillance over countries with floating currencies—surveillance that was clearly necessary to guard against the danger of a degeneration into competitive exchange policies.

On the question of convertibility, the report recognized that the mechanism of the Bretton Woods system, (with most major currencies being convertible into the dollar, and the dollar convertible into gold) had broken down and needed to be replaced with something else. The old system had placed the dollar in a special position which gave the United States authorities more rights and obligations than the managers of other currencies. (Whether the rights outweighed the obligations, or vice versa, depended largely on the negotiating viewpoint.)

New arrangements would have to work more symmetrically and put the United States dollar in a position more similar to that of other currencies. A system of asset settlement was proposed, whereby international imbalances would be settled exclusively by the transfer of assets and not also, as could happen under the Bretton Woods system, by the expansion or contraction of liabilities. But while asset settlement might impose on the United States a greater discipline that the Bretton Woods system, the question was whether the discipline might not be too great. If a reserve centre country got into balance of payments difficulties, an asset settlement mechanism would only work if the country were allowed to take strong external measures. Only if this could be guaranteed could the United States be expected to embrace the asset settlement system.

The report's chapter on reserve assets betrays a wide diversity of views. General lip-service was paid to the need to have an internationally accepted and controlled reserve asset: the role of the SDR was, therefore, to be enhanced. Gold and national currencies were to have a diminishing relative role; but how fast that role should diminish, and what rules should govern transactions in these assets while their roles were being diminished, were questions that did not receive any satisfactory answer.

The last two chapters of the executive directors' 1972 report concerned, respectively, capital movements and the developing countries. The mobility of capital does of course bring benefits for economic development, and these were recognized. At the same time, large amounts of volatile short-term funds can play havoc with a fixed exchange rate system. The report therefore suggests a number of palliatives designed to reduce the incentives for short-term capital flows, and to erect barriers to their occurrence.

The main issue for the developing countries was that of the Link between SDR creation and development. This proposal, which had a fairly lengthy history, found its first official expression in the 1972 report. The idea is extremely simple. Since the creation of liquidity generates spending power, why not give the new liquidity first to the poorer countries? As they used financial resources to acquire real goods and services from the industrialized world, the new liquidity would pass into the hands of countries which would wish to hold it as a permanent component of their reserves. There were a number of variants of this scheme, but the economic essence was in all cases the same. The report refrained from endorsing either the principle of the Link, or any of the particular schemes.

Soon after the executive directors began to prepare their report—perhaps even before—it became clear that the implementation of a monetary reform would require decision-making at a higher political level than the executive board of the Fund. The winter of 1971–2 saw a considerable amount of behind-the-scenes negotiation concerning the appropriate forum for such decision-taking. Some suggested that a world monetary conference under the auspices of the United Nations would allow the widest possible expression of opinion. The difficulty with this proposal, however, was that the width of opinion expressed might be too wide; and with no adequate provisions for weighted voting and majority decisions, the negotiations might be easily run into an impasse.

It was eventually decided that the executive board of the fund provided the most representative cross-section of national viewpoints, and that the forum should reflect this composition, but at ministerial level. In order to give a broader scope for the expression of national views, however, the 'members' of this Committee of Twenty should be accompanied by associates and advisers, which in total would bring the numbers of the deliberative forum to some 200.

To provide the technical backing for ministers to make political judgments, a deputies group was established, composed of senior-level officials from national capitals. This group was thought likely to be more effective than the Fund's executive board in preparing the ministerial discussions for two reasons. Firstly, they were at a higher level of responsibility, in the main, than the executive directors. Secondly, being based in national capitals they were thought to be more capable of accurately reflecting the particular preoccupations and concerns of individual member countries. To help guide the discussions of the deputies, an independent secretariat (or 'Bureau') was set up, consisting of a chairman and four vice-chairmen. These members of the Bureau were deputy-level officials, but gave up their national positions in order to work on monetary reform.

The chairman of the deputies (and head of the Bureau) was Jeremy Morse, formerly one of two British deputies. The vice-chairmen were Robert Solomon, Adviser to the United States Federal Reserve Board; Alexandre Kafka, Brazilian Executive Director in the Fund; Hideo Suzuki, formerly Japanese Executive Director in the Fund; and Jonathan Frimpong-Ansah, formerly Governor of the Bank of Ghana. The membership of the Bureau, it need hardly be said, was carefully calculated to provide the desired geographic balance.

The Committee began its work at the 1972 annual meeting. Meetings of the deputies were envisaged at two-monthly intervals, with meetings of the full committee of ministers perhaps half as frequently. It was hoped that an agreed outline of reform might emerge by the time of the following year's annual meeting in Nairobi. If this could be achieved, a further year's work was foreseen, mainly at a technical level, translating general principles into agreed legal texts.

The procedural arrangements of the reform discussions undoubtedly complicated the task of the Committee of Twenty. In the first place, the numbers participating in meetings inhibited productive discussion. In the ministerial meetings, the forty associates as well as the twenty committee members had the right to speak. In deputies' meetings, forty deputies and twenty executive directors had microphones. Both categories of meeting also had a number of observers, and well over a hundred advisers.

Despite these difficulties, success might have been achieved if the objectives of the various parties to the discussions had been reconcilable, and if the reform effort had not eventually been overtaken by events. The core of the disagreement centred on the nature of the exchange rate regime desired for the new system, and the mechanism by which balance of payments deficits and surpluses would be settled. On these questions, the continental European countries usually found themselves on one side of the controversy, and the United States on the other. In broad terms, it can probably be said that the United States was wary of being asked, as the major country in the system, to bear a disproportionate share of the adjustment burden. Other countries, on the other hand, did not want to be forced to accept United States policy as a 'datum' and to have to adapt their own targets and instruments to it.

In the early stages of negotiation it was possible, as is usually the case when skilled diplomats or officials are involved, to paper over the differences of view with sufficiently inclusive language. Thus, on the exchange rate mechanism, it was agreed that there should be 'stable but adjustable par values with provision for floating in particular circumstances'. This kind of statement is useful to sustain the momentum of progress, but does not define any meaningful agreement unless the circumstances are defined in which rates shall remain fixed, be adjusted by a given amount, or allowed to float. Clearly those who value fixed rates regard floating or par value changes as rather a last resort. Thus countries are expected to accept at least some measure of unwelcome domestic policies before resorting to the exchange rate weapon. This was probably moderately reflective of the European view, and reflected a feeling that the balance of payments should exercise at least some discipline over the formation of domestic economic policies.

If, on the other hand, 'stable exchange rates' was merely intended to demonstrate a vague preference, *ceteris paribus*, for fixed rates but a willingness to abandon par values whenever their maintenance became difficult, then the conclusions would be quite different. This would not truly be a fixed exchange rate system, and the balance of payments would not really exercise any significant effect on domestic policies. The United States probably took this rather more flexible view of the Committee wording.

Disagreement over the nature of the exchange rate system had its counterpart in the differing views of the settlement mechanism. On the other hand, European countries preferred a 'tight' system of asset-settlement, whereby there would be a fixed stock of international liquidity, and imbalances could only be settled by transferring claims on this stock. Thus a country in persistent deficit would be forced to take corrective action at an early stage. What the European countries had particularly in mind, of course, was the avoidance of prolonged deficits by reserve currency countries (such as the United States) financed by an accumulation of reserve liabilities.

The United States saw asset settlement as potentially imposing far greater burdens on deficit than on surplus countries. As a nation which had had deficits (on an official settlements basis) continuously for more than a decade, the United States authorities were naturally more sympathetic to the problems of deficit countries. The deficit countries, particularly the reserve centres, would have to adjust almost immediately to a payments disequilibrium, under the pressure of shrinking reserves. The surplus countries, on the other hand, could continue to accumulate reserves with no particularly compelling pressure to change their policies.

In order to accept asset settlement as a principle, therefore, the United States sought several modifications in its application in practice. In the first place, the United States sought assurances that it would be able to accumulate reserves when the American balance of payments was in surplus. Otherwise, the United States might find it was being paid dollars in settlement for its surpluses, and being asked for gold in settlement for its deficits. Next the United States asked that the pressure to adjust be brought to bear equally hard on surplus countries as on those in deficit. Deficit countries had the threat of an exhaustion of their reserves. Furthermore, since reserves were often small in relation to trade volumes, and it was difficult to allow any significant decline without provoking a crisis of confidence, deficits usually required corrective action within a very short time-span. Surplus countries, on the other hand, could contemplate an almost indefinite continuation of their disequilibrium, with the only measurable cost being the relatively low yield on their reserve holdings. To introduce greater symmetry to the mechanism, the United States introduced the idea of objective criteria for assessment of reserve adequacy. Broadly, this involved setting a 'norm' for reserve holdings with bands on either side. When a country's reserve holdings moved outside these bands (either above or below) corrective action would be indicated. There could, of course, be a series of bands which would indicate different kinds of response on the part of the international community. The first band might require only consultation, for example, while the next would imply a presumptive need for adjustment and the last, sanctions against the country concerned.

Although these two issues, the exchange rate regime and the settlement mechanism, were at the core of the reform of the system, there were disagreements on other subjects, too. On liquidity, for example, there was no agreement on how the system might move towards its ultimate objectives, namely, gradual demonetization of gold, the phasing out of reserve currencies, and the replacement of these two assets by an internationally created and controlled asset. This asset, which would be the SDR, in modified form, would be under international supervision, and new allocations would be made strictly in accordance with the world's need for reserves.

Few countries were prepared to accept these objectives as a short-term goal, however, and there was much disagreement on interim measures. The holders and producers of gold naturally wished to preserve a stable demand for their asset, and they were joined by those who preferred the arbitrariness of gold to the possibilities of abuse inherent in any managed monetary system. In practical terms, this translated into a difference between those who preferred to accept the market price of gold as a *fait accompli*, and those who would have preferred to hasten gold's departure from the monetary system by prohibiting transactions at other than the official price (then less than half the market price).

As far as reserve currencies were concerned, there was considerable support for a continuing role, both from the issuers of the reserve currencies, and from a number of major holders. The issuers of the reserve currencies (i.e. principally the United States and the United Kingdom) did not want to undertake the substantial burden of repayment of currency holdings, unless over a very extended period. Indeed, the United States probably felt that over time it was more appropriate that official dollar holdings should be maintained and even increased. Some of the major holders of dollar and sterling balances, too, were unwilling to see them converted into SDR. Their reason was simply that they feared the yield which would be offered on the SDR would be considerably less than that obtainable on short-term United States and United Kingdom Treasury paper.

On the question of capital movements, there was also a basic philosophical difference, cloaked in the ambiguities of official language. While everybody could agree that mobility of resources was good, and disruptive capital movements were bad, it was much more difficult to come together on what constituted a disruptive capital flow. They could not simply be dismissed as capital flows which undermined an existing parity, for if the parity was wrong then it could be argued that it was the official intervention that was preventing a true equilibrium from being reached.

The continental European countries were on the whole much more prepared to interfere with the free movement of capital. This was partly because they set greater store by the maintenance of exchange market stability but mainly because they saw themselves has having suffered from the previous freedom of capital movements. Some, such as Germany and the Netherlands, felt they had suffered in having their freedom of domestic monetary policy circumscribed. Inflows of short-term funds *via* the euro-dollar market were greater than they could conveniently offset with the conventional tools of monetary management. Other countries, such as France and possibly Canada, felt the greater disadvantage to lie in the gradual extension of American control over large sectors of their domestic industries. The fact that this extension of control was financed, not by a transfer of real resources via a current account surplus, but by an accumulation of short-term liabilities, only made the situation harder to accept.

The American position was much more favourable towards freedom of capital movements. This attitude reflected partly a philosophical bias towards the marketplace and partly a feeling that, as a technological leader, it would be in the interest of the United States to sponsor the free movement of American knowhow.

The final major area on which there was substantive disagreement was on how to achieve a greater flow of real resources to the developing countries. In practice, the debate boiled down to whether or not to implement the Link. Since most of the other issues in the reform were of somewhat peripheral interest to the poorer nations, they focused their attention on securing a Link between SDR-creation and development assistance.

As noted above, the Link idea involves giving the benefit of 'seigniorage' to the developing countries, either directly or indirectly. The analogy is drawn with a national banking system, where bank credit is extended to deficit units, who spend the resources so acquired on goods produced by the surplus sectors. The surplus sectors then hold money balances as an increment to their liquid reserves and to finance a growing volume of transactions.

The seigniorage could be distributed to the developing nations in one of a number of ways. The most straightforward, and the method favoured by the majority of the developing countries themselves, was simply to allocate them a disproportionate share of any new SDRs created. An alternative, more favoured by developed nations, would be to allocate new SDRs to development finance organizations, such as the World Bank and the regional development banks, which could use the resources thus acquired in their normal operations.

Despite the obvious attractions of the Link scheme from a development point of view, and the strong advocacy of most less-developed countries, there were firm objections from a number of developed countries. These feared that the mixing up of development goals with monetary objectives would lead to a compromise in which neither was achieved. Specifically, too much liquidity might be created out of a misplaced desire to foster development; while the aid extended via the Link might simply be offset by a reduction in other forms of development assistance. The Link issue was therefore shelved in most of the C-20 discussions in the hope that it could be reviewed as part of a grand compromise package at the dénouement of the negotiations.

The collapse of the Smithsonian Arrangements

While the reform discussions were proceeding, events did not stand still. In fact the two years of existence of the Committee of Twenty were among the most turbulent in post-war monetary history. The monetary arrangements which eventually emerged from the reform were at least as much a product of these events as of deliberate planning.

The first indication that the Smithsonian agreement of December 1971 might not provide a lasting basis for currency relationships came in June 1972, when the British government allowed the pound sterling to float. As in 1967, the depreciation of the British currency proved to be a prelude to renewed pressure on the United States dollar, as the American balance of payments was disappointingly slow in responding to the competitive advantage gained at the Smithsonian. Early in February of 1973, there was intense speculative pressure against the dollar, which could only be resisted by substantial intervention on the part of central banks in Europe and Japan. This was not a sustainable situation. The surplus countries were increasingly perturbed at the inflationary consequences of capital inflows on their already inflation-prone economies. Exchange markets were closed and the United States Under-Secretary for Monetary Affairs, Paul Volcker, set off on a mission to renegotiate the Smithsonian agreement, and achieve a further significant depreciation of the American dollar. The package that was agreed involved a further revaluation of the Japanese yen and German mark, and a devaluation of 10 per cent for the dollar. However, the specifics of the agreement turned out to be of little importance since, when markets reopened, it quickly became evident that private dealers had little confidence in the new rates and further pressure against the dollar built up. By this time, private dealers had become so confident in their own capacity to force the hands of central banks, and the central banks had become so doubtful of their ability to choose an appropriate rate (and once chosen, to defend it), that the markets had to be quickly closed again.

There followed a series of meetings in Paris and Brussels over three successive weekends, in which the major industrial countries considered whether and how to put back the pieces of a fixed rate system. But the will to make the sacrifices required by fixed exchange rates had largely evaporated, and it was judged impossible to find a set of rates that would avert speculative pressure more than temporarily. As a result, all the major currencies elected to float, with the exception of the group of countries participating in the European narrow margins agreement.

Although these developments in early 1973 were a serious blow to the reform effort, they did not really deflect the discussions from their chosen goal. It was felt that the existing uncertainties sprang largely from ignorance concerning the degree to which, and the speed with which, the United States balance of payments would respond to the exchange rate changes of the previous eighteen months. Once this massive adjustment had worked its way through the system, it would be possible to identify with greater confidence the pattern of exchange rates which would be appropriate in the medium term.

However, other events in 1973 were also complicating the task of those who hoped for an early return to an ordered system of fixed exchange rates. In the first place, the dramatic acceleration of global inflation sharply reduced the time perspective within which it made sense to aim at fixed parities. When national price levels had such substantial scope for divergence, it was clear that the 'smaller and more frequent' par value changes to which references had been made might have to become very frequent indeed—so frequent, indeed, that there might be little substantive difference from a regime of managed floating.

The second, and more dramatic development, was the tripling of oil prices in the closing months of 1973, coupled with the oil embargo following the Arab–Israeli conflict in October of that year. These developments had profound effects on balance of payments prospects, whose magnitude could not be estimated with any degree of precision. Following the announcement of the embargo, it was felt that the United States, as the industrial country closest to self-sufficiency in oil, would be best placed to withstand a cut-off of imports. As a result the United States dollar appreciated by some 25 per cent in the exchange markets against the European currencies between September 1973 and January 1974. Later, however, when it became clear that oil would continue to flow, though at a higher price, more importance was attached to the fact that the United States was the largest single importer of oil, and therefore the direct impact on its balance of payments would be greatest. The United States dollar proceeded to decline by 20 per cent against the German mark between January and July 1974.

These fluctuations served to re-emphasize the difficulty, indeed impossibility, of a meaningful return to fixed exchange rates in the foreseeable future. As a result, the Committee of Twenty, which at its meeting in Nairobi in October 1973 had given itself nine months to complete a comprehensive reform, at its next meeting in Rome, in January 1974, modified its objective to that of reporting on the desirable features of the ultimate reform and proposing a number of 'immediate steps'.

The 'outline of reform' which emerged from the final meeting of the Committee of Twenty in June 1974 was not formally endorsed by the ministers. It was a document prepared by the Bureau of the Deputies, under Mr Morse. It did, however, represent the widest consensus that could be found concerning the desirable features of the monetary system in the long term. The exchange rate system was to be based on 'stable but adjustable parities with provision for floating in particular situations'. Settlement was to be based on the transfer of reserve assets, but with suitable safeguards to preserve flexibility; liquidity was to be based on the SDR, with the gradual phasing-out of reserve currencies and gold; and 'full account' was to be taken of the specific needs of the developing countries. The details of how effect might be given to these broad principles were contained in a series of four reports by technical groups formed to examine the technical aspects of possible new arrangements.

Of greater moment than the outline of reform, however, were the 'immediate steps' on which agreement was reached in the final meeting of the Committee of Twenty. This meeting endorsed an 'evolutionary' approach to monetary reform, which effectively terminated the ambitious attempt to design a complete system which could be instituted at one go. Perhaps the most important step in this evolution that was taken in the June 1974 meeting was the agreement on a new method of valuation for the SDR. The SDR had initially been linked to the official price of gold, but since transactions in gold no longer took place, the SDR's value was actually defined in terms of the official gold price of the dollar. The agreement reached by the Committee of Twenty was to relate the value of the SDR to a weighted average of the exchange value of the sixteen major trading currencies. This gave the SDR a readily calculable market value which was much more acceptable to member countries than the old valuation, and which was likely to fluctuate less in value. The precise method by which the SDR is valued is described in more detail in Chapter 7 above.

The other main point on which the Committee of Twenty agreed was essentially procedural, but may well have a lasting impact on the mechanism of international monetary cooperation. It was agreed that a permanent forum should be established at ministerial level to undertake the management and surveillance of balance of payments adjustment and the working of the monetary system. In effect, the Committee of Twenty was perpetuating its own existence and widening its terms of reference. Initially, the Committee would have purely advisory functions, and would therefore be called an 'Interim Committee', but eventually it was envisaged that an amendment to the Articles of Agreement would bestow decision-making powers on the new organ, which might then be called a 'council of governors'. In essence, however, the membership and procedures of the two bodies would be quite smilar to those of the original Committee of Twenty.

The other tangible legacy of the reform work was a series of subjects on which it was agreed that draft amendments should be prepared. Those unfamiliar with the workings of bureaucracy should beware of reading too much into this development: agreement that amendments should be drafted in no way implies a willingness to accept the draft (or indeed any draft) when it is prepared. It is simply a technique which allows a meeting to close with the appearance of agreement without anybody having to sacrifice his position or lose face.

In the case of the list of amendments prepared at the final meeting of the Committee of Twenty, it was a matter of putting together most of the subjects on which one or more countries had expressed a desire for a change in the Fund's Articles of Agreement. The most pressing matter on which amendment was needed (though not the most important, substantively) was the question of gold payments to the Fund. The Bretton Woods Articles of Agreement required payment of gold by member countries to the Fund in certain specified circumstances. The most important of these, quantitatively, was the payment of the 25 per cent gold tranche portion of quota subscriptions and increases. Since there was general agreement that quotas should be increased at the review due to be completed in early 1975, some amendment to the existing provisions was clearly needed if the quota increase was to take effect. No members were willing to supply gold to the Fund at the official price of SDR 35 per ounce (the only price the Fund could legally pay) while the free market price was approximately four times as much.

The Jamaica Accords

The next stage of the reform discussions was reached in January 1976, when the Interim Committee agreed on a list of specific amendments to the Fund's Articles, which should be put to members. After some final drafting work by the executive board, the amendments were approved by the board of governors in April 1976. Formal ratification by member governments is a somewhat more long-drawn-out affair.

As noted above, the agreement embodied in the amended Articles is something less than a complete reform of the system. But it does represent a legalization of the existing situation concerning exchange rates, and affords the Fund a better change to exercise surveillance over its members' policies. A reduction in the role of gold, changes in the characteristics of the SDR as a reserve asset, simplification and expansion of the types of financial transactions to be conducted in the Fund's general operations, and the possible establishment of a permanent council as a new decision-making organ of the Fund are among the other provisions of the amendment.

The two issues which proved most difficult to resolve, and which were mainly responsible for the delay in reaching agreement, were those of the exchange rate regime and gold. It is therefore worth considering the compromise that was reached on these two matters in a little more detail.

Concerning exchange rates, certain countries, particularly the developing countries and France, had stressed the importance of stability and had wanted the Articles to embody the idea of stability, or par values, as an ultimate objective. The United States and a number of other industrial countries, on the other hand, were wary of any formal endorsement of fixed exchange rates, even as an ultimate objective.

The amended Article IV provides that members should be free to adopt any exchange arrangement they choose (except a peg to gold). In this, it reflects substantially the position of the United States and most industrial countries. However, it stresses the importance of 'orderly underlying conditions', and encourages countries to manage their domestic economies in such a way as to promote internal and external stability. In the words of the United States Treasury Secretary, William Simon ' ... the new system seeks to *develop stability from within*, through attention to responsible management of underlying economic and financial policies in individual member countries.'[3]

Of more significance is the Fund's role in the exercising surveillance of members' policies under the new Article. This surveillance is to be based on 'specific' principles for the guidance of all members with respect to their exchange rate policies. At the time of writing, these principles have yet to be worked out, but it seems likely that they will give the Fund stronger and broader powers of surveillance than under the Bretton Woods Articles.

Gold has always been an emotional issue, and in the reform discussions, too, it proved difficult to obtain agreement. Under the Bretton Woods Articles, central banks were free to sell gold at or above the official price, but they could only buy gold at or below the official price. Since the market price had been well above the official price for some time,[4] this meant that while central banks could sell their gold in the private market, they could not exchange gold amongst themselves nor could they buy gold in the private market.

A further complicating factor was that, under the Bretton Woods Articles, 25 per cent of quotas had to be paid in gold at the official price. Unless this provision was repealed, the prospects for implementing a quota increase would be slim, and the Fund would become increasingly less able to meet the demands on it to lend.

The obvious solution was to abolish the official price of gold, and this is in fact done in the amendments. But such a solution still leaves a number of loose ends. The United States was concerned that a *de facto* official price should not be re-established by central banks undertaking to exchange gold amongst themselves at a fixed price. To prevent this, the Group of Ten countries entered into an understanding, for two years, not to peg the price of gold and not to increase their combined stock of monetary gold. This understanding runs to February 1, 1978, when it will be reviewed by the parties concerned.

Another question raised by the abolition of the official gold price is what to do with the gold paid by members to the Fund as part of their quota subscriptions. The Jamaica agreement was that one-sixth of this gold should be returned to members; one-sixth should be auctioned to private purchasers and proceeds used to benefit developing countries, and the remaining two-thirds retained, for the time being, by the Fund. However, it is provided that these remaining holdings may, by 85 per cent vote, be disposed of in a number of approved ways.

Another important result of the Jamaica meeting of the Interim Committee, not related to the amendments, was the agreement that drawing rights under credit tranches should, in the period before the pending quota increase became effective, be expanded by 45 per cent. This development was important in itself for its impact on the availability of conditional liquidity. Beyond that, it emphasized that the Interim Committee was playing a role beyond simply negotiating amendments. The involvement of ministers in supervising 'the management and adaption of the international monetary system, including the continuing operation of the adjustment process and developments in global liquidity',[4] is essential if the Fund is to play an effective role at the centre of the international monetary system.

---

[1] Technically this took place because the SDR had a fixed gold value, and gold continued to be the numeraire for Fund operations.
[2] *The Role of Exchange Rates in the Adjustment of International Payments*, Report by the Executive Directors, IMF, Washington, D.C., 1970.
[3] Testimony of Mr Simon before the United States House of Representatives' Subcommittee on International Trade, Investment and Monetary Policy, June 1 1976.
[4] The private and official markets for gold were separated in 1968, but it was only after 1971 that the price in the private market rose substantially above that in the official market.
[5] From Draft Amendments, Schedule D, related to the establishment of a ministerial council.

Selected Further Reading

Deane, Roderick S., *International Monetary Reform: Content and Perspective*, Reserve Bank of New Zealand.
De Vries, T., 'Jamaica or the non-reform of the international monetary system', *Foreign Affairs*, April 1976.
Fleming, J.M., *Reflections on the International Monetary Reform*, Princeton Essays in International Finance No. 107, 1975.
International Monetary Fund, *Reform of the International Monetary System, Report by the Executive Directors*, IMF, Washington, D.C., 1972.
International Monetary Fund, *International Monetary Reform: Documents of the Committee of Twenty*, IMF Washington, D.C., 1974.
Journal of International Economics, *The International Monetary System: A Symposium*, September 1972.
Underwood, T.G., 'Analysis of proposals for using objective indicators as a guide to exchange rate changes', IMF *Staff Papers*, 1973.

Index

Absorption approach 41, 50–52
Accommodating flows 39
Adjustable peg 9–10, 75–81, 152
Adjustment mechanism 6–10, 20–27, 93–111
Adjustment, speed of 21–24
Aid 103
Alexander, S.S. 50
Allocations (of SDRs) 131
Amendment (to IMF Articles)
  First Amendment 120
  Second Amendment 74, 87–88, 156, 242–45
Annual Report (of IMF) 142–43
Arbitrage 158–59
Articles of Agreement of IMF
  Article I 207
  Article IV 87–88, 214, 243–244
  Article VI 159–160
  Article VIII 213
Asset settlement 148, 234–35
Asymmetrical basket 126–27
Asymmetries (in adjustment) 21–27, 197–202
Asymmetries (in surveillance) 81
Autarky 14, 81
Autonomous flows 39

Bagehot, Walter 57 fn.
Balance of payments 2–4, 38–57
Balance of payments constraint 65–66, 189–191
Band proposal 82–83
Bank for International Settlements 165, 212
Bank of England 32, 157, 159, 163
Bardepot 162
Basket (of currencies) 106–07, 124–28
Basle 155

Benign neglect 26–27, 34
Bilateralism 15, 207
Blocking (currency balances) 33
Bretton Woods System 4–18, 75–81, 117–18
  breakdown of system 20–37, 100, 226–27
Buffer stock facility 220–221
Bureau (of Committee of 20) 232

Cambridge, new view (see New Cambridge view)
Capital controls (see also capital flows) 96, 141
Capital flows 21, 30–33, 77, 89, 96, 141, 150–66, 236–237
Cassel, Gustav 44
Central rates 83
Chicago school 52
Churchill, Winston 45
"Clean floating" 86
Clearing arrangements 12–13
Clendenning, E.W. 183 fn.
Committee of 20 131, 164, 211, 232–33
Commodity reserve standard 124
Common margins (see narrow margins)
Compensatory financing facility 220
Competitive depreciation 9, 133, 229
Conditional liquidity 120–121, 142–44
Conditionality (of Fund lending) 216, 218–20
Confidence (in exchange rates) 105
Consultations (between IMF and members) 214–15

Index

Controlled flexibility (of exchange rates) 9–10, 74–91
Convertibility
  introduction 1958 153, 169
  collapse of 230
Council of Governors 208, 241–2
Crawling peg 83–85
Credit arrangements 12–13
Credit creation 172–73
  multiplier 173–76
Credit tranches 217–224
Currency unions 68–72
Current account 40

Delegation (of powers in IMF) 209
Demand for money 52–55, 193–195
Demand for reserves 135–39, 189, 195–96
Demand management 50–52, 61
Demonetization (of gold) 235
Deputies (of Committee of 20) 232
Destabilizing capital flows (see capital flows)
Devaluation of sterling 154
Developing countries 102–110, 172, 219–220, 237–38
Development finance institutions 129
Direct controls 159–62
Direct investment 151, 160–61
"Dirty" floating 86
Discipline (of fixed rates) 93–97, 185, 202
Dollars (in reserves) 13–14, 27–30, 118–19, 230–231
Domestic credit 54–55
Drawings (on IMF) 215–224
Dual markets 162–64

Economic Policy Committee (of OECD) 35
Effective exchange rates 90–91, 106–107
Elasticities (approach to balance of payments) 41, 47–50
Elasticity pessimists 50
Elections (of IMF directors) 209–10
Euro-currency market 31–32, 164–65, 167–83

European Economic Community 72, 100
Exchange control 15, 33, 159–62
Exchange rate policies 58–91
Executive Directors (of IMF) 79, 85, 105, 128, 201, 209–10, 226
Extended facility 222–23

Facilities of IMF 217, 224
Federal Reserve Bank of New York 157
Financial integration 69
"Financial Market" for foreign exchange 162–64
Fiscal policy 95–96
Fixed exchange rates 59–64
  and inflation 184–204
Flexible exchange rates (see floating exchange rates)
Floating exchange rates 8–9, 64–68
  and inflation 184–204
Forward exchange market 158–59, 193
Fractional reserve banking 54, 114
French franc devaluation 77
Friedman, Milton 22, 68, 190, 192
Fundamental disequilibrium 75–79

Galbraith, J.K. 131 fn.
General Agreement on Tariffs & Trade (GATT) 213
General Arrangements to Borrow (GAB) 158
Gliding parity (see crawling peg)
Gold 6–8, 11–12, 114–118, 235–244
Gold-exchange standard 4, 113
Gold standard 6–8, 42–44, 113–18
Gold tranche 218
Governors (of IMF) 208–09
Gresham's Law 30, 118, 122
Group of 10 35, 158, 244
Guidelines for floating 74, 87–90

Halm, G.N. 91 fn.
Harmonization of policies 34, 35, 154–156
Harrod, R.F. 50, 57 fn.
Hart, A.G. 132 fn.
Heller, H.R. 149 fn.
Hidden-hand 16

Hot money 157
Hume, David 19, 40–43

Import restrictions 77
Incomes policy 96
Independent floating 108–110
Inflation
  and euro-markets 167, 180–81
  and international monetary system 184–204
Interest Equalization Tax 33, 161, 169, 180
Interest rates 43–44, 152, 155–6
Interim Committee 241–42
International Bank for Reconstruction and Development (*see* World Bank)
International Monetary Fund 206–225
International liquidity (*see* liquidity)
International Trade Organization 213
Intervention (in exchange markets) 66–68, 74, 86–91

Jamaica Accords 242–245
J-curve 97–98
Johnson, Harry G. 49
Joint floating 100

Kaldor, N. 132 fn.
Kenen, Peter 71
Keynes, J.M. 13, 46
Kindleberger, C.P. 37 fn.

Laffer, A.B. 60
Lags
  in monetary policy 56
  in adjustment 97–98
Lanyi, Anthony 166 fn.
Leads and lags 164
Less-developed countries (*see* developing countries)
Liberalization
  of capital controls 150–51
  of payments arrangements 213
Link (between SDRs and development aid) 128–31, 237–38

Liquidity 11–14, 27–30, 112–49, 156–58
  and euro-markets 172
London capital market 8, 12

Majorities (in Fund voting) 209
Managed floating 10, 58, 85–91, 97–101, 144–145
Management (of monetary system) 16–18, 34–35
Managing Director (of IMF) 210
Manipulation
  of exchange rates 87–88
  of capital flows 96
Margins (of exchange rates) 75, 81–83
Marshall Plan 34
Maturity transformation (in euro-currency market) 170–71
Meade, J.E. 57 fn.
Mercantilism 19 fn.
Mix (of policies) 95–96
Monetary approach (to balance of payments) 52–55
Morse, Jeremy 232
Multilateralism 14–15, 207
Multilateral surveillance 35, 87
Multinational corporations 32, 169, 171
Multiplier 173–176
Mundell, R.A. 23, 95, 153

Nairobi (meeting of the IMF) 233, 240
Narrow margins arrangements 72
National income analysis 50
New Cambridge view 42, 55–56
New York capital market 33
Nixon, President 226
"norms" for exchange rates 89
  for reserve holding 235
Nsouli, S.M. 110 fn.
Numeraire 82, 113

OECD 35, 155, 210
Objective indicators 229–230
Officer, L.H. 57 fn.
Official settlements balance 40
"Offshore" banks 176–78
Oil facility 221–22

Index 249

Oil price increase 86, 195, 240
One-world system 15, 21
Oort, Conrad 23, 36 fn.
Operation Twist 154
Optimum currency areas 68–72
Outline (of reform) 240–41
Overall balance 40, 52
Overshooting (exchange rate equilibrium) 97–98

Par value system 9–10, 41, 42–44, 58, 75–81, 187
Pass-through 70
Phelps, E. 204 fn.
Phillips curve 196–97
Policy mix 95–96
Portfolio investment 162–64
Precious metals 54
Price flexibility 64
Price-specie-flow mechanism 42–44, 187
Primary producing countries 109
Principles for exchange rate policies 88
Program loans 222
Public sector deficit 56
Purchasing power parity 39, 45–47
Purposes (of IMF) 207–208

"Q" (Regulation of Federal Reserve) 177
Quotas (in IMF) 120, 142, 157, 209–210

Radcliffe Report 23
Ratchet effects 197–200
Real money balances 52–55
Reconstitution 120–21
Reform (of International Monetary System) 226–245
Regional Development Banks 129
Regulation
  on banks 169
  on euro-markets 181–82
Regulation Q 177
Remuneration 122
Replenishment 216
Repurchases 216
Reserve creation (in euro-markets) 172

Reserve currencies 118
Reserve discipline 189–91
Reserve needs 106, 135–145
Reserves (*see* liquidity)
Reserve standard 10–14
Resources of the IMF 215–217
Revaluation 128
  of mark and guilder 77, 157
"Revealed preference" in reserve holding 135–37
Rhomberg, R.R. 91 fn.
Rome (meeting of C-20) 240
Roosa, R.V. 204 fn.
"Rules of the Game" 44

Scarce currency clause 25
Schacht, Hjalmar 14
Schiller (Professor) 86
Seigniorage 128–29, 237–38
Simon, William 243
Smithsonian agreement 227
  collapse of 238, 242
Snake (*see also* narrow margins) 101, 144
Sovereignty 71, 72
Special drawing rights 14, 30, 121–31, 231, 241
Speculation 31–33, 68, 78–79, 82–83, 152–54
Spot exchange market 158–59
Stabilization policies 56
Standard basket 124–26
Sterilization (of monetary inflow) 187
Subscriptions 209
Suez crisis 153, 157
Super-gold tranche 218
Surveillance 80, 87–88, 214–15, 243–44
Swaps 157

Tower, E. 71
Traded goods price effects 185–186
Trade-off (between inflation and unemployment) 71, 196–97
Transfer of real resources 128–31, 151, 237–38
Transmission mechanism (of inflation) 185–191
Triffin, Robert 119

"Twisting" of yield curve 95, 154
Two-tier gold market 122

UNCTAD 212
Uncertainty (in exchange
  rates) 191–93
Unconditional liquidity 120–123
Uniform change in par values 117

Valuation of SDR 123–28
Vehicle currencies 194
Vietnam War 20

Volcker, Paul 239
Voluntary program (of foreign
  investment restraint) 169, 180
Voting (in IMF) 209

Wage-price spiral 200
Weighted majorities 209
Wider bands 81–83
Willett, T.W. 71
Williamson, J.H. 91 fn.
Working Party 3 35, 155
World Bank 129, 209, 212